Academic Success
and Social Power

Academic Success and Social Power

Examinations and Inequality

Richard Teese

MELBOURNE UNIVERSITY PRESS

MELBOURNE UNIVERSITY PRESS
PO Box 278, Carlton South, Victoria 3053, Australia
info@mup.unimelb.edu.au
www.mup.com.au

First published 2000

Typeset by Syarikat Seng Teik Sdn. Bhd., Malaysia in Sabon 10/13
Printed in Australia by Australian Print Group

National Library of Australia Cataloguing-in-Publication entry

Teese, Richard.
    Academic success and social power: examinations and
    inequality.
    Bibliography.
    Includes index.
    ISBN 0 522 84896 6.

    1. Curriculum planning—Social aspects—Australia.
    2. Education, Secondary—Australia—Curricula. I. Title.
373.2380994

Contents

Figures

Acknowledgements

TO MY CO-WORKERS in the Educational Outcomes Research Unit of the University of Melbourne I owe a special debt of gratitude. Our survey programme during 1994–97, covering the whole of Australia, has been drawn on liberally in this book, while the many parallel lines of historical research which are pursued in the book have frequently diverted efforts from the survey and from the many other commissioned projects on which academic survival has come to depend. For their continued support and help, thanks to John Polesel, Margaret Charlton, Merryn Davies, Kate O'Brien, Chris Agius, Samantha Unger, Anne Walstab and Amy Maughan. Much of the analysis of the datasets used in this book relies on training and advice given generously over many years by Dr Ian Robinson of the University of Melbourne Information Technology Services. Betty Mastenbroek of the Education Resource Centre located materials that were often critical to the project. Thanks too to my colleagues in universities around Australia who recommended this project to the publisher, to Teresa Pitt of Melbourne University Press who commissioned the work, to Jenny Lee, who edited a long and complex manuscript, and to Gabby Lhuede on the production side. Finally to my family for their support throughout.

Permission is gratefully acknowledged to reproduce Figure 26 from 'Curriculum hierarchy, private schooling, and the segmentation of Australian secondary education', *British Journal of Sociology of Education*, 19 (3) 1998, p. 405, published by Taylor and Francis Ltd, 11 New Fetter Lane, London EC4P 4EE.

1

The Age of Curriculum

THERE IS A STRIKING parallel between the poverty experienced by many workers denied opportunities to work, but kept in the workforce, and the failure experienced by many students denied opportunities to achieve, but kept on at school.[1] The economic system should create real chances to earn; the education system should create real chances to learn. But today the institutions through which wealth is produced plunge large numbers of workers into poverty every year, and the institutions that create academic success condemn large numbers of students to failure. Each system, it seems, sets limits on the diffusion of economic and cultural benefits so as to prevent the dilution of quality and protect a narrow social enjoyment, which amounts to the same thing.

There is more than a mere parallel between the poverty of many unemployed workers and the failure of many students in school. Often enough, these groups are drawn from the same populations. Scholastic failure leads to casual, poorly paid work. Economic failure leads to frustration, loss of self-respect, loss of commitment, loss of means—all fatal to the confident sense of purpose, the inner integrity and personal well-being on which childhood learning most readily builds. Where economic institutions no longer protect against poverty of a material kind, educational institutions might compensate by reducing the poverty of intellectual means that constitutes failure. No doubt they do, up to a point. Many poor children complete school today who were unknown in senior forms twenty years ago or even ten. And many make good their

1

chance, thanks to teachers whose devotion is recognized only grudgingly, if at all. But the new populations who have been compelled to extend their time at school as jobs for young people have disappeared have paid a heavy price for their academic temerity.

In the urban regions where working-class and migrant families are highly concentrated, every third girl can expect to receive fail grades in the least demanding mathematics subject in the curriculum. Among boys—whose attraction to mathematics is even more fatal—failure strikes more than 40 per cent.[2] The better students gravitate to the mathematics subjects that lead to university. But here too failure awaits them, one in three. This is the same rate of failure experienced by preparatory mathematics students as a group in 1960.[3] To attend school in the western suburbs of Melbourne is to be more than three decades behind in relative terms. To be educated in the up-market inner east is to leave history behind, for here only 12 per cent of boys and 8 per cent of girls fail in preparatory mathematics. It is the same story with chemistry— the more democratic of the physical sciences. In this subject, four out of ten girls from the most depressed urban environments receive the fail grades of E+, E or UG (zero grade), as do more than three out of ten boys.[4] This is despite lower levels of participation and survival to the end of school in the first place. To take refuge in less academic subjects is not the answer. Girls in the north-west can expect to fail Human Development 36 per cent of the time, boys in the outer west to fail Legal Studies 31 per cent of the time.

These fatalities are the results for geographical regions, in which populations are somewhat mixed and attainment is averaged through aggregation. They are mild compared with the depth of failure recorded at individual schools where families lack the cultural and economic advantages to manage the intellectual demands of the curriculum. Poor achievement on a large scale is a recurring fact of life, never officially acknowledged—except back-handedly to justify cutting funds to government schools, to impose punitive testing programmes and to demand ever greater contestability and transparency from the schools already most exposed to failure. And it is endured with the same resignation as the poor prospects of work that await school leavers in these same areas. It is a sad irony that the young people who most need to succeed if they are to counteract the economic breakdown and degradation that surround them are instead the most likely to fail.

The contrast could not be sharper between the academic insecurity of the economically most vulnerable populations and the success enjoyed by the economically most powerful groups. There are sites within the school system where failure has been abolished by years of public and private investment and also by the most careful management of curriculum reform—sites where it is a socially legitimate aim to eliminate failure altogether. Fewer than two in one hundred girls attending private non-Catholic schools are placed in the lowest fifth band of English. In a system of relative merit, however, failure cannot be eliminated, merely exported. The curriculum system that grants honours to every second boy attempting preparatory mathematics in the most insular and richest sector of schooling—and spares 91 per cent of them the humiliation of an E+, an E or a UG—must find failure somewhere else and in abundance.

The fortification of strong sites in the school system—through fees, public subsidies, social and academic segregation, the market ideologies of government and the venality of low-life talkback radio—presents only the more visible aspect of generating success and exporting failure. Less visible is the long-term process of investment in the curriculum. School subjects are codified, authoritative systems of cognitive and cultural demands.[5] The nature of these demands weighs more or less heavily or lightly on different families, depending on their historical experience of academic schooling and the extent to which formal education infuses their life-styles and values. It depends too on their economic strength and capacity to act collectively. As economic reliance on completed secondary school grows, it is not only selective schooling that becomes more valuable as a way of preserving or extending social advantage. The curriculum also grows in importance, with its hierarchy of opportunities and its ability to determine academic merit. It is through the curriculum that the financial and cultural reserves of educated families are converted into scholastic power—the ability to differentiate one group of children from others on a socially legitimate and authoritative scale of general worth. To understand the regularity with which social inequalities occur in school achievement and hence in access to higher education, it is not enough to lay bare the processes that accumulate wealth in certain schools and impoverish others.[6] How the curriculum is constructed over time, the values that animate it and the demands framed within it are all crucial in the production of social inequality. From one point of view, these processes are even more important because of the illusion of impartiality and neutrality created by a curriculum that is authoritative and coercive.[7]

The post-war period has seen large increases in average levels of schooling and significant improvements in access to some of the most demanding areas of the curriculum. Yet successive reforms in English, mathematics and chemistry—key subjects whose history is examined in this study—have not led to a reduction in social inequalities.[8] Overall growth has occurred without weakening the advantages enjoyed by the most well-educated families. On the curriculum side, this is because the focus of reform always tends to fall on underlying quality of learning—not simply more modern content—and this presents a major pedagogical challenge, pursued under very unequal conditions.

Syllabus writers have an implicit view about the ideal student, and the pursuit of this ideal governs their choice of content, the relative stress placed on different tasks, the compression of content and the implied pace of teaching. Whether in English or chemistry, mathematics or modern languages, an image is formed of the young scholar–intellectual. Exams and other tests require students to project this image: to display an ability to understand principles, to apply rules correctly, to handle novel situations, to manage form or genre, to decipher code, to reason soundly, and in general to manipulate the properties of the materials entrusted to them, whether symbolic, lexical, mathematical, grammatical or logical.

These requirements on higher-order conceptual growth span the different disciplines and are often formulated in very general language that is not easily interpreted pedagogically—the capacity for abstraction, the ability to synthesize, analytical skills, creativity, imagination, the capacity to develop perspective and so on. Teachers aim to cultivate these behaviours, but are constrained by the cultural demands implicit in them, which many students cannot satisfy under routine classroom conditions. Language facility, attentiveness, achievement motivation, self-confidence in learning, personal organization and self-direction, capacity to learn for intrinsic satisfaction rather than extrinsic interest—these elements of the scholarly disposition are fundamental to success in the more academic areas of the curriculum. But they are linked closely to an educated life-style and arise from the continuous and informal training given by families rather than explicit and methodical instruction in school.

The academic curriculum reaches through the cognitive architecture of the school subject, with its conceptual richness and masses of data, to these sustaining personal attributes, which it then shapes into a scholastic identity—the mathematics student, the writer, the science student, the historian. The pursuit of expertise is the process through which intellectual training is conducted. While this is often overtly linked with careers and economic gain and appears as a goal in itself, the real object is cultural. Secondary education, as Durkheim told intending teachers in 1905 returning to the closeted world of the lycée, is not about producing mathematicians, literary critics, physicists or biologists. The aim is to train the mind, the spirit. The field of expertise—literature, history, mathematics or science—is merely a setting in which to create intellectuals, thinkers.[9] So the task for the curriculum is to stimulate conceptual growth, independent reasoning, the capacity to see the whole picture, to detect relationships, to find new ways forward.[10] Syllabus writers and examiners have accepted this mission, and teachers have correctly drawn the fundamental implication that they are to mediate between the conceptual demands laid up in the curriculum and the family cultural resources available to the average student in their class.

Given the basic concern of the curriculum—to create thinkers able to regenerate knowledge—conceptual growth has been the priority of syllabus reform over the whole period since Durkheim, during which secondary education has evolved into a mass system. Indeed depth of understanding and theoretical insight have become more emphasized as knowledge itself has become more complex and prolific, breaking down disciplinary boundaries and appealing to a general intelligence. Teachers as a result have been stretched ever further between conceptual structure and family culture. They it is who have to compensate for the gaps between what the curriculum expects to find in students—conceptual depth and a scholarly outlook and habits—and who students really are.

The sharply varying conditions under which teachers work often undermine the intellectual ideal that drives the syllabus writer and the examiner. Moreover, the competitive context tends to accentuate those aspects of the ideal that enable good students to be compared and ranked against each other, whether this involves the simultaneous management of complex concepts and numerical operations in chemistry or the felicitous blending of philosophical and stylistic virtues in English. So the ideal is continually refined against a diminishing image of the merely average, the mediocre student, drawn almost inevitably from the new populations completing school. The mediating role of the teacher becomes ever more onerous. Too frequently corrupted by the search for academic distinction in privileged settings, it is too frequently overwhelmed by the scale and persistence of scholastic failure in others.

If curriculum reform always tends to re-create an intellectual ideal, ignoring the implicit historical and cultural basis on which this ideal has taken form, it has also been conducted largely without reference to the school system as a social structure within which the ideal has to be realized. Examiners have known at least since the 1940s that there are marked and systematic differences in student achievement, for example between city and country, but successive revisions to senior school programmes have not been made with a view to improving the quality of learning of the weakest groups.[11] Until the late 1980s the emphasis was always on improved knowledge in the syllabus, not improved learning in the student.

Not only has the social map of achievement been ignored—thus compelling teachers to make do with the design or abandon the student—but the syllabus has usually been planned for upward integration into university studies, even though most students completing school from the mid-1960s onwards did not enter university. Programmes to integrate schooling with work or vocational training, such as the school-based Technical Year 12 courses introduced in Victoria in 1982, have been confined to the margins or have disappeared. Vertical integration has not only meant that syllabus content is constantly displaced downwards from university to school, but has also indefinitely prolonged the principle according to which universities alone have power over the curriculum, while schools alone have responsibility for student learning. Universities, through positional politics and prestige rather than formal authority, effectively control the programmes taught in senior secondary school, but they accept no responsibility for quality of achievement at this level. Conversely, teachers are accountable for how well students learn, but have no control over the design of the programmes they teach. Universities select students on the basis of prediction of success. Schools have to produce success to serve a university teaching regime that is as archaic as it is authoritarian. The vertical relationship between university and school, and the tendency towards hierarchy and pedagogical uniformity within the university system itself, aggravate competitive pressures within the school curriculum, reinforcing those aspects of form and content that offer academic discrimination, not intellectual growth.[12]

Curriculum reform without structural reform leaves institutional power relationships intact and simultaneously subordinates the teaching task in schools to the prestige needs of universities. Equally, the failure to evaluate school programmes in terms of the relative social outcomes they produce sustains the fiction that there are no substantial resource differences between schools, or that any such differences are irrelevant. All that disadvantaged students need are good teachers.

This is exactly the opposite of what parents think. They know that a hierarchical curriculum demands a stratified school system, containing fortified sites where the advantages of education and culture can be deposited, pooled and pedagogically multiplied, and exposed sites where failure will and must accumulate to balance its eradication from the strongholds of selective schooling. It is not the intellectual demands of the curriculum as such that are problematic, but their imposition without parallel improvements in how the weakest students learn and without controls over how power is exercised by the strongest students and their institutional patrons. Without reforms to the conditions under which working-class, rural, migrant and Aboriginal children learn and to the structures that split curriculum control from pedagogical responsibility, even the most thorough revision of syllabus content and assessment methodology will tend to reproduce social inequalities of achievement and subordinate individual development to social domination.

In the past, popular access to secondary education was blocked by lack of provision and lack of means. Children from poor families could climb the narrow ladder of opportunity offered by a handful of scholarships, but they could win these only by displaying academic qualities that were uncharacteristic of their origins and more typical of the social ranks they would enter through education. They had to pass a cultural test to compensate for their lack of income and modest social position. Imposing cultural tests on children was a way of preserving the integrity of the dominant social strata, whose ranks were fed from different streams (landed wealth, mercantile wealth, the liberal professions), which were unified and distinguished by their shared cultural life. Scholarships were thus tests of fitness to enter a way of life, not simply to enter a school. The Schools Inquiry Commission of 1869 argued the case with elegant simplicity when it rejected the notion that the poor should not have to compete with the rich in scholarship exams. On the contrary, the Commission said:

> [The] best test of all is that the competitors should be pitted against [others] of the very class into which they are to make their way . . . If the son of a labourer can beat the sons of gentlemen that goes a long way to prove that he is capable of using with advantage the education usually given to gentlemen.[13]

Today access to secondary education is universal, but this has only tended to amplify the role of cultural selection, not abolish it. The poor now have to demonstrate their capacities by rising up the curriculum rather than by passing scholarship tests. Equally, the rich must and can prove their academic superiority through the hierarchical structure of the curriculum and the stratified systems of selective schooling serving it.

The reforms of the curriculum over the past half-century, while modernizing the content of programmes, have preserved the principle of cultural selection. This is not because reformers were seeking to resist the social effects of mass secondary education, though more than one prophet of cultural doom has risen from the ranks of examiners.[14] Rather it is because reforms or revisions were made without regard to the learning experience of different student groups and the pedagogical experience of teachers working in different settings. Nor did reformers adequately consider how school subjects were used once put into operation in the school system. Most of the post-war changes to chemistry, for example, were made to improve the knowledge base of scientific research, but the best students in chemistry shunned research for more lucrative professions. Curriculum changes worked in practice to support an economically secure and culturally rich way of life, and they could work in this way because the intellectual demands stored up in school programmes were assumed to be equally manageable by all student groups, where in fact they could be managed well by only a minority. Given that no steps were taken to test this assumption, while at the same time policy measures were applied to economically stratify the school systems that delivered the curriculum, the conclusion is inescapable. Curriculum reform has been governed by a collective bad faith. Juxtaposing the intellectual investment in curriculum over the past fifty years with the social patterns of student achievement arising from it— the purpose of this book—captures this divided enterprise of framing the scholarly ideal, only to betray it. If curriculum is a test of students, what is the test of curriculum? Is it the ever-greater depth of understanding that describes the evolution of academic subjects? Or is it the ever-greater social spread of learning without which societies cannot cohere democratically, and without which theory must remain the servant of privilege?

2

English in the 1940s: A Service Course for the Professions

English in the utilitarian tradition

In 1943 the University of Melbourne created a compulsory subject, English Expression, to examine the powers of thought and expression of its matriculation candidates. It thus banished the literary heritage to a specialized domain of the curriculum and settled on an unambiguously technical view of English as an instrument of logic and rhetoric.[1] This reversion to the earliest utilitarian impulses behind the teaching of English challenged the stronger current, running from the seventeenth and eighteenth centuries, that defended the place of English literature in the curriculum as the 'poor man's Classics'.[2]

In colonial Australia, the English taught to the children of educated families was indeed a child of classical education, emphasizing moral reflection and the cultivation of judgement and discrimination through the study of great works.[3] The training of the mind through grammar, then through logic and rhetoric, reached a still higher plane when human purpose was explored through literary and dramatic art. The new subject of English Expression would be content with more modest objectives. It was about the skilful use of the machinery of language for examining ideas, assembling arguments and making them persuasive. Clarity, precision and direction were its principles, correctness in language, punctuation and spelling, and coherence of thought. Style was defined mainly by orderliness: simplicity of construction, the proper use of paragraphs, connectedness of ideas and thematic integrity—features that distinguished a good and serviceable prose, engineering rather than art, academic rather than literary work. Beyond this, the business end of English, lay the imaginative world of literature, with its themes, heroic and malevolent, which gave human experience depth. This was a world created not by the journeyman's craft of plans and paragraphs, precept and precision, but by a magical art of parable and allegory, metaphor and illusion. Literature, loved by many, could be taught to few.[4]

Tempting as it may be to see this retreat from the morally formative powers of great literature as the renunciation of a cultural ideal, the writers of the new subject had, on the contrary, found in the technical facilities of English a more functional and vigorous way of reasserting this ideal and imposing it on all matriculants, whatever their professional destinations. In reviving the older utilitarian tradition, they would not abandon literary culture. Indeed they expressly reminded teachers that 'satisfactory progress in the writing of English is not possible where the study is divorced from the reading and appreciation of English literature'.[5] But by focusing on logic, comprehension and composition, they could expose the whole of the senior school population to the discipline in logical and moral reasoning that these skills involved. Literature, whose authentic course lay beyond the classroom, could not play this role. When forced to do so, as when it was assessed under examination conditions, it quickly degenerated into artificiality.[6]

Nor was the formal emphasis of the new subject—its preoccupation with order, coherence, correctness and precision—an admission that the cultural level of the average matriculant was too low to demand more noble qualities. A Harvard inquiry, begun in 1939, had reached this conclusion, not only about students, but about their teachers as well.[7] But secondary education in Australia was not an emerging mass system; the 10 per cent of the teenage population who presented themselves to the examiners in the 1940s were future leaders and professionals. There was an implicit pact between them and the university that in exchange for the scientific or humanist training that they sought, they would raise themselves to the ideal of the liberal thinker upon whom the whole of scientific and humanist culture ultimately rested.[8] The formal properties of English were a measure of progress toward this goal. When candidates submitted themselves to the requirements of structure, logical development, thematic integrity, accuracy and precision, they showed that they could transcend their own narrowness as individuals and begin to think and write in a universal capacity. This justified their claims on a university education.

Examinations and professorial expectations

The creation of a subject in which logical and grammatical rectitude were paramount meant that the examinations in English Expression would be tests of the whole person.[9] Skills of argument, exposition, organization and expression needed suitable material to be displayed to a high degree, and that material was the topic chosen by the candidate in the test of composition.

The scale of topics was a guide to intellectual level. The candidates described by the examiners in 1944 as the 'most immature' chose to write about Safety First—'lacking ideas, they laboured the point of the dangers of modern traffic'.[10] Ascending the scale, the topic on the 'state of education' attracted a large group, many of whom had read their newspapers but could not synthesize the material—they 'failed to develop one central or unifying idea to which the details might be related and subordinated'. Others, writing on the topic of a referendum, could not develop a position and were merely 'reproducing arguments caught up from the papers or fireside discussion and not fully understood or seen in proper perspective'. At the apex were the candidates who announced truly intellectual qualities by addressing topics that provided the greatest scope for learned reflection and skilful use of language—the proposition that 'every man is the architect of his own fortune' or the claim that 'it is not the form, but the administration of government that ultimately matters'.

If the seriousness and the complexity of topics chosen for composition enabled candidates to be measured on a scale of maturity, so did their attitudes to the use of language. Most candidates, the examiners complained in 1944, 'were absurdly severe about anything which at all approached persuasive language'.[11] The dangers of emotive terms having been drummed into their heads, they had not learnt how to infuse argument with interest and feeling. Rhetoric was the most dangerous terrain for school students to enter because it taxed both language and culture. When required to reveal a breadth of thought and a capacity for sustained argument that could not mature in a classroom alone, they took refuge in a dogged insistence on rules laid down by Fowler and Herbert 'which had to be observed at all costs', attacking the prescribed samples of 'clear thinking' in exclusively logical rather than literary terms.[12]

Labouring under the 'delusion that all emotionally coloured language is a BAD THING', the average student renounced emotional appeal and psychological effect as incompatible with sound thinking.[13] Only those candidates who had acquired a different attitude to language and who had learnt to use it in more generous measure could avoid the pedantry that arose from exclusive reliance on classroom instruction. 'The best candidates wrote freely and with imagination, but at the same time produced work that possessed the qualities of relevance, order and coherence.'[14] They knew how to balance reason and emotion, to dissect with words, but also to entice with words.[15] In the quality of their language, in their appreciation of the form of an academic exercise, and in the posture of intellectual detachment on which the management of form rested, these students set themselves apart. Meanwhile, the mass of candidates, for whom academic writing was too obviously artificial, betrayed their lack of refinement by their 'laboured, wordy and repetitious manner' or by 'lack of order', 'garbled information', 'muddled' argument, 'wild claims' or rigid sticking to the rules.[16]

The examiners were explicit about the virtues that the best students in English should exhibit—'capable and sincere expression', 'evidence of wide and thoughtful reading', 'orderliness and systematic treatment', 'clear, discriminating and critical thinking'. These they saw coming together in the key attribute of 'maturity'. A candidate displayed maturity in choosing serious topics to write about, in careful arrangement of the essay, in the fuller view of language as a servant of both logic and rhetoric, in the tone of the essay (again serious and sincere), in balance and impartiality (but also in resolution and conviction) and finally in originality of ideas or perspective.

The tendency for these different attributes to cohere, producing a summary impression of the person, can be seen in how the examiners calibrated the scale of performance in English composition in 1944. The top 10 per cent of candidates presented ideas that were 'original', but also 'well-illustrated' and in a style that was 'pleasing'.[17] Those in the middle band were undistinguished but 'consistent' in their efforts and 'competent' in writing. Below this group came the one in five candidates who had an 'immature' outlook and could write with only limited success. At the bottom of the scale was a large group—one in four students—who were two years below matriculation standard. Their effrontery in attempting the exam gave the Chief Examiner ample scope for delicious ridicule, as with the luckless candidate of 'true Malaprop genius' in whose school 'capital punishment had proved an excellent method of building character'.[18]

If maturity expressed a complex of traits representing the high point of achievement in English, it also implied a complex process of personal development. The kinds of language behaviour it arose from eluded methodical treatment by the teacher. The weakest students, certainly, could be saved by 'Much drilling . . . not only in the cultivation of clarity and precision . . . but also in the elementary mechanics of good composition'.[19] Teaching to prescribed texts was effective and produced the great crop of students who knew the contents of their books thoroughly and were aware of the human significance of the topics that the books addressed. But to advance beyond a knowledge of the facts, beyond the all-too-rehearsed justifications of a theme, required an attitude to the material and a use of language that could not be instilled in the classroom, however closely the examiners' demands were studied, codified and subjected to routine.

Breadth of reading, for example, was the key to transcending an 'immature outlook'. But in which social settings were students most likely to change their tastes, giving up comics, adventure stories and romances for novels of psychological depth and moral tension? Certainly English teachers and school libraries supported the shift in reading preferences towards 'serious' literature—for leaving school early meant being trapped in adolescent tastes, the adult equivalents of historical romances, *Biggles*, Charteris, Cheyney and Westerns. But it was also the homes in which history, biography, travel and the modern novel were part of a reading culture that would anticipate and prepare this shift.[20] When the English examiners demanded 'imagination harnessed to a definite purpose', they were looking to the results of a sustained apprenticeship in the art of framing thoughts for an educated audience, a training that made language flow confidently and freely, not only because of a learned vocabulary acquired precociously, but because of an inner confidence in playing an adult role.[21] Like a foreign tongue, the language of ideas required continuous personal interactions with educated speech partners and the shaping of a disposition to use speech as a mark of education. Only then would its characteristic signs of 'sincerity' and 'connectedness', of 'ease, grace and precision' appear in place of the 'dullness' and 'laboriousness' that signalled an initiation confined to the classroom. Mastery of academic form was indeed a matter of maturity. But what mattered was not so much the years of a child's growth as the social and institutional climate in which growth took place. Maturity, as judged by the literary and intellectual values enshrined in the curriculum, owed much to personal experience of a style of life in which facility with words and concepts was an explicit and continuing point of culture.

Children who had learnt 'proper speech' only at school could not manage academic prose. Encouraged by their poorly educated parents, who were anxious to see them do well, they wrote in a characteristic stilted style.[22] They could not meet the academic demands of 'ease' and 'naturalness' because, not having incorporated the lexis, tones, subtleties and distinctions of essay language into everyday speech, they tended to view the essay as a kind of showcase for literary display and affectation. Nor did their choice of topics qualify them as 'serious' scholars, for serious topics demanded an appropriate register of language, a formal vocabulary of Latin and Greek roots, a literary-posture and dialectic, without which candidates would produce only a stumbling, confused caricature. 'Modes of speech', Ballard observed in his *Teaching and*

Testing English (1939), 'cannot be learnt *in abstracto*: they can only be learnt in conjunction with the ideas they are meant to convey'.[23] Style of language was a servant of the intellectual level of the home.

Focusing the English syllabus on formal strengths of composition, logic and comprehension did not relieve students of aesthetic demands. Rather it privileged the qualities most highly prized by teachers of academic English, not the values sought after by novelists, dramatists or poets. English style, interpreted academically, had to be 'natural', emotions had to be carefully controlled (though not absent), the links between ideas had to be explicit, structure rather than mood or psychological experience was important. In short, it was an aesthetic to mark the difference, sometimes subtle, sometimes sharp, between scholar and artist, pedagogue and poet. To write in the vein of a teacher—inspirational, yet formal—was an art learnt from masters of rhetoric in the salon–theatre of the classroom, but by apprentices whose language and love of words had been fashioned at home so that they should grow in the esteem of their masters.

It was not only in the criteria of literary quality that the examiners betrayed their cultural allegiance. Their choice of how to assess student learning was equally revealing. Just as classical education found its measure in the epigram aptly quoted, so modern education needed a touchstone, a test of those properties of intelligence and expression that cohered inextricably in the trained mind. This was the essay, the favoured instrument of assessment in English—and in other subjects, such as history, that demanded discussion. The place of essays in the armoury of the English examiner shows that the stress on formal properties over literary accomplishment was only half-hearted. Reading essays, markers wanted 'imagination' and a 'pleasing' or at any rate 'agreeable' style,[24] along with good architectural qualities that converged on narrative. They sought the signs that the candidate lived conversant with a world of books, and like every reader of a story they also demanded feelings, the evidence of 'sincerity' without which they themselves could feel no involvement. These many virtues originate in conversation rather than writing, and can only be coaxed from their origins by literary art. Without them, the immature scholar's essay becomes a confused drama of production and a nightmare of assessment.

Although the teaching of English emphasized 'intellectual training' not art, the examination of student learning in English steadfastly refused to follow suit.[25] Examiners clung to the essay—poor sampler of learning criteria, subjective in standards, unreliable—because it allowed them to see in a candidate's work exactly what they wanted to see: the person of the candidate, the whole story. Because essays tested so many aspects of student learning—but above all the ability to create a single, coherent and compelling argument—they measured the extent to which the student writer fulfilled a cultural ideal. It was not the qualities of thought and expression taken in isolation that mattered, but the unifying powers of intelligence and feeling behind the work. Mastery of particular knowledge and skills in English could have been measured using short, focused tests (for vocabulary, sentence construction, punctuation, grammar), as could logical abilities.[26] But the cultural ideal towards which the whole of secondary education worked was a creative and independent thinker, a mind whose capacity to formulate ideas, marshal argument and evidence, and engage human feelings could not be measured except through a whole work of intellectual production. To the examiners, the essay was a unique vehicle for fashioning this cultural ideal in schools and testing its realization at the end. So it was the very uncertainty of the essay that ensured it would be retained.[27]

Exam results and the performance of schools

Essay writing testified to the completion of a certain style of intellectual training in which powers of synthesis and exposition were paramount, but this cultural ideal was not equally attainable from all sites within the school system. Furthermore, the framing of the ideal itself was influenced by the examiners' personal experience as former teachers and method lecturers at work in some of the most privileged locations of the system. The cultural ideal of the good English student was not an empty hypothesis, but a historical model built upon a real institutional basis. The notion that it could be diffused beyond this base represented the hypothetical element, as can be seen from the distribution of English results over different types of school.

The standards of literary and intellectual judgement imposed by the University of Melbourne examiners worked well for students in the oldest-established secondary schools, whether public schools of the English type or selective state high schools. In the main, these were great urban foundations, and their students' success in English partly reflected the fact that living in a large city gave their students access to literary and artistic pursuits—pursuits that could also be reproduced in a boarding-school environment. By contrast, students living in country districts could expect below-average results, and boys had a greater risk of failure. But it was in qualifying for the highest praise of the examiners that country students were distinctly disadvantaged. No less active readers than their city cousins—in fact, more avid consumers of newspapers[28]—they betrayed their remoteness from academic culture by their weaker success in gaining honours. Those who attended Victorian country schools rather than boarding in the city represented 27 per cent of all full candidates for the matriculation certificate in 1947, but gained only 18 per cent of first-class honours.[29]

The top students in English attended a small group of private and selective-entry public high schools located in Melbourne. More than half of all first-class honours given to full candidates for the matriculation certificate went to just five schools—Melbourne Boys' High School, Wesley College, Scotch College, MacRobertson Girls' High School and Presbyterian Ladies' College. Together with Geelong Grammar, the Academy of Mary Immaculate and University High School, these accounted for more than two-thirds of students gaining the highest marks in English Expression.

The distance between these large establishments, with their socially selected intakes, and the many small schools, especially district high schools and Catholic colleges, was most marked among boys. Aiming at careers in engineering, agriculture, architecture, medicine, dentistry and science, boys tended to focus their efforts on physics, chemistry and mathematics. Because these subjects were savagely marked in the late 1940s, students could not give the same attention to English in the final crucial year of examinations. The small groups of boys from lower middle-class or skilled

manual workers' families who attended local high schools or
Catholic schools had few cultural or linguistic advantages and
were heavily dependent on success in mathematics and physical
sciences. Upper middle-class boys, oriented more to the professions of law and medicine, commonly did a 'second Sixth' for
broadening and leadership, and their cultural background enabled
them to excel in the humanities—or at least to dabble in them
without fear of failure. But in provincial Ballarat or Geelong, in
rural Shepparton or Castlemaine, in industrial Northcote, casualties were frequent, and failure sometimes more common than success. At Northcote Boys' High School, 37 per cent failed English
Expression; at Geelong High School, 40 per cent of boys; at
Ballarat, every third boy, at Dandenong, 31 per cent, while at St
Pat's in the country town of Sale, 53 per cent dipped out. Some
small high schools proved exceptional. These were schools with
locational advantages or those such as Bendigo High, which had
usurped the role of the provincial grammar school and could
boast outstanding results. But these few schools were eclipsed by
the very much larger institutions—public and private—that could
take whole classes of boys to a standard in English approaching
the achievements of girls (see Figure 1).

Schools: the institutional basis of a cultural ideal

If such a small number of schools tended to monopolize high academic honours in English, this was because the curriculum as interpreted by the university examiners implied a cultural model of
the successful student towards which these schools could realistically work. The characteristics of high achievement in English—
creative and independent thought, mature and confident use of
language, mastery of the essay as a unified and persuasive argument—were built into the curriculum as authoritative expectations. While these expectations were doubtless tests of what had
to be achieved in English, they were also resources—assets—for
those students whose life-style and school ethos supported the cultural ideal of the liberal intellectual.

Figure 1: Matriculation English results for boys, 1947, by school

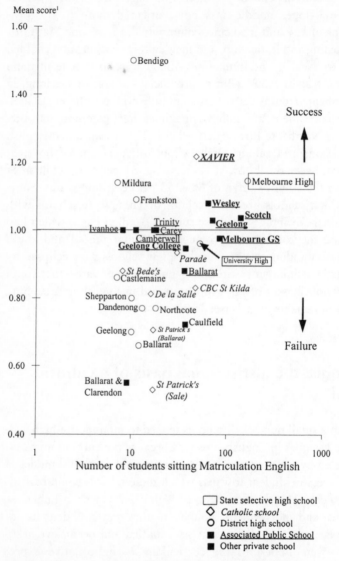

Mean score[1]

Number of students sitting Matriculation English

☐ State selective high school
◇ *Catholic school*
○ District high school
■ <u>Associated Public School</u>
■ Other private school

[1] Scale: 0 = fail, 1 = pass, 2 = 2nd-class honours, 3 = 1st-class honours

Source: Unpublished Matriculation results for 1947 matched with individual school records. See R. Teese, 'Curriculum hierarchy, private schooling and the segmentation of Australian secondary education, 1947–1985', p. 406.

In pursuing this ideal as the standard of excellence, the examiners were building up the curriculum as a historical infrastructure, designed implicitly for students whose cultural characteristics enabled them to exploit it. But students could not expect to do so acting in isolation. The social effects of examinations do not lie simply in the cultural model of the successful student imposed by examiners through their preference for one set of learning criteria over others. Equally vital are the schools established to conserve a life-style and a community of interest. Many families, Findlay wrote in 1932:

> attain a standard of culture by which they set great store, let it be the merest social veneer or the more solid attributes of good taste ... every such family, as a stock, prizes these elements as a valuable part of education, and is solicitous that schooling shall promote their continuance or at the least shall not destroy them.[30]

By pooling their resources in schools, the most educated families and those with the greatest social prestige create an environment that not only presents their own children with a binding model of behaviour, but promotes this model as the only legitimate end in education. Selective schooling enables parents to combine their resources and organize their efforts around the model of the successful student installed in the curriculum. These schools, by the standards they set, vindicate the examiners' expectations, which are always formulated in terms of what individuals should achieve, but in reality are based on what institutions routinely achieve for particular groups of students.

How schools mobilize pupil and teacher resources—especially those that impart particular strategic advantages—reacts on the curriculum in the way learning requirements are interpreted and enforced. Was it simply a good understanding of the demands of the English curriculum that led J. S. Darling, headmaster of Geelong Grammar School, to impose 4000-word essays on his matriculation boys?[31] Or did he also influence the examiners' own requirements by presenting them with candidates who had been drilled in the philosophical high end of the curriculum by a master of divinity and rhetoric?

'Authority has its source in God and not in man', was one of Darling's sixth-form essay topics: 'no man and no group of men has in itself the right to govern others'.[32] Such a topic struck deeply at the maturity of the class, transcending the narrower requirements of the syllabus and calling on the cultural training that his Anglican boarding school dispensed to future political and civic leaders. The cultural training provided through such vehicles as the Public Affairs Society and the Areopagus made the most academic tasks an integral and successful part of school life. Darling's charges would often do well in English because the school's classical emphasis provided many outlets for fine speaking—from the routine chapel services through to the Shakespearian productions and the pageant plays.[33] Writing too was given every encouragement—by the poet masters, the librarians, the literary editors (*If*, *If Revived* and so on). Geelong Grammar School could be proud of its string of poets, writers and historians as well as its Prime Ministers (with their oratorical predilections).

Not that the culture of fine words was confined to this school, with its rural acres and its provincial lassitude, which Latin, art, music, drama and oratory, sacred and profane, were called upon to dispel.[34] The great boarding schools that were members of the elite Associated Public Schools might have needed the arts to bond their communities together, but other academically powerful establishments—above all the selective-entry senior public high schools—also promoted a literary and intellectual culture. University High School—a practice school for the training of teachers—had its Modern Languages Club, its Green and Tan Dramatic Club (for past pupils), its Debating Club, History Club, Dramatic Club, United Nations Club, Literature Society, Gilbert and Sullivan Society, Public Questions Society, its *Ubique*, its form dramas and school plays, its enviable music programme and its annual Shakespeare Day.[35] These activities belonged to an age when the culture of eloquence and its corollary, the training of the voice, were a fuller, more overt and more conscious part of the task of social refinement through education. English was never merely a subject, never merely the language of instruction: it was an end in itself, an explicit object of art and personal culture as well as a badge of academic honour.

3

Cultural Ideal and School Systems: English in the 1970s

> *Socrates:* To make the common people philosophical was never my aim: I dared not hope for that. I left them crude, corrupted, wallowing in error, and confined myself to educating some few disciples, cultivated minds in search of the principles behind sound morals. I never wished to write anything, and I found that teaching was best done by the spoken word.
>
> *Fénelon*, Dialogues des morts

The academies where the art of the essay flourished in a circle of intimacy were far removed from the pauper schools of the 1960s where essay-writing was also to take root.[1] At Brunswick Girls' High School in inner-city Melbourne, every second student beginning school was at least two years behind the reading standard and every third was three years behind.[2] The school was not for 'academic' children but for working-class migrant girls, for whom the pinnacle of studies was the commercial stream. But they too studied English, and from a syllabus framed in an academic tradition that had been no part of their historical experience. Their teachers had been introduced to English as a firm body of school knowledge, ascending from the rudiments of grammar to the principles of good style and the architecture of the essay. As pupils in secondary schools, they had been presented with the edifice of rules and principles confidently set forth in the *Handbook of English for Junior and Intermediate Pupils in Victorian Secondary Schools* (at least seven printings) by Aughterson, Aughterson and

Stirling, the principal author for many years senior examiner in Matriculation English Expression.[3] Form and taste, feeling and intelligence were inherent in the codes elaborated by the syllabus writers of English and transposed into the classroom by teachers, often using the driest techniques in the most unpromising contexts.[4] But as the ambit of English widened, the settings in which post-war teachers went to work diverged radically from those in which their subject had acquired its historical force.

The curriculum, with its stress on the intellectual and artistic strengths of good English prose, drew its implicit standard from the achievements of an institution such as the Collegiate School of St Peter in Adelaide. In the depths of the 1930s Depression, St Peter's guided its pupils towards the 'right choices' in literature and ensured that they could 'make explicit the grounds of their judgements'.[5] This was decades ahead of the slum school of the 1960s, with its low standards of literacy. The curriculum, however, not only demanded that teachers bridge this gulf, but also denied its own complicity in consolidating and legitimizing the great historical divide between such schools.

Destitute schools undermined the pedagogical illusion of a curriculum without history. Trends in teaching in the 1960s—wide reading, drama, creative writing, thematic studies—were reactions to the twin abstractions demanded by the English syllabus. Meaning had been sacrificed to form, and personal experience to intellectual role (the good thinker, the capable writer).[6] It is a measure of the deep, socially specific roots of this philosophy that, when confronted by a growing and diversifying school population in the post-war years, English should disintegrate at the most exposed sites in the school system. In not a few schools—but especially the junior technical schools—English disappeared as a separate timetabled subject. Its traditional rhetorical emphasis on 'insight and fluency' proved unsustainable as class sizes rose, migrant and working-class children took their places in ramshackle accommodation, untrained teachers took charge of overcrowded classrooms, and cloakrooms and corridors were pressed into service.[7] Teachers could not retreat into the conceptual order of English. Despite its book codifications, it had no real hierarchy of branches, no indubitable truths or principles that could confidently be defended against change, no redoubts on which a kind of intellectual resistance could be mounted. Lacking the calm interiority of mathematics or the majesty of science, English had no inner recess, no vaults of facts to be emburdened upon unwelcome pupils crowding in on its circle.

Doubts about English spread well beyond the despised enclave of the technical school. More than one-third of all English teachers (37 per cent) believed that their subject had 'no content of its own', and a further 8 per cent could not be sure if it did. They doubted whether English should be preserved as a separate discipline, rejected the idea that literature should be the central purpose of the subject, and dismissed examinations as incompatible with pedagogical objectives. They placed a strong functional emphasis on English, wanted correctness in speech and writing, but on the other hand refused to accept that 'practical writing' should dominate lessons. The poetic or imaginative use of writing was the most important element.[8] Hesitant, the English teacher would not renounce the love of literature learnt at school nor betray it by assessing it through exams, would not abandon rectitude of form (knowing the consequences) nor rule the classroom with it. Fluid over these many dimensions, English threatened to slip away into Drama or Integrated Studies or Communication or Media Studies. If it kept its name and place in most schools, this was because it was a symbol of pedagogical order to conservative-minded parents and the most transparent medium through which to view student achievement, or at any rate to construct a view of it that had the most transparent appeal. But inside school, English would never be fully respected as a subject. Source of shame for pupils who could not speak or write correctly or who had no taste for ideas, it lacked the solid architecture of facts and principles on which the prestige of the sciences rested.

Reasserting the place of academic English

The turbulence of classroom experiment and social change shaking the lower forms of secondary school did not spare the matriculation syllabus. While control over the syllabus remained firmly in university hands through a Board biased towards the academic schools, bureaucratic power alone could not protect the subject. The very fact that English lacked the firm, hierarchical structure of science or school mathematics or languages worked against the top-down assertion of the discipline's authority and exposed curriculum committees to professional influences rising up from below. After all, there was no university department of English Expression. Departments of English were concerned with literature, or were dabbling with linguistics, not with the menial tasks of how to write properly and reason well.

In the mid-1960s these stirrings turned to action, and in 1968 a revised syllabus was issued. The big departure was the emphasis on wide reading, anchored to a major theme. Previously, students wrote on a topic of interest to them and read three out of a prescribed eight books. The number of books was now lifted to seven out of thirteen, and these were trained on a unifying theme—'The Family' (1968), 'The Dedicated Life' (1969), 'Authority and the Individual' (1970).[9]

There was now greater freedom for students to read and develop their interests, and also more unpredictability, which the syllabus writers insisted upon to promote authentic learning rather than exam preparation. To the frustration and disappointment of teachers, however, the core of the examination was still made up of a short essay, clear-thinking exercises and a mix of questions on comprehension, vocabulary and prescribed books. Had not the intellectual integrity of the clear-thinking task been irretrievably undermined by research and criticism, local and overseas?[10] Where was the response to international research on language achievement and socio-economic status, and the recognition that the old course had failed so many working-class students, especially those in technical schools?[11] To some it seemed that no real progress had been made at all.

But in fact the syllabus had moved much further than the structure of the examinations might suggest. The centrality of the organizing theme shifted attention from the text as a vehicle of expression to the social or psychological phenomena addressed by the text. To leave no doubt about this, teachers were reminded in February 1969 that the examinations required essays, not about the books—literary objects—but about the topics themselves.[12] This emphasis on the student as observer of the world brought forcefully to the surface the English examiners' long-standing concern for the intellectual quality of the student. The examiners wanted the measure of the student as a thinker and communicator, not the student's measure of the quality of books. English reasserted its historical mission of training the intellectual. If it demanded corporate respect for its values, which breached all discipline boundaries while erecting none of its own, it would also demand cultural adherence from the populations now colonizing secondary education, whatever the price and however little they might share its vision or accept its mandate.

In 1971 the Chief Examiner, looking back over the decades, saw that English—the only compulsory subject, but one that was not taken seriously—would continue to occupy an insecure place in the curriculum so long as its technical or 'service' orientation was stressed. The name of the subject was changed. Expression was dropped from the title. English was a cultural heritage. That was why all students had to study it.[13]

English was a radical concept in the curriculum. It aimed at the transformation of the learner, not just an expansion of knowledge and comprehension. The cultural heritage that it contained could not be communicated without changing the student. That was the point. By enlarging the individual's field of experience through literature—fiction and non-fiction—and by exposing this experience to analysis and interpretation, English created a new person with wider sensibilities, greater depth and range of feelings, heightened perception, acuteness of thought and judgement. English was about the transmission of a cultural ideal—the mature thinker, the builder of perspective, the maker of ideas, the speaker and the listener in whom the thoughts and feelings of others could run, freed by sympathy, but abated by judgement.

The cultural project of changing the person could be represented with greater confidence in the 1970s because of sweeping changes in outlook. The relative calm and provincialism of Australia in the early post-war years had gone. Authority and institutions, the limits of moral and political obligation, the exercise of social and political power were widely questioned. Candidates for

English were set to work on topics that reflected the new social and political consciousness—conscription for the Vietnam war, women's liberation, the generation gap. More, not less, would be demanded of students by way of intellectual training, because they themselves demanded a more influential role in society.

English moved more explicitly towards moral discourse. Underlying the issues that candidates were expected to discuss were fundamental ethical questions. The examiners set these out in their 1977 report so that teachers should be in no doubt about the final aims of English: 'What is our basic nature? What is the extent of our responsibility for our actions? What is the extent of our responsibility for the actions of others? By what means should we fulfil our responsibilities to others, whatever their relationship with us? What courses of action are open when various responsibilities conflict with one another?'[14]

Candidates in the 1940s had been expected to display philosophical sensitivity—the capacity to see broader issues of principle beyond particular topics—but the examiners now wanted to see a more active philosophical engagement with books. Texts were selected to enable students to reason about human purpose and behaviour, about social order and responsibility. English was a source of philosophical training, and if no classical texts were recommended for reading, the examiners might well offer candidates crumbs from the philosopher's table. These, like the epigram from the first chapter of Rousseau's *The Social Contract*, distinguished the students who understood that they were to reason about high purpose from those who could not transcend the pettiness of their own particular concerns—the candidates who chained man to the 'speed limit and social etiquette'. The better students understood the tone of Rousseau, and only required the tone—not the text, which they had not read—to expatiate upon themes as lofty as the original, whatever that might happen to have been. They 'rose . . . to consider the presence and power of "spiritual" chains in contemporary society'.[15] Similarly, the tone of the topic on the 'seventies as the era in which man was pursued by evils of his own creating' stimulated the best writers to adopt a trans-historical perspective, leaving behind the majority of students who could see no further than environmental pollution. The philosophically sophisticated, correctly reading the tone of the topic, viewed the seventies as a 'time of reckoning, or point of no return'. They summoned future historians to agree, or abstracted from the decade to give a mature, even metaphysical assessment of it as 'one in which no more evil had been created than in earlier epochs'.[16]

Writing in 1951 about *The Road to the Sixth Form*, an anonymous Ministry of Education author observed that 'the power to abstract is one of the supreme aims of a good grammar school education; a pupil must learn to see through the momentary externals of circumstances to the principle beneath'.[17] Philosophical abstraction as a task in English counterposed the personal world of the school student to the vicarious world of experience embodied in books, imaginative and factual. Discovering the deeper principles beneath this ever-varied objectivity—the motives of human behaviour, the dynamics of social order, the verities of history—the student could not claim a maturity of lived years. He had to stand on the authority of philosophical perception. Only a precocious student who recognized the examiner's interest in the wider view could justify this claim by skilfully exposing the philosophical dimensions of a literary or historical experience, using a natural and sincere style of language that suggested a habitual inclination to reason at this level. The scale of philosophical and literary values put into play by the examiners in search of the student–intellectual rewarded precociousness. Signs of maturity testified to a culture of mind in which the work of reading, discussion and writing made up for what the slender years of youth denied. For students to receive the highest accolade—a Special Distinction—they had to distinguish themselves in a global way, to exhibit strengths of thought and language that marked them apart—an 'alertness of mind, a maturity of thought and ability to conceptualize ... a sensitivity which is capable of probing a topic or responding to a book or an idea in a complex ... fashion, a capacity to write in an organized and developed manner using words intelligently and creatively ... overall, a quality of distinction rather than competence'.[18]

If only precocious individuals could fully attain the cultural ideal of the mature and independent thinker in the school setting, this was not because the gifts that led to such an early flowering of talent were too thinly distributed among the population or too poorly recognized. Rather the ideal itself presupposed a pedagogy of cultural immersion, without which there would be competence but not distinction. The contexts in which such a pedagogy could be practised were socially reserved. The ways in which the best students were distinguished from the merely competent reflected cultural advantages of life-style and institutional segregation. To minimize their reliance on set texts—as high achievers knew they should—meant participation in adult discussions or wide and independent reading, which they owed to the emphasis on early literacy in their homes and the libraries and reading policies of their schools. Their literary facility came from the developed lexical and syntactic complexity of their language training at home and the continual exercises in writing demanded by their teachers. They wrote with confidence because from an early age they had been taught to verbalize and to manage their demands on others through the resources of speech. They wrote with precision and liveliness because their educated speech-models gave them superior access to the technical and philosophical register of Graeco–Latin roots and because they had been trained to vary their speech to make it attractive and persuasive. They could appear in their writing as mature and perceptive thinkers because they were often raised in a culture of ideas and because they attended schools where the serious use of speech in prayer, oratory and debate was a means of social bonding beyond any narrower function. Precocity as the flowering of an individual ahead of his time had its false counterpart in the illusion of precociousness that children from culturally advantaged families could impose on others entering school at the same time. Was it this illusion that moved the examiners to complain of the tendency towards pomposity and prolixity among candidates receiving high grades?[19]

Both the particular characteristics of philosophical and literary merit—'acute insight, personal liveliness and vitality'—and the blending of these virtues that defined quality of mind—the 'combination of excellence in content and style'[20]—called for a pedagogical relationship that was intimate, continuous and total. To surround the individual on all sides, to restrict the code of communication to a certain style, to make learning proceed from affection as well as function, no doubt recalls the seminary in which 'the master imposes his authority by the double prestige of his piety and his knowledge'.[21] Yet the pedagogy of cultural immersion had its secular parallels, especially in boarding schools where piety still played a role in prayers and chapel and where robed masters still exercised the 'magistracy of learning'. The socially restricted setting of the fee-charging school—the architecture and the devices that verified its history, the rituals of assembly and speech night, the livery of the pupil and the black gown of the master, the rhetoric of leadership and service, compulsory sport and community work—closed the circle on the outside world and steeped the pupil in 'tradition'. Academic learning, especially the more theoretical and abstract sciences, could be cultivated to a high degree in this context of immersion. The special and defining task of the school was as a nursery of intelligence. Here precocity was not the random manifestation of talent in an individual, but a reproducible group characteristic related to the school's specific cultural emphasis and the social conditions under which it worked.

Patterns of attainment

When the first great wave of growth towards mass secondary education came to an end in the mid-1970s, most high schools had been offering senior classes for at most twenty years or so. Pioneering this level of schooling, they had done so with meagre resources—temporary and unqualified staff, large classes, dilapidated buildings or 'portables', few libraries and often no science laboratories. Students with the fewest family advantages entered schools with the fewest facilities and encountered the least experienced staff. Unsurprisingly, few high schools could offer the academic security that most of the large private establishments could boast. At the English exams in 1975, and looking just at boys' results, only fourteen of the high schools fielding twenty or more candidates were placed in the band of performance where most private schools lay (see Figure 2).[22]

High schools—still in their infancy as a system leading to university—were expanding in an institutional environment dominated

Figure 2: English honours grades in private schools and public high schools, boys, 1975

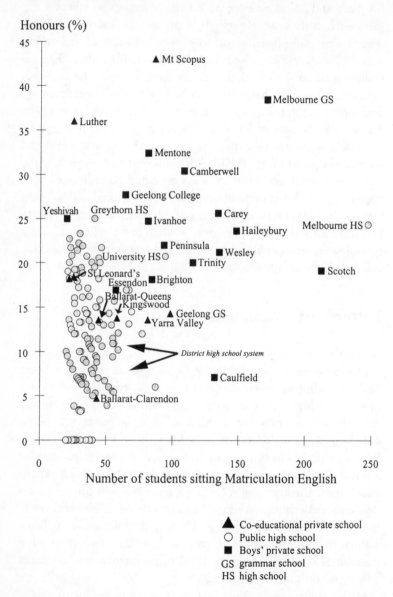

Source: Unpublished HSC results, 1975.

by large, socially segregated and academically powerful establishments. While not all private schools had made significant progress in the standard of boys' attainment in English, in most of the larger schools every fifth boy at least was awarded a first-class or second-class honour at the Higher School Certificate exams. Some of the lesser-ranking schools whose results had been undistinguished in 1947 had now moved ahead, securing honours for every third or fourth boy. These establishments enrolled large numbers of students and their honours rates point to a trend towards 'excellence for all'—globally competitive success—that would be consolidated over the next two decades. This outcome was already evident at Melbourne Grammar School and the recently opened Mt Scopus, where 40 per cent or more of boys gained honours in a subject ranked low on the scale of institutional worth.

Established at every point in social space—small rural communities, provincial cities and the urban agglomerate of Melbourne, with its extremes of wealth and poverty—high schools and many Catholic secondary colleges operated on fundamentally different lines. Private organization could surmount or exploit the constraints of social space. 'No schools are wealthy', claimed a conservative politician in 1969.[23] But in the early 1970s the typical independent school in Australia was spending 40 per cent more on teacher salaries per pupil than the average government school, and some used 'well over twice the volume of resources'.[24] Private schools could boast very favourable pupil–teacher ratios.[25] Since 1964 they had received capital grants to build science laboratories, and since 1969 to build libraries; in Victoria, they received per capita recurrent grants from 1967, and the federal government began to pay recurrent grants on a uniform per capita basis in 1970.[26]

Public subsidies gave the wealthy schools security against the risks of corporate venture, redoubling the advantages of private organization—fees to filter intakes, administrative autonomy, a poorly unionized workforce and patronal control over staff. The choice that only wealthier parents could exercise was underwritten, partly through direct payments by state and federal governments, partly by taxation relief.[27] A sponsored system of private schooling was forming—not a market system. But market freedoms there were, and these were protected by the way grants were paid and by the lack of any but the narrowest concept of financial accountability. As competitive pressures were heightened by the greatly increased number of students completing school and the scarcity of university places, private schools had little choice but to become efficient and more academically effective, and the means had been made available for them to do so. The creation of a sponsored market of private schooling through generous and thinly regulated public grants enabled the old system of grammar schools and 'public schools' to modernize without surrendering any of their autonomy.[28]

The beneficiaries of this system can be studied from the surveys conducted by the private schools themselves during this period as they sought to check mounting public hostility and threats to reduce subsidies. Looking at the sector as a whole, about 61 per cent of parents in 1975 were from senior management, farming and grazing or upper professional backgrounds. Middle managers and teachers made up a further 22 per cent. About 15 per cent of fathers were described as 'office employees, skilled workers, sales representatives' (see Figure 3). Only about 2 per cent of fathers were in semi-skilled or unskilled manual jobs or were retired, on pensions or unemployed.[29]

This social profile shows that the growth of mass secondary school systems was being countered by the segregative strategies of the most economically and culturally advantaged families. Segregation was greatest in the medium and high-fee schools, where 84 and 88 per cent of students respectively had fathers drawn from the ranks of managers and professionals. These represented the sector as a whole, for they recruited about 86 per cent of all students in private non-Catholic education.[30]

While these schools consolidated and augmented individual advantages of income, education and culture, disadvantage was accumulated and concentrated in the high schools, poorer Catholic schools and technical schools of the industrial suburbs. Among the parents of Sunshine West High School in 1979, 86 per cent of mothers had received only compulsory schooling, 69 per cent of fathers were from non-English-speaking backgrounds, and more

Figure 3: Fathers' occupations of students in private schools, Victoria, 1975 (%)

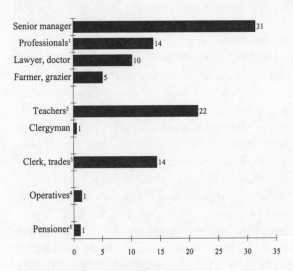

¹ Engineers, accountants, architects
² includes middle managers (original coding)
³ Clerical, sales, and skilled manual workers (original coding)
⁴ Semi-skilled and unskilled workers
⁵ Retired, pensioner, unemployed (original coding)

Source: AISV, unpublished survey of parents, 1975.

than 60 per cent were employed in factory jobs. At nearby Chisholm College, the figures were about the same, as they were at Tottenham Tech, which was in the same street, but was shunned by many migrant families and burnt down by its students.[31] Given the cultural demands of the curriculum, the intensification of advantages through social geography and selective schooling could only lead to an institutionalized pattern in which competitive success was reserved to the most educated or economically powerful strata, while failure was exported to the poorest communities, year in, year out.

The social geography of success and failure in English shows not only how the curriculum, through its learning criteria, implicitly valorizes attitudes and behaviours that are unequally available to the population, but also how the capacity of different sub-groups of the population to mobilize resources in schools is vital for exploiting the advantages stored up in the curriculum. Judged in the abstract, the ideal of the liberal intellectual that inspired the English curriculum no doubt seems sufficiently remote from the life-styles of many children in the 1970s to account for their failure and exclusion from school when measured against it. But it was the historical conditions under which children sought access to this ideal that gave it its particular potency as a culturally discriminating force. The distance between the ideal and those who aspired to it depended on the kinds of schools and the circumstances under which these operated, including the stocks of knowledge and the values of the families using the schools.

Failure rates in English rose from 23 per cent in the inner-eastern suburbs of Melbourne, which contained the highest proportions of professionals and senior managers and the lowest proportions of non-English-speaking migrants, to 36 per cent in the industrial, high-migrant-density north-west of the city (see Figure 4).[32] When the effects of gender are added in, the scale of differences becomes much greater. For girls living in the most advantaged regions, the failure rate in English was 14 per cent, while for boys living in the most disadvantaged regions it was 43 per cent. This threefold increase in risk was based in part on socio-economic and ethnic disadvantages and in part on the tendency for boys to discount the role of English. Their negative perceptions of the subject were reinforced by university science, engineering and other faculties, which stressed mathematical attainment far more than English. Girls, whose access to mathematics and physical sciences was still very limited, relied much more on the humanities and turned in better results whatever the region.[33]

Ironically, the cultural ideal of intellectual independence underlying the English curriculum had little chance of being realized to its full potential in those communities where it was most needed to compensate for lack of economic power. On the contrary, the ideal of the independent and mature thinker flourished in regions where economic power could be translated into intellectual ascendancy, thereby legitimizing itself and assuring its transmission over generations. Those who could create perspective, balance

Figure 4: English failure rates by labour-force region, Melbourne, 1975

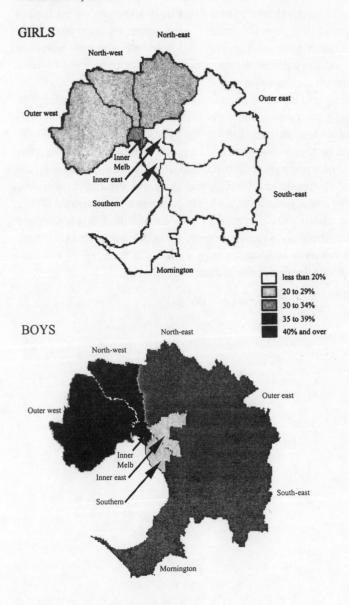

GIRLS

BOYS

Source: Unpublished HSC results, 1975.

arguments, see through the externals and migrate across history beyond shallow and immediate concerns might well do so. Trained often enough to think of themselves as bearing special leadership responsibilities, they did indeed stand apart, entering the world of work only after a long delay and only from the high points of economic and cultural detachment from which they could exercise the greatest claims upon it.

Corresponding to the points on the scale of distinction in English, whether grammatical, literary or philosophical, were zones of social geography and institutional prestige. The academic behaviours demanded by the examiners could be more intensively cultivated, the more urban residential stratification and institutional segregation worked to elevate and homogenize cultural level and disposition, language fluency and style, and proficiency in examinations. Whole cohorts of students prepared on this basis would display all the characteristics of an early maturity, a precociousness for their age, that in reality was no more than an illusion founded on the cultural and institutional dominance of their class.

4

English under the Victorian Certificate of Education

POWER THROUGH THE CURRICULUM becomes a more urgent imperative when the ranks of students completing school swell to include the whole age group. It is then that the implicit cultural demands of the curriculum as well as its higher-order concepts acquire both the constructive force needed to transmit social status across generations and the destructive force to check and negate competing aspirations. After many years in force, the curriculum becomes stamped with the characteristics of its most successful users. They have adjusted to its requirements through the teaching, testing and preparation strategies of their schools. The syllabus is dismembered into the components that are habitually examined and those that are merely educational. Schools run exam rehearsals, using papers privately prepared by associations of schools. The real exams, set by universities or assessment boards, are carefully monitored for recurring questions, as are the examiners' reports. Senior teachers are enlisted in the official subject committees and examiners' panels; they are active in professional subject associations; those who write textbooks are promoted, and the students who cannot read these works are weeded out or forced to sit the exams as private candidates. In time, the curriculum is domesticated. To each new cohort of students it is something new and imposing, but to the schools it is a recurring cycle, a business that can and must be reduced to routine, especially where success is expected as a matter of routine.

At the Methodist Ladies' College in Kew, only one in ten of the 242 girls who sat for English in 1975 could expect to fail—about half the rate for girls across the school system as a whole. The 100 girls from Melbourne Church of England Girls' Grammar School were equally insulated from failure, while the 170 girls at the Presbyterian Ladies' College who took the exam were still further removed (8 chances in 100) and those at Mt Scopus almost immune (1 in 100). It was a very different matter at Richmond High School or Moreland or Keilor Heights, all in migrant working-class communities. The children of these communities could not compete effectively, but they also could not renounce their claims on the curriculum, for education was their best hope of relieving their economic powerlessness. But the risks of failure were five times as great as in the most prestigious private schools—among girls at Richmond, 44 per cent, at Moreland 50 per cent, at Keilor Heights 49 per cent.[1] Migrant working-class students faced the same risk of failure as the average candidate for English had in the mid-1940s. They were thirty years behind. The girls at MLC, for their part, were decades in front. They failed, not at the rate of the average candidate ten years ahead, but at only half that rate, and they were not particularly distinguished.

Among migrant and working-class students, academic insecurity would soon be joined by deepening economic insecurity. The first oil shock in 1973–74 shattered the youth labour market. Within a few years, schools were absorbing economic refugees as high unemployment among teenagers became the norm (Figure 5).[2] But the academic curriculum offered only the most volatile material for rebuilding their employment chances.

When a new curriculum authority began its work in 1978, under the darkening cloud of economic downturn, reform took the path of creating space within the curriculum for students not planning to enter university. That they were a majority of those finishing school had been clear a decade earlier.[3] There would be new subjects, developed and assessed by schools themselves, and running parallel to the mainstream. At the same time, the structure of the curriculum for intending university students was also revised. Schools would be able to choose among options of study within

Figure 5: Unemployment among teenagers, 1964–1985

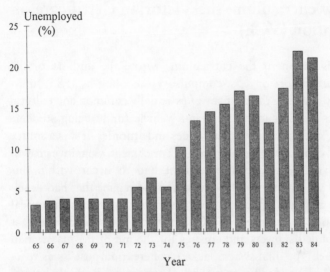

Year

Source: Peter Stricker, 'Statistical appendix on youth unemployment', in
R. F. Henderson (ed.), *Youth Unemployment*. Proceedings of the Second Academy
Symposium, Institute of Applied Economic and Social Research, University of
Melbourne, and Academy of Social Sciences in Australia, Parkville, 1977; ABS, *The
Labour Force Australia. Historical Summary 1966 to 1984*, Catalogue No. 6204.0,
Canberra 1986, pp. 30–1.

subjects and to assess components of their students' work. External exams would carry less weight.

This two-pronged approach—creating parallel streams and
broadening assessment practice within the mainstream—would be
pursued into the mid-1980s. Many new subjects made their appearance, and the 'core and options' structure compelled revisions of
the syllabus in university-preparatory subjects. Progress was made
in allowing teachers to assess the quality of their students' achievement. But within a few years, the tensions created by duplicating
curriculum streams—a university track and a terminal track, with
multiple and competing credentials—and the push to give more
assessment weight to schools against the wishes of the universities

would usher in another, more sustained and more bitterly fought-out period of reform.

A new curriculum: the Victorian Certificate of Education (VCE)

'Any discussion of the curriculum', wrote the authors of the Blackburn report on post-compulsory schooling in 1985, 'must begin by asserting the primacy of essentially common and cultural purposes'.[4] The curriculum was a vehicle for bringing students together and for shaping their values and attitudes. It was a source of social cohesion as well as personal enrichment. Cognitive growth and private economic advancement had to occur within this broader programme of objectives. The old regime that had developed as a system of competitive advantage had lost its historical justification in the selection of elites. But piecemeal reforms that simply added subjects and courses for the use of the masses had also failed. The dual system lacked 'coherent purpose', was reactive, and had ended up as a form of streaming. Radical changes were required.[5]

The curriculum was now to be reintegrated. The problem of diversity would have to be managed within the framework of one certificate. This would not be through formal streams, but through flexible curriculum design and multiple approaches to testing student learning. There would be room for schools to choose some of the content in all disciplines, and they would contribute to student assessment through 'take-home' work projects, with less reliance on exams. The curriculum would extend the freedom granted to schools in the early 1980s into the new, unified certificate, while avoiding the dangers of having a low-prestige track, segregation and lack of comparability of student work.

This was an ambitious programme. Previously, it had been a matter of manipulating the elements of a structure—adding a parallel track, differentiating options from core, dividing and balancing assessment components. Now the challenge was taken up to the content of subjects, their purpose, the pedagogical role of assessment, and the teachers' capacity to use flexible design to manage greatly varying classroom settings. At stake was quality of learning for all students. The archaic tools of selection and segregation were thrown aside.

English was proposed as one of the two major common elements in which students from all backgrounds would be brought together. Australian Studies was the other. There would no longer be separate English subjects for low and high achievers, for university aspirants and those heading for work. All would tackle a common and compulsory subject. This was to draw on the approaches that schools had developed independently of universities or of mainstream HSC English. The review committee, through its working party on credentials, outlined in a general way what it meant by English:

> In communication, we do not simply mean knowledge and use of the English language, although this must be a major part. We also imply a familiarity with elementary logic and analysis, structure of language and the creative use of both the spoken and written word, supplemented by some knowledge of literature.[6]

But the underlying cultural importance of the subject—and thus its justification as a compulsory element—was only fully brought out in the committee's main report. Other subjects could strengthen functional skills in English, but this would always be ancillary to their more specialized roles. 'The study of English', the committee argued, 'provides a more open focus for wide reading and for the consideration of human and personal concerns than is possible within the logico-rational requirements of other studies'.[7]

There was also a public perception that high literacy standards could only be met by having a specific subject in English, a notion the committee appeared reluctant to endorse. It was the broad cultural role of English that it wanted to affirm, not the notion of 'standards', which it considered narrow and problematic. English was a source of sustained and personal reflection, undertaken in common through shared themes, shared materials and the discipline of language skills and literary form. It dealt unashamedly with moral and behavioural issues, which it could approach through the conventions of imaginative literature as well as print journalism and electronic media. English centred on the learner's moral sensibility and logical and expressive skills, and it aimed to cultivate both the domain of art and the domain of philosophy.

In terms of design and assessment concepts, English under the VCE represented a major advance. Learning objectives were explicitly defined. The programme was organized over two years into a sequence of semester units, each with a range of carefully specified and varied work requirements; in the second year, these built into Common Assessment Tasks, which allowed students to report their learning over continuous stages and against clear goals. The assessment criteria were published and incorporated into the test material issued to students. There was greater integration between the programme of work and the assessment programme. The rationale for the study of English was fully laid out in the official study design document. The design itself was flexible and allowed schools to select material of particular relevance to their students. The range of assessment instruments engaged teachers more fully in judging students' work, and provided a variety of channels for achievement to be expressed.

The English curriculum became much more transparent as a programme of study and testing. Both teachers and students could have greater confidence about what they were trying to achieve, thanks to the strength of the design concepts. The focus on 'purpose and audience' in the assessment task on the 'presentation of an issue' exemplified transparency by showing how 'form' in the writing of English could be functionally interpreted.[8] Overall, the curriculum was made more an instrument of teaching than before, more open to teachers' skills and energies. It also became more tractable to students' demands for tasks that could be accomplished and were worth accomplishing. English advanced towards communicable, meaningful and achievable standards.

The reforms of the curriculum promised to advantage no particular group of students. Transparency of design improved the potential learning experience of all individuals because it enabled both teacher and learner to direct and monitor their efforts more effectively. But would this in itself, unsupported by other measures of reform beyond the curriculum, improve outcomes for disadvantaged students and reduce the burden of failure that they had borne so unequally for so long? To judge from the fears of conservative vice-chancellors and headmasters, the cultural ligaments that had bound English teachers together across the divides of public and private school, industrial and middle-class suburb, preserving the integrity of the subject over successive reforms, were about to snap. English would degenerate into a mix of degraded media materials incapable of providing spiritual elevation. But such complaints left open the question of how student work would be judged, quite apart from the issue of the range of texts from which they would really have to draw. To design an English programme in such a way that Shakespeare might not be studied at all did not free students from the cultural world in which Shakespeare was venerated. Just as it is not possible to rig the curriculum downwards in favour of the weakest users—since this merely relaxes the efforts required of the strongest—so the removal of the most canonical texts from the curriculum does not purge it of the values materialized in these objects.

Achievement in utilitarian English

The reformers of English sought to lay bare the intellectual requirements of their subject and to subordinate its underlying cultural values to a pedagogical challenge that was socially unrestricted. They did not, however, abandon their values. The reactions of assessors and teachers to student work in the functional tasks of journalistic logic and expression show that the qualities of thought and expression that mattered before the reforms still mattered. Showing distance from the content of a text and focusing on form and function required students to detach themselves from the substance of a communication and concentrate on literary and psychological effects, on style and strategy. They were being trained in abstraction and analysis, giving up the naive standpoint of the reader, and learning to develop the skills of criticism habitually exercised by intellectuals. Nor was it enough to read through the message to its artistic or technical principles. The student had to write and to explain, and therefore to have mastered the categories and the vocabulary of a second-order relationship to English in which meanings were subordinated to form.

Reporting to teachers in 1994, the assessors warned: 'Students need a language to discuss language, so that they can say precisely what they mean'.[9] Nor was analysis enough. They had to build arguments—as they had always been required to do—and to enlist the adherence of the reader, not only through persuasiveness of language, but through depth of thought. Called on to assess the 'wider implications of an issue', they would need to draw on wide reading and active participation in discussion and debate.[10] It had long been recognized that, in essays on contemporary topics, it was 'often a matter of chance whether a student has sufficiently detailed knowledge to present or analyse a closely argued point of view'.[11] Thus, even in the more modern side of English—media studies, with its practical emphasis—the assessors continued to search for intellectual disposition and the evidence of developed cultural interests. Though the test on issues in the media had very explicit design concepts—based on audience and purpose—there was sufficient richness in the task to enable students from well-educated families to draw well ahead of those from working-class families. Girls from professional and managerial backgrounds were more than twice as likely as the daughters of blue-collar workers to receive an A+ or an A grade from their teachers, and the social gap was even greater among boys (Figure 6).[12]

Transparency in curriculum design and school control over components of assessment did not redistribute results in favour of socially disadvantaged students. These features strengthened the curriculum for all users, including those with the greatest linguistic and cultural resources. Educationally important though they were, they would not rebalance social patterns. Indeed, as conservative critics pointed out, there was a real danger that the extended assessment tasks, which were done at home and marked by teachers, would advantage students from upper-status families and well-endowed schools.

Putting teachers in charge of assessment tasks was meant to link testing more closely with teaching. The tasks in which this was to happen were carried out over an extended period, enabling all students to interpret requirements, organize themselves and apply their knowledge in a more manageable time-frame than the traditional exam allowed. But in a competitive environment where all

Figure 6: Grades for the 'presentation of an issue' in the media by socio-economic status and gender, 1994

(A) GIRLS

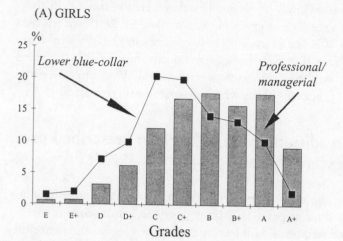

(B) BOYS

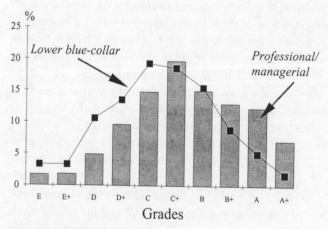

Source: Unpublished VCE results 1994.

marks count, pedagogical emphasis is readily diverted into the struggle for academic supremacy. The time made available to the weakest students to pace their learning more effectively and to utilize relatively meagre resources is used by the strongest students to exploit a greater abundance of resources and to produce highly refined work capable of maximum possible marks. Thus, while girls with tertiary-educated parents could expect to gain top grades in the external examinations in English more than twice as often as girls from lower-status families, they were five times as likely to be given the highest grade in tasks marked by their own teachers (Figure 7).[13] The extended take-home assessment tasks were abandoned after they were too conspicuously abused.[14] Yet the abuse lay not with the schools whose students stood most to gain pedagogically, but with those who had most to gain strategically.

The traditional side of English: prescribed text and external exam

Writing about contemporary issues in the media or utilizing journalistic skills in practical writing provided ample scope for well-read and well-trained students to display their logical and rhetorical strengths and the educated qualities of their language, both architectural and stylistic. With external examinations came the more conservative content of the set text. Here the cultural reserves of the good student were called into play. If exams left little time to write, those candidates who could write well countered by exploiting the subtle and diffuse requirements of the traditional essay to impose their own interpretations and pursue their own themes. Poor students would signal their mediocrity by writing on 'popular texts', just as in the 1940s the weak students wrote on childish topics.[15] Good candidates went for hard texts. To choose Camus' *The Outsider* was to lay claim to philosophical sophistication and tap into the wealth of secondary literature that made existentialism part of academic culture. In the case of this novel, the examiners observed, text and topic 'allowed for considerable complexity of thought in response . . . in general responses to this text were of high quality'.[16] There can be no better illustration of the dilemmas of curriculum design and assessment in an age of mass secondary schooling than the debate among the English examiners themselves as to whether weaker students should be encouraged to tackle harder texts—on the chance of getting better marks—or whether they should stick to 'short and fairly accessible texts' and thus protect themselves from the very low marks they could expect if they did tackle difficult works.[17]

Figure 7: What grades do upper-status students get in English compared with lower-status students?

Differences on a school-assessed task and an external examination.[1]

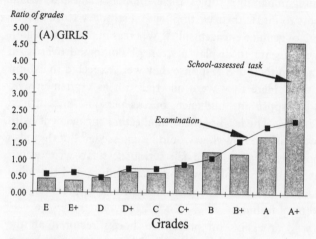

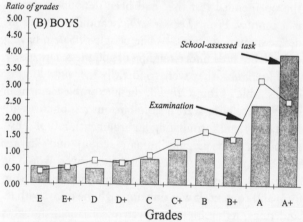

[1] Reading the chart: girls from upper-SES families are five times more likely than girls from lower blue-collar families to receive an A+ in the school-assessed task, but only about 2.2 times more likely to receive an A+ at the external exams. Relative advantage is calculated by dividing the percentage of upper-SES students receiving a given grade by the percentage of lower-SES students receiving the same grade.

Source: Educational Outcomes Survey, Victoria, 1994. For the sample (n = 6405), see R. Teese, M. Charlton, J. Polesel and M. Davies, *Catholic Secondary School Students in Victoria: Attitudes, Achievement and Destinations*, Educational Outcomes Research Unit, University of Melbourne, Parkville, 1996, p. 105.

Beyond the seriousness of the text, which implicitly favoured a raising or lowering of the grade of the candidate, other equally traditional criteria came into play. It was not enough to master interpretation: students also had to convey the right attitude. Continual training in handling topics, the examiners suggested, would help students to infuse their writing 'with a stronger sense of purpose, a sense of genuine engagement'.[18] Whereas in practical English students were meant to display a *strategic* command over form and language, in their text response they were expected to exhibit 'authenticity'.[19] Here they were on trial, not as craftsmen who understood purpose and audience, but as persons, uncontrived and spontaneous. The level of their 'intellectual engagement' with the topic was basic to how they would be assessed.[20] But they also had to show that theirs was a felt seriousness. To write about serious themes involved an elevation of the mind, and the mind rose not simply by levels of logical and precise expression, but through steps of feeling.

Setting student essays on prescribed books restored all the dangers of the open-ended test that had been denounced by researchers for a century. From *The Crucible*, candidates were instructed to define human goodness—'The people of Salem have a strong sense of evil, but little understanding of goodness. Discuss.'[21] From *Pride and Prejudice*, they were to identify the 'right kind of pride [that is] desirable'. From *Othello*, the inexorable element in human tragedy.[22] These tasks were a simultaneous test of creativity (constructing an essay and formulating an argument), moral sensibility (understanding and judging human action) and literary powers. Here, once again, it was the whole person who would be judged—not the sum of disparate skills, but the mind reflected in the play of form and content. It was only through the essay, with its leisured meanderings, its multiple perspectives, its tonal thoughts and thoughtful feelings, its moods and tensions, crescendos and cadences, that the examiner could encounter a like-minded spirit. If there were also 'flashes of brilliance or flair with language', then that was the 'very best', proof that even the hardest tasks could be mastered and therefore could be set, and that English was right to search in all students for the ideal of the literary intellectual.

Exams on set texts were no kinder to working-class students than the extended take-home tasks in practical English. Among girls, only 9 per cent of working-class students were awarded A+ or A grades, compared with 18 per cent of girls from professional and managerial backgrounds. At the other end of the scale, boys from lower working-class homes were twice as likely as those from the most highly educated families to receive E+ or E grades (see Figure 8). To upper-status students, exams did not present the same advantages of sustained preparation and refinement as extended projects marked by teachers. But such students were much better prepared over the long term to manage a more culturally rich task through their language training, early reading habits, the greater rhetorical emphasis of the schools they attended, and their developed disposition to use language as a form of personal discrimination and style. Exams compressed the time available to draw efficiently on this training, but as it had been acquired over many years in a sustained and continuous way, it was also readily and spontaneously available, to say nothing of formal practice in essay writing and exam rehearsals.

The reforms that led to a newly integrated curriculum in the early 1990s produced results that scarcely deviated from patterns under the old syllabus, the regularity of which was the hallmark of social engineering conducted over the long term. Neither in the more limited practical tests, which called for 'authenticity', 'engagement', 'seriousness' and 'sophistication', nor in the traditional exam on composition, which called for 'intellectual complexity' and 'imagination', could candidates escape the cultural demands of English.[23] Transparency of learning criteria, robust design, greater pedagogical freedom, better links between assessment and teaching and greater breadth of assessment methodologies all made English more accessible, more amenable to teaching and to learning. Its underlying values, now potentially more communicable, were meant to be shared and to act as the intellectual bonds of community. When transmitted by teachers from very different sites in the school system, however, they would serve to divide. How well English lent itself to discrimination can be seen in the great distances separating the schools at the

Figure 8: Grades on the external exam on set texts by socio-economic status and gender, 1994

Percentage
of students

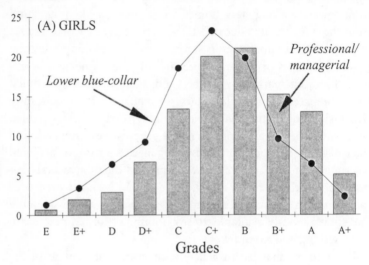

(A) GIRLS

Lower blue-collar

Professional/ managerial

Grades

Percentage
of students

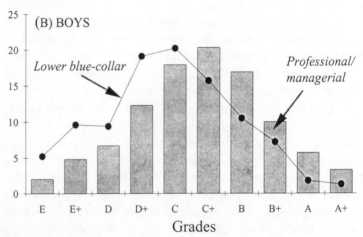

(B) BOYS

Lower blue-collar

Professional/ managerial

Grades

Source: Educational Outcomes Survey, Victoria, 1994.

missionary edge of the curriculum in working-class, migrant and rural communities from those located in its traditional heartland.

In 1994 the average school with at least twenty candidates attempting English gave around 17 per cent of them an A or an A+ on the school-assessed media test and could expect 9 per cent to receive A or A+ on the externally examined text response task. The great majority of public high schools lay below both these averages, but almost all private schools lay above them (see Figure 9). While in many cases high schools gave none of their students an A or A+ on the teacher-assessed task (horizontal axis) and had none who received these top grades at the external exams (vertical axis) many private schools awarded at least 40 per cent of their students A or A+—a few more than 50 or 60 per cent—and a good number could boast at least 25 per cent receiving top marks from the external exam.

The new curriculum and the school system

The competitive advantage of the traditional users of secondary education was carried over by the new curriculum into a context of deepening social dependence on school, first after recession in 1982, and then again after a severe downturn in 1991. Young people now needed school more than ever. Between these two points in time, the proportion of students completing school doubled, and a mass system of secondary education became definitively established. Most of the growth in school retention rates occurred in the public system and to a lesser extent in Catholic schools. These establishments were faced with a widening social front just as the new curriculum was being implemented. The lowering of private-school costs as a result of state and federal government grants allowed a flow of more academic or ambitious students to move out of high schools into the private sector, but did not redistribute the social tasks of upper secondary education more evenly among the sectors. The private schools at this level remained largely insulated from social exposure, while their financial position during the decade became more advantageous

Figure 9: Schools ranked by percentage of girls with an A/A+ in the take-home media test and in the external exam on set texts, 1994

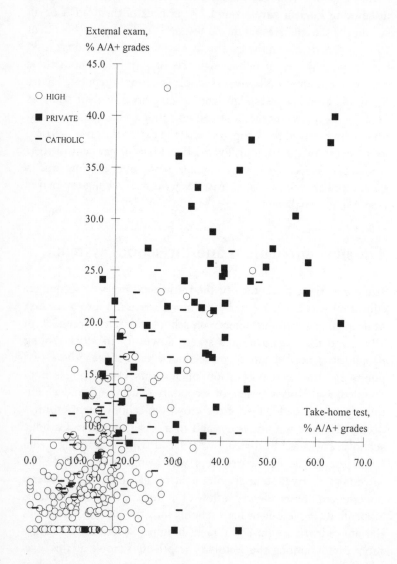

Source: Unpublished VCE results, 1994.

than ever before. By 1985 income received by the model independent school from private sources, including fees, donations and contributed services, represented the equivalent of average expenditure per pupil in government secondary schools.[24] Subsidies received from government thus allowed private establishments to *differentiate* their efforts from those of government schools. This occurred at a time when government schools most needed resources to manage the increasing differentiation of the populations to which they were exposed.

The new curriculum did not lower the vulnerability of the high-school population to failure, for the cultural ideals of literary sensibility and intellectual maturity had to be pursued within geographically and institutionally segregated systems that were growing apart. One in four girls living in the working-class north-west of Melbourne and attending public high schools could expect to be placed in the bottom fifth band of performance in English. For girls living in the upper middle-class suburbs of inner-eastern Melbourne and attending private non-Catholic schools, the figure was only four in a thousand. Among boys—who, as a group, made no virtue of English—less than 2 per cent failed if they lived in the best suburbs and attended the best schools, compared with 44 per cent of those living in the outer west of Melbourne and enrolled in high schools. The extent of segregation in the evolving school system is tellingly captured in the patterns of failure: private school students, whatever their geographical region, were the least vulnerable, followed in turn by Catholic school students, whatever their region, then finally public high school students, the most vulnerable group, with each sector virtually sealed off from the others (see Figure 10).[25]

If the reforms of the English curriculum led to no discernible improvement in relative social outcomes, this is no argument against their educational and pedagogical merits. It is consistent with rising absolute levels of attainment, based on higher general levels of schooling. But it *is* an argument against pursuing major curriculum change in the absence of structural reform. From one side, the new integrated curriculum brought all students together. From the other side, in the schools they attended, they were drawn apart. Taught in settings that divided them on socio-economic,

Figure 10: Failure in English by region, school type and gender, 1994[1]

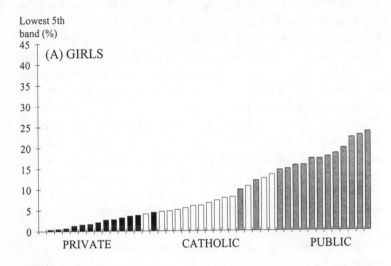

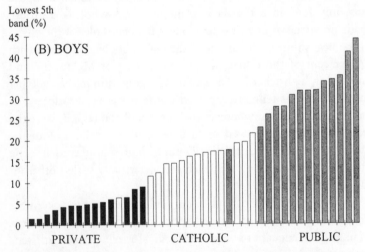

[1] Each column represents the schools of a particular type in a labour force region. The height of the column represents the percentage of students attempting English who were placed in the lowest fifth band of achievement (regional 'fail rates' for the relevant type of school and gender).

Source: Unpublished VCE results, 1994.

cultural and academic lines, they were made to meet in the same programme and exposed to the same set of learning demands. If an argument for commonality of civic culture seemed to justify bringing all students together, the values expressed through the common assessment tasks would tend to reinterpret 'civic' as 'academic'. How were students to escape the hierarchy that ranked Camus over *Doctor Strangelove* or the aesthetic that placed pleasure in words ahead of mundane purpose, that demanded originality, synthesis and imagination?

Even in the transition from the functional tasks of media analysis and practical writing to the interpretative work on imaginative and serious texts, no doubt was left about the order of things. Utilitarian English was assessed by teachers, literary English by examinations. This corresponded to the institutional hierarchy that subordinated schools to universities. In turn, academic power *over* the curriculum was a vehicle for the exercise of social power *through* the curriculum. To improve individual learning and reduce the burden of failure carried by the most disadvantaged groups, curriculum reform had to be backed by structural reforms— diversification of tertiary education to relieve vertical and homogenizing pressure on the school curriculum, integration of post-compulsory education and training across institutional levels to end selection by academic rank, funding arrangements to support the populations most dependent on effective teaching. Instead the technical schools—long the scorn of academic culture—were closed down and the colleges of technical and further education forbidden to enrol young people who would normally be in school. Structural diversity was thus removed at the same moment as the school curriculum was integrated. The circle was closed.

5

Searching for the Scientist: Post-war Chemical Reform

CURATORS RATHER THAN CREATORS, the science staff of Australian universities in the late 1940s were condemned by penury of means and provincialism of culture to serve out their days teaching over again the little enough that first-year undergraduates had failed to learn at school. Lecture theatres and laboratories were filled, not with budding scientists, but with the great class of future professional men ambitious for worldly advancement—engineers, surveyors and architects, physicians and dentists, agriculturalists and veterinary scientists. The science staff were servants of these young men, and the courses they taught were service courses. The idea of science as a vocation to fundamental knowledge, as a profession of experimental method and discovery, set academics apart from undergraduates only in theory. It formed a kind of celibacy on which authority and respect for learning might be based, but was in all other respects a useless virtue, fruitless and frustrating.

Harnessed to the machine of technical training—for they were preparing their young masters to apply old knowledge, not discover the new—university staff could do little research. There was no time, no relief from the year-round cycle of lectures and exams, 'prac classes' and 'supps', marking and preparation.[1] Their published work was thin—in chemistry, less than one paper per staff member per year on average between 1947 and 1949—and waited the arrival of new professors to make world contributions.[2] Their teaching was unadventurous and uninspiring, and indifferent to the poor progress of many students.[3]

Conservers of knowledge, the chemistry staff would take each
new class of undergraduates—and there were hundreds of them—
back to the archive of descriptive and analytical chemistry that
had been badly covered at school, imposing memorization on the
weakest students and boredom on the brightest.[4] Behind them lay
the authority of the textbook and the examination rather than
their own discoveries or published insights. Those who would
make a mark on the world of scientific learning—like John Stuart
Anderson, Professor of Inorganic Chemistry at the University of
Melbourne—demanded an audience of talented students. The
long sentences in which Anderson delivered his lectures were of
such 'perfect structure and subtle vocabulary [that they] often
concealed from the unprepared students the key principle essential
for the understanding of the chemistry'.[5] Men of science, they
assessed their students in the spirit of British academics, whose
classes were for the potential research worker.[6] In the public examinations to which school students were subjected, university staff
would also search for the evidence of scientific acumen, deeper
understanding and grasp of principles, hoping to rediscover the
researchers that too often they themselves could only wish to be.

The old regime of punishing facts

In the syllabus for matriculation chemistry in the late 1940s, the
old knowledge was stored up for transmission, little changed
in scope since 1906, though somewhat in emphasis.[7] Chemistry,
perhaps the more pedagogically conservative of the sciences, made
a 'sound basis of factual knowledge [the] first essential'.[8] The
periodic system supplied the framework for studying the elements
and their compounds, the chemical properties of which had to be
mastered (though not the electronic structure of atoms). The syllabus listed all the elements to which detailed attention was to
be given, went on to quantitative analysis, then molecular and
atomic theory (including Dalton's law of constant and multiple
proportions, and Dulong and Petit), chemical reactions and equilibrium, electrolysis, and finally some organic chemistry. It was recognized that some students needed a technically oriented training for

work in extraction and processing industries, the importance of which had grown during the war. So the chemistry of major industrial applications was included in the syllabus, though far less prominently than in the 1930s.[9]

The syllabus—a simple listing of content—offered little guide to what the university required by way of balance between factual recall, comprehension of principles and theoretical application. Teachers would have to glean this from the examination papers and examiners' reports. If contemporaries (and later critics) chided the university for having an excessive interest in testing knowledge of facts, the examiners must accept responsibility for this perception.[10] The detailed sections of their annual reports were replete with examples of candidates' factual errors, and the examiners went to much greater lengths to document ignorance of basic chemical facts than to define the higher kinds of knowledge and understanding that they wished schools to teach. Paragraph after paragraph of the reports from the 1940s and 1950s waded through the lush and endless errors that the matriculation chemistry student frequently made. 'Many candidates showed deplorable ignorance of even elementary chemical facts, and such inexcusable statements as "zinc and phosphorus act on caustic soda and precipitate sodium" were common'; 'As usual, many [candidates] treated "superphosphate" as a chemical compound'; 'there is little evidence of study of the oxygen compounds of the halogens'; 'the question on the preparation of methane was answered best, but it was rarely stated that the sodium acetate should be anhydrous'.[11]

The chemistry curriculum of the early post-war decades was later described as a triumph of fact over principle, particularly by reformers in the 1960s who sought to distance themselves from the past and justify their innovations.[12] But this simple polarity does not help to describe the concerns of university examiners in the 1940s and 1950s. They wanted facts, but as part of an understanding of chemical processes and principles. Either side of learning presented in the absence of the other earned their scorn: 'assiduous memorization' of facts was as blameworthy as the 'recitation' of theory.[13] While they did include mainly descriptive topics in the exam papers—for they believed strongly in the need for solid factual grasp—they wanted to see theoretical comprehension of chemical processes and set questions to test application, conscious that this was 'difficult for any but really good candidates'.[14] It was one thing to describe an experiment for determining the number of atoms in the ozone molecule, another to 'state and explain'—not *recite*—'the laws involved in the interpretation of [this] experiment'.[15]

Year after year, the examiners focused on weaknesses in students' intellectual grasp of the properties and behaviour of chemicals. In 1946, they detected a definite improvement in 'theoretical matters'.[16] But each exam brought new and disturbing evidence of lack of theoretical depth. The class of '48 was ignorant of the effect of pressure on equilibrium, the class of '49 had not learnt the method of equivalents and confused Henry's Law and Dalton's Law of Partial Pressures; the class of '51 had not grasped kinetic principles and could not explain how Dalton's atomic theory was supported by experimental results.[17] The good student, in short, was expected to move from descriptive to physical chemistry, even though the examiners were slow to make this explicit and schools were often unable to support such an emphasis.[18]

The examiners were aware that there were not enough good teachers. How could students evince a theoretical interest in chemistry when their teachers had not been trained in research? To derive intrinsic satisfaction from experimental chemistry and from the elaboration of chemical laws was a matter of culture, something that demanded models of human behaviour and values. Students in country schools were under a particular handicap, as successive examiners' reports documented.[19] Even within Melbourne, advantages of culture and size were not widely enjoyed. In some schools, most students—not a handful—turned in 'very poor results'.[20]

Quality of learning suffered from pedagogical and discipline weaknesses, a professional culture centred on the classroom and exam, and the career and cultural narrowness of students themselves. But it was the lowly place of the science laboratory that captured the schools' remoteness from the research values and expectations of university chemists. Facilities were generally poor, despite being approved as adequate, and training in experiments and laboratory techniques was frequently either not seen as important or neglected through want of training. The majority (62 per cent) of schools submitting student record books for examination in 1946 fraudulently certified that laboratory work had been completed individually by students (a formal examination requirement). Inspection of the books showed that entries were being copied; in one school, the results had been dictated to the class.[21] Without real involvement in laboratory work, the awakening of theoretical interest and understanding through discovery would be rare, and learning would degenerate into the memorization of textbook facts.

The gap between professorial values and instructional experience, aggravated by frustration on both sides, transformed the annual examinations from a ritual of habilitation—the election of new scholars to the ranks of the old—into a trial by summary judgement and execution. Every second candidate attempting chemistry in 1947 was failed (see Figure 11). The same occurred in 1948; in 1949, 61 per cent were dispatched; in 1950, 51 per cent; in 1951, 48 per cent; 1952, 44 per cent; 1953, 43 per cent; 1954, 46 per cent.[22]

These savage rates of failure were the university's answer to the high levels of participation in senior school science and mathematics. More than 60 per cent of candidates attempting a full matriculation in 1947 enrolled in chemistry and physics. While these students represented only a tiny proportion of their age group—in the case of chemistry, 4 per cent of boys and less than 1 per cent of girls—they did not constitute an academic elite in professorial eyes.[23] To sort the wheat from the chaff, a heavy thrashing was administered. Even those candidates who survived were by no means protected from failure once reaching university. For the 'slaughterhouse' method applied to matriculation was simply an extension of the traditional organization of university teaching, with its lecture theatres, one-way communication, poor supervision of learning and professorial disdain, manifested in the heavy culling of weaker students in final exams.[24]

With undergraduate failure running high, a combined university–schools conference on careers was asked whether it was the schools or the university that was deluding students, for only 'one in three would get through first-year Science, and one in four through first-year Medicine'.[25] There was in fact a large gap between the official university entrance requirements—the formal

Figure 11: Distribution of grades in chemistry and physics, and enrolment rates in 1947[1]

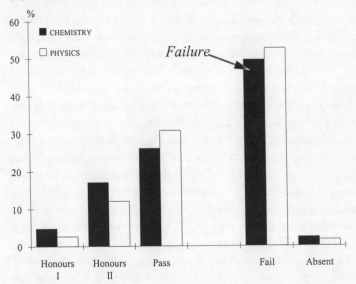

(A) GRADES

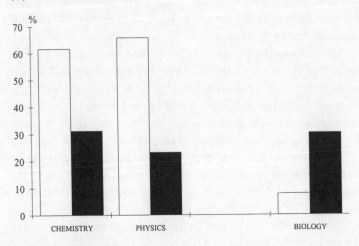

(B) ENROLMENT RATES

[1] Grade distribution for full candidates only.

Source: Unpublished Matriculation results, 1947.

entry level—and the level of performance deemed necessary to continue beyond the first year. Even before the war, science students had to satisfy a higher effective entry level than their colleagues in Arts, thanks to a policy of low pass rates in first year. This policy favoured students who had completed the Honours year of the old Leaving Certificate—an additional year, assessed by external exams—over students who matriculated with the minimum standard of a Leaving Pass—one year less and often assessed by schools.[26] Science professors demanded higher standards of their incoming students. So attached were they to these standards that during the war, when places were reserved for the academically most able groups, science pass rates did not shift up in line with the more stringent selection policy, but remained stable.[27] The practice of eliminating a fixed ratio of undergraduate students had become institutionalized: it operated as a seemingly 'unconscious' measure, indifferent to changes in the quality of students.[28] By regularly failing a high proportion of first-year undergraduates, the professors of science signalled to the outside world that only the best students could claim a place in departments under their control. At the same time, they rewarded themselves by admitting into their company only students who had the marks of future professors. These were the 'self-taught', who in second year and later would overtake the merely 'taught', as C. 'Pansy' Wright, the physiologist, was to recall.[29]

Before the new Matriculation Certificate was instituted in 1944 —requiring six years of secondary school and sanctioned by external exams—science courses had already ascended the hierarchy of academic disciplines. These could be ranked on the one hand by *academic mix*—the proportion of incoming university students who had completed an Honours year at school—and on the other hand by *progression*—the proportion of undergraduates who completed their degrees. Contrary to expectations, the richer the academic mix of a university course, the *lower* the rate of progression.[30] The dual principles of initial selection ('entry level') and continuous selection (fail rates) worked cumulatively rather than correctively. Instead of failure diminishing in line with the academic richness of student intakes, it actually rose. As the educationalist R. F. Butts was to observe in 1955:

It struck me as odd that the very best and most able students regularly go into science and mathematics in the secondary schools, but they are the ones most likely to fail in the university. This must mean either of two things: the best Australian boys are not bright enough to become good scientists, or the 'standards' set by the university are arbitrary and unreasonable.[31]

Across Australia, science undergraduates typically fared badly at first-year exams—49 per cent passing in 1951 compared with 59 per cent in agriculture and veterinary science, 61 per cent in medicine and dentistry, 63 per cent in engineering and architecture, and 66 per cent in Arts.[32]

Science-based courses such as engineering, architecture, agriculture and medicine had the highest academic mix of incoming students, thanks to career benefits, type of school attended and social background.[33] Students aiming for these courses had the ambition, the advantages of private schooling and the benefits of superior socio-economic status to achieve a higher level of qualification—six years, or Honours standard—and also to gain the scholarships and exhibitions that went with high marks.[34] Once admitted to science courses, however, they encountered men of science with a predilection for students with an intrinsic attachment to their discipline. Science professors might not all have been as dismissive of mediocrity as the Dean of Medicine who alleged in 1956 that one in three of his undergraduates were 'lame ducks right through their course'.[35] But they were concerned to promote the cause of science. Though their salaries might depend on giving 'service' courses along the way, their priority was the fostering of able students who would dedicate themselves to scienctific thinking and research.

The search for these budding scientists required the professors to perform a harsh process of elimination. The Melbourne dons allowed only 40 per cent of full-time science students enrolled in 1951 to graduate, compared with 67 per cent at Adelaide, 74 per cent at University College, London, and 84 per cent at Liverpool.[36] Thus it was not the academically weakest pools of incoming students (as in Arts) that would be most heavily culled, but the richest. Concluding the studies that laid this bare, Hohne noted the 'strong suggestions that examinations sought to identify, and teaching to nurture, the potential brilliant specialist graduate in preference to the less outstanding, or less ambitious student'.[37] The greater rejection of science undergraduates, despite their more severe initial selection, pointed back to curricula and to the professorial values at work in examinations that were preoccupied, not with knowledge of scientific facts, but with grasp of principles, experimental orientation and theoretical depth.

Theoretical chemistry triumphant

From the mid-1950s there were moves to rectify a situation in which the chances of failing matriculation chemistry were as good as the toss of a coin. Though no formal overhaul was made of the chemistry syllabus until a decade later, design and emphasis were made stronger and more explicit, the examination papers became more technically sophisticated, and in 1963 pass rates were fixed for all subjects at 67.8 per cent.[38] The power of the Chief Examiners was cut back and the status of mathematics and the physical sciences in relation to other subjects began to receive attention.

The schools' capacity to get students through chemistry also improved. This was partly because of curriculum and assessment changes, but partly also because the emphasis on science was drawing more and more resources into schools. The sciences were becoming increasingly secure investments. Their profitability, as measured by the relative likelihood of gaining honours, would convert them from prestigious but dangerous subjects into a prestigious and lucrative business. This transition had already started in the 1960s, when the curriculum of all the sciences was upgraded in favour of a more theoretical and experimental approach aimed at student understanding. The intellectual emphasis imparted to chemistry, physics and biology came, in other words, at the very time when the relative value of these subjects as sources of high performance in exams—especially physics and chemistry —was being strengthened.

The new matriculation chemistry syllabus implemented in Victoria was presented as a radical break with the past. Its authors were reformers who looked disparagingly on the condition of science in schools. Chemistry was no more than an academic routine. Teaching and learning had been reduced to 'memorizing ... apparently unrelated factual information [as the] prime object'.[39] No doubt examinations were in part to blame. But the root of the problem lay in the syllabus, which was focused on assimilation of facts rather than comprehension of theory. Students were 'sadly lacking in understanding of fundamental principles and [in] the ability to organize coherent, logical chemical arguments'.

Comparison with chemistry programs being implemented in the United States and Britain—the Chemical Bond Approach (CBA), CHEM Study and Nuffield—showed that the deficiency lay in physical chemistry. A sub-committee of the Standing Committee on Chemistry of the Victorian Universities and Schools Examinations Board (VUSEB) appointed a working group, which solicited views from science educators, and the results confirmed their judgement. The new syllabus would have to 'provide a much better insight into the nature of chemical bonding within the framework of a reasonable physical model, an appreciation of stereochemistry ... and a realization of the importance of energy in chemical reactions'.[40]

The shift to a syllabus based on physical chemistry had already been undertaken at Year 11 level, the penultimate year of secondary education in Victoria. This made reforms to the matriculation syllabus inevitable, as an end to a process rather than the beginning. Teachers were already coming to terms with a 'principles-based' approach to senior school chemistry and beginning to grasp what it implied both about their own grasp of fundamentals and their students' capacity to meet the challenge. Chemistry, as presented to students, was elaborated from first principles—the atom, sub-atomic particles, chemical change, the reactivity of metals (to illustrate molecular structure), gases, electrolysis, atomic weight (using mass spectrometry), solids (the carbon atom), acids, bases and salts, redox reactions, the properties of nitrogen, sulphur and chlorine and the mole concept.[41] The matriculation syllabus would entrench this approach, in which the internal architecture of the discipline dictated the pedagogical order of its treatment.

Under the reforms, chemistry was viewed as a language to describe and measure change in matter. If this definition tended to resolve chemistry into physics, this was very much the thinking of the syllabus reformers. In their textbook for the matriculation course—*Chemistry, A Structural View* (1965)—chemistry was described as a branch of physics.[42] Chemistry was an academic discipline. It was concerned with 'one very important aspect of the behaviour of matter—the way in which atoms behave when they cluster together'.[43] From this point of view, chemistry was a step along the path leading to physics, and was 'in a sense . . . a part of physics'. To leave the question in no doubt, students were introduced to a hierarchy of the sciences—including the human sciences —which was shown to proceed from physics as 'the rigorous study of the fundamental laws governing the behaviour of matter' (see Figure 12).

Chemistry was thus reoriented away from the description and analysis of chemical substances based on experimental procedure to a theorization of physical relationships based on structural hypotheses. The impulse behind this, shared by contemporary British and American curriculum reforms, was the desire to create a new type of science student. Physical chemistry, proceeding from modern atomic and molecular theory, aimed to establish a conceptual universe in which entities—always assigned hypothetico-deductive status—were described in symbolic form and manipulated mathematically. Chemistry was no longer a world of tangible realities, familiar to the student by sensory properties of colour,

Figure 12: Hierarchy of the sciences: the chemistry reformers' view in the 1960s

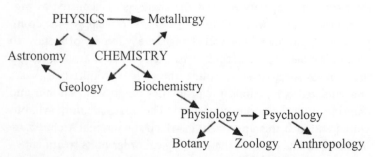

Source: D. S. Stranks, M. L. Heffernan, K. Lee Dow et al., *Chemistry: A Structural View*, Carlton, 1965, 2nd edn 1970, p. 3.

smell and taste.[44] The new science student had to stand back and abstract from the experiential order of attributes that had imbued chemistry with its traditional character as alchemy, to abandon the marvellous world of substances under the magical command of the laboratory. The objects that were now to be worked on were conceptual, and progress through the chemistry courses written for upper secondary school required continual abstraction from chemical phenomena to underlying physical structure and process.

The notion of chemistry as a formal language was one of the first lessons encountered by students following the Chemical Bond Approach in the United States. To read that chemical equations carried more information than natural language statements was also to see that the plain of naturalistic chemistry had to be abandoned.[45] The student's perspective was to be elevated to the point where it became a matter of habit to condense meaning into complex, abstract expressions; theoretical progress depended on gaining structural focus. As in mathematics, the compression of meaning through symbolic concentration of concepts was essential, and indeed mathematics itself was the means to achieve this. Training the research scientist—someone who could *produce* knowledge—was the ambition, so the focus had to be on mastering generative principles and their mathematical language.[46]

Less exclusive in spirit, Nuffield chemistry also aimed to give school students the experience of the scientist's world. Not all students—even from the academic band for whom the programme was planned—were expected to continue as research scientists. But the growth of knowledge would come from cultivating the scientific method and turning away from the old pedagogical model of assimilating facts. School science should be exploratory and enable students to discover, instead of being force-fed for exams. Experimental work in the school laboratory was to be the medium for 'creative speculation', for 'training in the disciplining of speculation'.[47] The cultural ideal of the scientist represented the very opposite of the pedagogue. But whether this cultural ideal could be pedagogically implemented, given the pressures of examinations, was another matter.[48] There were also doubts about whether the required mathematical proficiency could be achieved, given results from the trial Nuffield O-level exams.[49]

The aesthetic of wonderment and creativity that animated Nuffield would not translate to the matriculation syllabus designed in Victoria. The latter was a hard-nosed document for a course that had no room for sentiment. Canonical, it laid down objectives in crystal-clear fashion. Students were to understand basic principles of chemistry, gain insight into modern chemical terminology, appreciate how theories develop and progress, learn careful and critical thinking, develop practical skills, interpret experimental results critically, and understand experimental design. Factual learning was to be subordinated to grasp of fundamental principles. The course was organized around three 'themes'—the mole concept, the electrostatic nature of all chemical bonding, and the equilibrium law.[50] Pedagogically, the new matriculation chemistry made few concessions. There was no room for historical treatment of concepts, despite explicit reference to this in the list of objectives.[51] Classical experiments behind atomic theory were not to be taught. There was no room for applied chemistry. In spite of students' known weaknesses in mathematics and with relative concepts of atomic or molecular weight, the dangers of an excessive concern for measurement were ignored.[52]

From the beginning, the emphasis of syllabus reform was on the language of quantifying the fundamental concepts of physical chemistry—chemical stoichiometry and the mole concept. Measurement and chemical structure, grasped through the study of change, were the overriding concerns of the new course. This had major implications for how well chemistry could be taught, by whom and to whom. For the weight given to physical concepts, their exact expression in the condensed form of chemical notation, and their algebraic manipulation demanded an abstract stance, a theoretical disposition and mathematical facility and confidence. These implicit social demands on the culture of students—and the more overt expectations on teaching quality, training and aptitude—would reveal their discriminating effects in the sharply varying patterns of participation and achievement once the syllabus was implemented.

6

Structural Chemistry and its Social Beneficiaries

UNFOLDING AS THE DECADE of greatest post-war growth, the 1960s would burst the seams of the industrial economy built up since the war and drive the swelling ranks of baby-boomers into salaried middle-class jobs based on education. A tide of rising aspirations broke on the antique structure of academic schooling, weathering down its outworks—the lower-level examinations (Proficiency, Intermediate, Leaving) and the elaborate passages between them —till checked by the harder walls built up around the university itself. Within the cultural world enclosed by these fortifications, academics could reason freely about the scientific training they would demand of matriculants. In a social sense they knew few students, could not tolerate many they did know, and were ignorant of the economic and social pressures that filled their lectures to overflowing. Devoted to science as monks to prayer, the science academics knew only two kinds of students—the ones who reached university and the ones who merely wanted to.[1]

The syllabus reformers, knowing the kind of chemistry they wanted taught, framed the definition of the learner accordingly. The good student could manage the theoretical demands of physical chemistry well, had manipulative dexterity in mathematics, logical strengths and experimental appreciation. Chemistry knew no other student. If every third candidate for the chemistry examinations failed in the mid-1960s, this terminal group—as they were called—were still to have the same chemistry as the candidates who passed. Better for them, the reformers asserted, to 'emerge from their course with a sound appreciation of the manner in which chemical theories are developed, tested and revised in the light of experimental evidence' than to have something else contrived for them.[2] It was of no account that the terminal group, having failed the examinations and dashed their hopes for university, would not be leaving school with a 'sound appreciation' of theoretical chemistry or a love of experiments or a passion for science. The syllabus would no more have served them well than the great majority of students who, turned back by the academic curriculum, never reached matriculation or had been streamed out of mathematics and physical sciences along the way. The refusal to contemplate anything but a single chemistry subject was a declaration not only about chemistry itself, but about the nature of the students who had rightful access to it.

Selecting material to suit only aspirants for university, the syllabus writers also circumscribed the social space of the chemistry curriculum. All the factors that predicted entry to university—early success at school, confident aspirations, type of school attended, and capacity to pay fees or win scholarships—were linked to socio-economic status. It was a very meagre view of who could benefit from science teaching in upper secondary school. On Fensham's estimates, only about 6 per cent of the cohort of boys starting secondary school reached university science courses in the late 1960s (with a further 5 per cent entering technical institutes); for girls, the proportion commencing science-type degrees was only about 1 per cent.[3] By giving pre-eminence to physical chemistry and quantitative concepts and measures, the reformers filtered the student population not only for university aspirations, but for the sub-groups who could manage physics and preparatory mathematics, even if many would not take up physics or would drop it before their matriculation year. The chemistry curriculum thus acted as a form of social engineering in which a particular concept of science and of the ideal science student constrained the nature of the population capable—under contemporary teaching conditions —of satisfying the requirements of the curriculum.

The capacity to relate to chemistry as an abstract science of fundamental concepts and principles—not the laboratory craft of description and analysis, with its industrial applications—to manage complex notational systems, to comprehend high-level measurement concepts, and to manipulate algebraic and geometrical relationships called for a detached scholarly posture that was indifferent to time and surrendered purpose to the internal architecture of the discipline. If creativity as such was not called for—objectives were not so ambitious as in Nuffield—inventiveness was demanded in posing hypotheses for experimental testing. All senior students could be expected to work with abstractions. The question was how many could sustain an image of chemistry that increasingly withdrew into its theoretical and mathematical recesses, treating the earthly phenomena of chemical substances as mere illustrations of higher-order principles. In place of the traditional chemistry of fact and process, the stress was now placed upon students discussing *'unknown* chemical systems in terms of their basic understanding rather than upon a regurgitation of memorized, but apparently unrelated chemical "facts"'.[4]

But the flight to theory also posed risks to the future of chemistry in the school curriculum—to long-term demand for the subject, to the adequacy of its social base, and to the attitudes and priorities of the students who did take it. The academic crafting of the chemistry curriculum would deter new populations, entrenching the subject as the domain of the traditional users of secondary education. For the potential of chemistry to be exploited as an economic and strategic tool was enhanced just when the need for competitive advantage through the curriculum was increasing. Satisfying the private goals of academic success—high marks, access to elite courses, social esteem, professional incomes—was by no means consistent with the philosophical objective of spreading scientific culture or the policy goal of training more research scientists. If these notions of the public value of chemistry supplied the ultimate justification of the reforms, the direction of the reforms raised the market value of the subject as a vehicle of private purpose.

Chemistry as a theoretical discipline based on atomic structure, energy and bonding made a very suitable object of academic study. It was screened off from everyday life as an independent hierarchical system of abstraction, with its own technical vocabulary and internal 'problems' and 'topics'. Like an ancient or foreign language, it required students to master both its underlying grammar and its surface features of experimental production—basic physical concepts and principles, symbolic language, measurement and representational strategies (as with molecular structure), the 'rules' of chemical behaviour, the wealth of factual material about elements, compounds and reactions, and the laboratory framework that tested both the generative theory and the knowledge of detail. The new chemistry had all the attributes needed to make it an academic discipline without producing a single scientist–remoteness from life, the sense of election that it imparted to a select group of students, its prestige in the social hierarchy of knowledge, the complexity of its concepts and nomenclature, its mathematical bias, and the daunting mass of information that only the most hardened 'swots' could digest.

To operate chemistry as an instrument of strategic advantage, however, would require more than its conversion into a branch of physics. The traditional examination regime was an obstacle to improving the standing of the physical sciences and would have to be overhauled to support both the new demands made on students and their ability to derive career benefits from it.

Student quality and the academic status of chemistry

The high failure rates of the late 1940s and early 1950s had impressed on schools the need to limit the numbers of students taking senior mathematics and science. Participation in these subjects had fallen sharply from the end of World War Two as the population completing school rose rapidly. Schools and students were also being more cautious about entering zones that presented such clear risks (see Figure 13).[5]

Pass rates rose in the 1960s, in part because of this greater selectiveness, in part because the university examiners came under pressure to bring science rates into line with those in the humanities.[6] Standardization procedures introduced in 1971 would capitalize on the underlying trend in the relative quality of science students. To compare achievement across different subjects as a basis for selection to university, the matriculation examining

Figure 13: Chemistry enrolment rates by gender, 1947–90: full candidates taking Year 12 chemistry

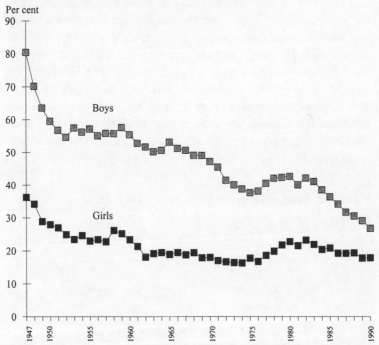

Source: Examination handbooks for successive years published by MU, Schools Board, VUSEB, VISE and VCAB.

authority adjusted distributions of marks so that, in effect, subjects taken by consistently stronger students would be scaled upwards, while those taken by weaker students would be scaled downwards. Standardization protected the high levels of achievement of students in subjects, notably mathematics and the physical sciences, in which individual performance was highly correlated. This system fortified the position of the most able students. Their distribution across the curriculum determined the relative profitability of the different subjects within it. Other changes, in particular the shift towards short-answer and multiple-choice formats in examinations, improved the reliability of assessment, thus channelling high-achieving students towards a restricted range of subjects that offered competitive advantage.

All these changes in the examination regime cushioned the students who were embarking on the new chemistry syllabus that had been implemented in 1966. Balancing its rigours as a theoretical and mathematical exercise was the security that hard work in this subject would contribute to good marks in the other subjects most frequently taken with it—physics and mathematics—and would be rewarded by a globally high result. The likelihood of gaining honours in chemistry—highly variable until the early 1960s, then comparable to biology for a few years—began to rise in line with the improving trend in student quality and the system of standardizing results to the advantage of the strongest students (see Figure 14).[7]

Figure 14: Honours rates in the sciences, 1947–85

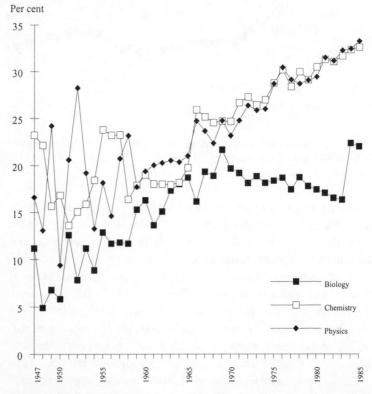

Source: Examination handbooks for successive years published by MU, Schools Board, VUSEB, VISE and VCAB.

Chemistry and physics—along with traditional foreign languages and mathematics—were being set apart as a separate channel within the curriculum, virtually a different system of schooling with a distinctive institutional base. Meanwhile, the great tide of post-war aspirations would flow into inferior channels subjacent to them—biology and human development, the larger humanities, the new business subjects, eventually technology. If the 'hard options' in the curriculum were attracting a declining proportion of students, this was because their social base was narrowing towards a select group of clients who needed *difficult subjects to settle affairs among themselves.*

Participation and performance in the 1970s

The new chemistry syllabus implemented in 1966 was to remain in place with successive modifications until 1978.[8] During this period, interest in completing school climbed steadily until checked in the mid-1970s by economic downturn. Growing diversity would see falls in participation in the subjects most frequently prescribed by university, sparking concerns over the drift away from science. But chemistry numbers were still at a very high level—around 6500 candidates presented for the exam in 1975—and the subject was widely available, taught in more than 350 schools across Victoria. Chemistry was a mass subject, a major vehicle of educational aspirations, indispensable for gaining a place in many science, clinical, paramedical, engineering and applied science courses. Yet, while it was indeed a mass subject, access to it remained socially restrictive, for it was highly discriminating of the attainment of those students who did attempt it.

The social geography of participation in subjects that are used to exercise power in the curriculum recapitulates the social history of mass secondary schooling itself. Thus in those urban regions inhabited by the populations whose historical presence in the upper secondary curriculum was longest, the likelihood of studying chemistry in 1975 was also greatest—41 per cent of boys and 19 per cent of girls in the wealthiest quarters of Melbourne. Where completing school was least likely—as in the inner, western, northern and south-eastern suburbs—the chances of studying chemistry were also poorest—around 30 per cent of boys (higher in the outer west) and between 12 and 17 per cent of girls (see Figure 15).[9] So great was the gender divide that even girls from regions with the most educated populations had lower participation rates than boys in the most disadvantaged regions.

If the last groups to embrace senior secondary school exercised the weakest claim to study subjects at the pinnacle of the curriculum hierarchy, they also fared worst when they did study them. In the north-west of Melbourne, every third boy failed chemistry in

Figure 15: Chemistry enrolment and completing school by region and gender, Melbourne, 1975

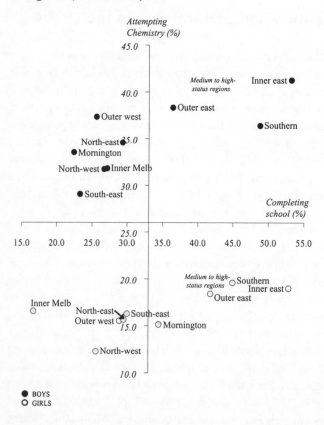

Source: Unpublished HSC results, 1975.

1975—though they were less likely than other boys to enrol—and every fourth girl, even though only 12 per cent attempted the subject. Conversely, in the high-status inner east of the city, around 37 per cent of boys gained either first-class or second-class honours, compared with 24 per cent in the north-west and 19 per cent in the south-east (see Figure 16). More 'firsts' were awarded to boys in the inner-eastern and southern suburbs than the total number of honours at any level received by boys in the western or south-eastern suburbs or in rural Victoria.

The double advantage enjoyed by students from professional and managerial backgrounds—higher levels of participation and superior performance—derived in part from family education and life-styles built on economic position, and in part from collective organization through private and other selective schools. Parents who were university-educated or had experienced higher secondary education expected their children to go to university—an expectation that had grown during the 1950s and 1960s as competition for places rose and quotas were imposed.[10]

Tighter access to university accentuated the strategic importance of science for boys from upper middle-class homes. They were also more likely to internalize science as a trajectory, and as a source of personal interest and satisfaction. In the mid-1970s, when every second qualified applicant for university was being turned away, the boys who displayed the greatest attachment to science in the middle years of secondary school were also those whose social background promised to deliver them a science-based profession.[11] In a survey conducted in Melbourne in 1979, 46 per cent of boys whose fathers were in the higher professions or senior management nominated the sciences as the subjects that most interested them, compared with only 26 per cent of boys from manual workers' homes.[12] What was, objectively, a medium of scholastic discrimination was also, subjectively, a medium of personal fulfilment. Early success at school paved the way for this harmonization of career destiny and psychological experience. It would also dictate the social sequence in which girls took up an increasing share of places in science. Students from educated homes could build on higher relative attainment in English and mathematics to relate to science as an academic discipline and to

Figure 16: Chemistry honours and enrolment in selected regions by gender, 1975

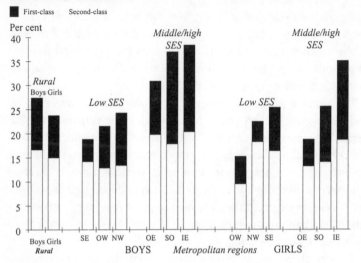

HONOURS IN CHEMISTRY

■ First-class   Second-class

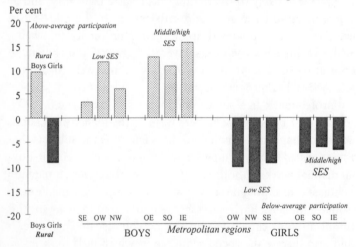

ENROLLING IN CHEMISTRY -- deviations from regional average (= 25.7%)

Notes: SE South-east, OW Outer west, NW North-west, OE Outer east, SO Southern,
          IE Inner east

Source: Unpublished HSC results, 1975.

manage its progressively more abstract demands as it became specialized into chemistry, physics and biology.

'Too complicated' and 'too difficult' were the most frequent complaints levelled against science.[13] But those students whose training in language and number at home had equipped them with the conceptual skills to master abstract principles and symbolic expression would escape the boredom that inevitably descended on a subject that had ceased to be an avenue of learning. Tests of cognitive style showed that chemistry and physics students were fluent in the skills of conceptual differentiation—classifying and distinguishing—that they could change perspectives and view issues and data from different angles, and with originality, and that they looked below the surface of physical objects to 'intrinsic qualities'.[14]

Schools for science

If the disposition to abstraction, analysis and classification took root in homes where word and concept were objects of explicit and reflexive training—the 'critical thinking' that the science curriculum prized as much as the humanities—this would grow or languish according to the intellectual culture and resources of schools. Establishments that drew narrowly from the educated middle classes did not merely act as a relay of family influences or a depot for like-minded families to pool their efforts. They assembled the specialist resources needed to teach science to a high standard and to ensure that it would be, if not the dominant educational endeavour (as in boys' schools), at any rate a major emphasis on which the prestige of the establishment would rest.[15]

Science teachers in private schools were very well trained. In Victoria in 1979, 44 per cent of secondary-school teachers working in these establishments had graduated from universities (rather than teachers' colleges) compared with 36 per cent of those in public high schools.[16] Mathematics departments were staffed almost entirely by graduates who had three-year majors in mathematics at a university or college of advanced education (90 per cent as against 70 per cent in the government sector). Their chemistry teachers had all completed majors in chemistry, though—in contrast to high schools—none held honours degrees. But it was in physics that private schools were especially selective as to whom they employed.

Every second physics teacher in a private school had an honours degree, while the remainder had all done three years of physics. The situation in high schools presented a sharp contrast—only 14 per cent had graduated with honours, and more than 40 per cent had completed only one or two years of physics.[17] The bias in private schools towards a high level of investment in physics answered a science curriculum that officially proclaimed the takeover of chemistry by physics (and the progressive assimilation of biology to physical chemistry).

The science culture of schools was also reflected in the attainment and attitudes of students themselves. In the IEA survey of science achievement in 1970, the average results for 14-year-olds in Victorian private schools in the combined biology, chemistry and physics tests, understanding science, interest in science, and word knowledge all clearly differentiated this sector from government and Catholic schools.[18] In the more discriminating context of public examinations, there could be no doubt that private schools were effectively capitalizing on the cultural and financial resources of parents, recruiting the most academic teachers and using all of these assets to capture the strategic heights of the curriculum.

The institutional geography of chemistry in the mid-1970s shows that the reformed syllabus found its natural home in private schools. Between these establishments and all other schools —public or Catholic, well-located or in poor suburbs—there were very substantial gaps, both in levels of participation and in competitive performance. Girls in working-class high schools had about a 6 per cent chance of gaining first-class honours in chemistry. This improved to about 8 or 9 per cent among girls in Catholic secondary colleges and in middle-class high schools. Girls in private establishments could expect to receive first-class honours at nearly double that rate. Their competitive advantage was also built on higher levels of participation (see Figure 17).

By the mid-1970s, chemistry was coming under siege from girls. The new syllabus ensured that it was girls from private schools—

Figure 17: First-class honours in chemistry and enrolment rates by school type and gender, Melbourne 1975[1]

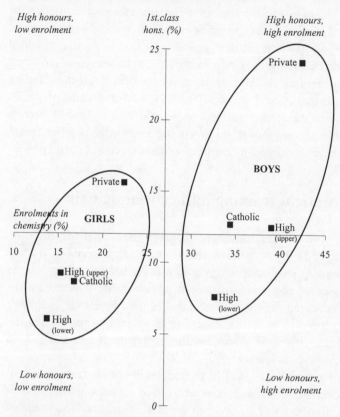

[1] High-school results are shown for middle to upper-status suburbs ('upper') and for working-class suburbs ('lower').

Source: Unpublished HSC results, 1975.

as well as from a few selective Catholic and public high schools—who would take the lead in colonizing this male domain. Its theoretical and mathematical orientation exploited the intensive language training given to girls in professional and managerial families, the encouragement and practical help that they received in mathematics, and the self-assurance that was nourished in them as a prelude to personal independence.

Boys from private schools were granted first-class honours three times as often as those in working-class high schools. Nearly every fourth boy in a private non-Catholic establishment could be assured of gaining the top grade in chemistry—and as many again a second-class honour. The severe risks that had once attended tackling chemistry were now in the past. Syllabus reform towards greater theoretical depth, examinations reform to lift the standing of mathematics and physical sciences, and a decade of public finance to modernize socially segregated and inefficient private schools had combined to transform the 'knowledge base' of chemical science into an academic base for the exercise of social power.

Theoretical training and economic gain

If the rationale for reform in chemistry had been the fostering of science as public culture, the institutional patterns of student achievement suggest that this goal was readily assimilated to the strategies of economic and social advancement pursued by the most educated families. These families used academic chemistry not to build careers in science, but to reserve to themselves the allocation of scarce places in elite professional courses and, in effect, to bypass science.

Only a minority of the best candidates in chemistry entered general science courses, and those who did so came from high schools and Catholic colleges, not private establishments. The students brought to the top by the hierarchical chemistry curriculum, with its stress on fundamental concepts and laws, were those who in the end did not want to be scientists. They used the conceptual hierarchy of chemistry as a means of relaying social advantage. Science as a vocation was served only after this function was filled, generally with students of lesser attainment and from more modest homes.

In the schools where relative advantage was greatest, chemistry was an avenue to the clinical professions. More than half of all boys in private schools who received first-class honours in chemistry in 1975 aimed for medicine, dentistry, veterinary science, optometry, physiotherapy and other paramedical courses (without counting pharmacy).[19] If law and architecture are included, then about 60 per cent of the top-ranking students from the private sector used chemistry to secure entry to the private-income professions, with only one in six aiming for general science (and sometimes then only as a bridge to clinical courses).

Girls with first-class honours gravitated more to science, which balanced their poor representation in engineering. But they were also even more narrowly focused on clinical sciences—from 54 per cent of the best students in Catholic schools and 60 per cent of high-school girls to as many as three in every four girls from private schools (see Figure 18).

Figure 18: Top chemistry candidates and their preferences for university science and medical courses by school type and gender, 1976[1]

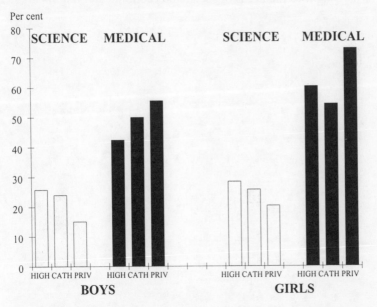

[1] Percentage of all school candidates gaining As in chemistry and expressing a first preference for general science or mathematics courses compared to those nominating medicine, dentistry, veterinary science, optometry and other paramedical courses (other than pharmacy, for which no information available).

Source: Unpublished VTAC data, 1976.

If reforms to the chemistry syllabus were made in the name of chemical science, in practice they operated to restrict social access to professional training by increasing the intellectual demands on students in a context where only a minority could meet those demands. The syllabus writers of the 1960s—and the curriculum authorities who would enforce their vision in the 1970s—had focused narrowly on internal changes in the discipline. They sought to mirror the theoretical architecture of chemistry in the curriculum, believing that logical structure determines cognitive growth in a discipline. They ignored quality of student learning experience, instructional standards in schools, and the values and aptitudes of teachers. Aiming at a better chemistry, not at a chemistry better taught, they constructed the syllabus in a pedagogical vacuum. Left to the strongest schools to interpret and exploit, the syllabus became a means not of spreading scientific culture, but of harnessing it to the needs of social and economic dominion.

7

Resisting Chemical Reform in the 1980s

> For them, the progress of the sciences is a secondary aim
> to the perpetuation or extension of their power.
>
> *Condorcet* (1793)

Over time, the academic curriculum comes to be moulded by the characteristics of its dominant users. Examiners shape their demands according to the performance of a large core of good students, and then stretch this group with more difficult questions in order to identify stronger individuals. Since the core of candidates who can satisfy the examiners' expectations is not drawn randomly from across the school system, the schools that are major suppliers of good students exercise a substantial indirect influence over what the examiners can reasonably expect and what they cannot. The style of teaching and the philosophy and policy of curriculum in these schools, and the academic and social characteristics of their students, become decisive for holding the curriculum in place as a workable system. Neither excessively harsh nor too lenient, manageable but discriminating, the curriculum must embody a feasible and fair set of demands to enjoy public confidence, especially among the families who count on its hierarchy of opportunities to advance or conserve their social position.

The severity of examinations, however, is relative. If a contemporary standard of fairness requires that one in five candidates should fail, but no more, this may stretch to two or three times as many at some sites in the school system and contract to half as many or less at other sites. Because the distribution of failure across schools is generally unknown, the test of legitimacy comes to reside in the failure rate experienced by the most influential users of the curriculum, among whom it tends to zero. To achieve this end, it is not enough for the most educated families to influence examinations indirectly and over the long term through superior quality of students. Nor are financial and cultural resources in themselves sufficient to maintain academic dominance. Because the strong performance of good students constantly tends to annihilate other groups, the curriculum as a system of coercive demands would lose legitimacy unless it was fortified on the outside. Power through the curriculum must be supported by power *over* the curriculum in order to give authority to intellectual demands and legitimacy to the arbitrary, unequal and grave effects these demands produce at the social level.

When the global economic environment weakened in the mid-1970s and youth unemployment escalated, it brought to a head the protracted conflict over control of school programmes that reached back to the inter-war years. Space had to be created in the curriculum for new populations, and the relationship of universities to schools had to change. Universities, however, would not readily cede or share their authority over school programmes. Their key strategic objective was to maintain the integrity of the selected science and humanities subjects on which their authority ultimately depended. The assertion of authority switched from the legal and bureaucratic instruments of examination boards, with their more or less narrow institutional membership and formal regulatory powers, to the politics of the academic discipline, with its hierarchies of intellectual authority, professorial rank and institutional prestige.

The structural syllabus revisited

In 1979 the old Victorian Universities and Schools Examinations Board was replaced by a more broadly representative curriculum body, the Victorian Institute of Secondary Education. Its task, carefully distinguished in statute from that of its predecessor, was to expand the upper secondary curriculum to serve a variety of needs beyond university.[1] The Matriculation Certificate had been renamed the Higher School Certificate in anticipation of the policies that would eventually be implemented by the new agency. These policies hinged on giving schools significant decision-making power over their programmes. In future, they would be able to decide which prescribed syllabus options they would teach in addition to core material. They would take over part of student assessment, and they would be free to design subjects that were not for university and over which they had complete control. These developments triggered a new round of reform in chemistry.

From a university perspective, permitting schools to choose options within the syllabus carried with it the dangers of diversity, lack of student comparability across schools, and uneven preparation for university courses. The relaxation of central controls thus required universities to work more closely with teachers to limit how the partial autonomy of schools would be exercised. This was particularly important in science and mathematics, which were closely sequenced across institutional levels. Extending pedagogical freedom to schoolteachers curtailed it among university academics. How lecturers designed and taught subjects would be constrained by what schoolteachers did, a reversal of the traditional hierarchical relationship, and one that threatened academic freedom and institutional authority in the most conservative disciplines.

Meeting in September 1975 in the lead-up to statewide changes in curriculum management, chemistry teachers took the opportunity to express their views about the structural course that had been set for them to teach ten years earlier. They wanted changes in emphasis, in style of approach, and also in content. Gravitating back to traditional chemistry, they wanted to see 'explicit references to [the] Australian chemical industry, its processes and problems'.[2] Less emphasis should be placed on 'numerical manipulation rather than chemistry', and there should be more descriptive and organic chemistry. The whole course should be interesting to teachers and students. Teachers felt that the objectives of the current course were satisfactory, if not presented as precisely and usefully as they could be. Significantly, they thought that the key concepts of chemistry were 'within the grasp of students'. The questions were the quantitative emphasis and the pedagogical framework within which the subject should be presented. More attention should be paid to how student interest developed. At least some topics should be presented historically. Materials should be attractive, and the social responsibility of chemists and chemistry should be addressed in the course.

Introduced on a trial basis in 1977 and offered selectively as an alternative course in 1978, 'newchem'—as the syllabus came to be known—was fully implemented in 1979. Setting the tone, the *Handbook* gave as the 'overwhelming reason for the revision of [the course] the belief that Chemistry must be seen by students to do with the world about them'.[3] The subject was no longer to be 'theory-dominated'. It was to be inclusive, not only of young people aiming for tertiary education, but also of those who would not continue with chemistry. This terminal group made up the majority of the population, and they were to be spared the 'extreme emphasis on "unreal" atomic and structural levels'.[4] They would benefit instead from the chemistry of everyday life substances.

Though organized differently, the new chemistry course had much in common with the old, particularly in the core areas of atomic theory, energy and chemical reactions (embracing stoichiometry, the mole concept and equilibrium). The major departure was the use of the biosphere as an umbrella concept to cover the elements and organic chemistry. This enabled everyday themes to be introduced, such as atmospheric and water pollution, fertilizers, insecticides and energy in human society. But these themes were not treated in depth: their place was to spark interest in theoretical principles of energy, reactions, bonding and equilibrium. Similarly, the coverage of industrial applications—petroleum, coal, ammonia, phosphorus, sulphur, extractive metallurgy—was intended to launch students into theory rather than technology. The textbook, *Chemistry, Key to the Earth* (1979), met the promise of attractive presentation and reintroduced a historical treatment of concepts (atomic theory, electrolysis, redox reactions and some industrial processes).[5] But it diverged little from the previous textbook in setting theoretical comprehension and a quantitative orientation as its major goal.

If 'newchem' was 'neither the innovative nor the radical change in direction' announced in text and syllabus, there was little reason to expect it to have been.[6] Continuity with the past was assured by the fact that all of the members of the editorial board responsible for the textbook were members of the standing committee in charge of the previous course, as were many of the writers, while the chief editor was also one of the five men who had written the structural syllabus for 1966. As in the past, the course had to satisfy the traditional client preparing for further chemical study at university or college of advanced education. It was tempered pedagogically to engage the interest of terminal students, for whom chemistry was treated as a form of general education. It had no direct or planned relevance to their employment or training destinations and took no account of their future possible exposure to chemical processes in different industries and occupations.

The new course did not have a vocational orientation. Its core–options structure was not flexible enough to generate multiple strands with a variable emphasis on industry or research. There was only one chemistry—fundamental chemistry. The order of presentation could be rotated and its components might receive different weight, but theoretical mastery remained the overriding objective. The lack of substantial choice in the chemistry programme and the continuing dominance of structure and measurement in the examinable syllabus effectively contained the wider reform process that had aimed to transfer significant curriculum control to schools. The integrity of the discipline had been preserved.

Student outcomes

Little change could be expected in social patterns of student achievement. The curriculum continued to be shaped by the performance of the strongest students and to respond to their need for academic distinction. At the 1976 examination, the Chemistry Standing Committee—soon to become the editorial board responsible for the revised syllabus—had resolved to reverse 'the trend over the past few years to easier examination papers' by increasing the number of questions that tested 'analytical and synthetic skills'.[7] Would such a philosophy, with its concern for standards, be left behind when the writers of the new syllabus were given their brief?

While retention rates climbed again in the early 1980s, placing renewed pressure on university places, the containment of reforms in chemistry prevented any break in the unequal flow of benefits to the established users of academic schooling. There was scarcely any change in relative outcomes following the revision of the syllabus. More than half of all boys in private schools took the subject in 1985—itself a major indication of the nature and role of the course—and every second one received a first-class or second-class honour.

The academic prowess of the private-school boy—the archetypal pupil on which examinations in the oldest disciplines, whether sciences or humanities, were modelled—had been built up over many years, if not over the 'century of excellence' claimed by some establishments. New populations were competing against the weight of history, for the settings in which they were being educated differed systematically from the 'greater public school' in terms of intrinsic and extrinsic motives for learning, deep and surface approaches, collaborative and competitive learning styles, confidence and self-esteem, mixed-sex classrooms, and liberal versus selective promotions. It was not simply that the social conditions under which boys in private schools competed were superior. Nor was it the result of much better facilities, such as the six science laboratories that Camberwell Grammar School could boast in 1983, or the five laboratories at Brighton Grammar in 1988, to name only second-string establishments.[8] Managed so well by this dominant group, the chemistry curriculum represented a successful educational enterprise that could remain aloof from the needs of new populations so long as the clients to whom the course authorities were most sensitive continued to experience almost complete success.

Failure rates in chemistry for boys in private schools were only 7 or 8 per cent. These students had little reason to fear exams, so long as they worked hard, and the social, physical, organizational and cultural conditions of their schools ensured that they did work effectively. Their schools had evolved a style of work based on the settled routine of the large class (filled over three or four years by successive testing and streaming), group-centred pedagogy geared to homogeneous classes and intensive training using work sheets, practice exams and cribs. Ultimately, it was the effectiveness of this technical–bureaucratic pattern of work that moulded syllabus and assessment around the private-school student as the implicit point of reference and the test of reality.

The shift to physical chemistry and to a 'theory-dominated' course in the 1960s and its continuation into the 1980s was managed by employing trained physics and mathematics teachers and by reducing the syllabus to an ever-varied but basically constant series of 'topics' that could be mechanically rehearsed and drilled until students reached a level of examinations competence, if not a deeper understanding. The abstract and mathematical character of physical chemistry could be surmounted because students had the necessary cognitive and language skills. Learning could be taken to the point of collective competitive success because, given social intakes and academic selection, instructional practice could be reduced to a technical–bureaucratic process, represented by Smith and Fox's 2500 *Questions in Chemistry* or Gardiner's 1218 'problems in physics', capturing as these do the contemporary pedagogical regime of Carey Baptist Grammar School and Melbourne Grammar School from the late 1960s up to the early 1980s.[9]

The shift to short-answer and multiple-choice formats for examination questions suited this production process and ensured its success. In the factory model of learning, the way in which students reported their knowledge was closely controlled, with a minimum of open-ended discursive answers (which risked imprecision and irrelevance and might betray gaps in comprehension). When Wesley College told its parents in 1987 that the school's 'concentration on academic excellence' meant that it was 'anything but "an H.S.C. factory"', it could only have sown confusion by adding statistics to prove that the school produced success for virtually all its students with an efficiency that had become routine.[10]

The modelling of the curriculum on the capacities of its strongest users can be judged from the distance opened up between them and students from the most vulnerable populations. In 1985, only about 16 per cent of girls living in the working-class west, north and south-east of Melbourne and attending public high schools attempted chemistry. Switching gender and shifting from public to private sector raised participation levels more than threefold. Though much more severely selected, girls in working-class high schools who took chemistry would be awarded first-class honours only four times in 100. Boys in working-class high schools, though nearly twice as likely to enrol in chemistry, were awarded 'firsts' three times as often. But the dominant male group, located in private schools, were eight times as likely to obtain top marks (see Figure 19).[11]

Marginalizing new populations

No mental experiment is needed to assess how long the chemistry syllabus would have endured had the high rates of failure experienced by the weakest students been transferred to those with the highest public profile. Back in the 1940s and early 1950s, when the science professors of the University of Melbourne were failing every second candidate for matriculation chemistry and physics (and ridding themselves of a further sizeable proportion at the end of first year), school protests eventually stripped the Chief Examiners of their excessive powers. Fail rates were reduced in line with other subjects. Eventually only a third of candidates would fail every year, and there would be later improvements over this. In those early post-war decades, the students who were failing often came from private schools, the major group from which the university then drew. Such high levels of scholastic mortality were unacceptable. Yet just such rates would be experienced routinely by newer populations some forty years later, even after official adjustments had been made to fail only about 20 per cent of students in total in any subject.

The institutional invisibility of these newer groups protected the chemistry syllabus from more fundamental change than was implemented in 1979. In the north-west of Melbourne, where only 13 per cent of high-school girls sat for the chemistry exams, as

**Figure 19: First-class honours and enrolment in chemistry by
school type and gender, 1985**

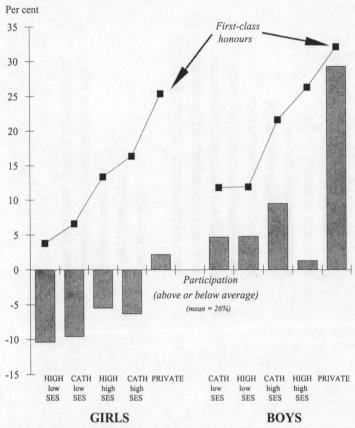

Source: Unpublished HSC results, 1985.

many as 37 per cent were failed (see Figure 20). This was the level
experienced by mainly male candidates from non-government
schools in the late 1950s. The chemistry syllabus, devised without
regard to the quality of learning of the newest populations to
complete school, retarded their historical progress by thirty years.
Conversely, the syllabus offered each new cohort in the top private schools a head start of two decades over the average student.
The rate of honours results obtained by the elite Headmasters'

Figure 20: Chemistry failure rates and enrolment, high-school girls by region, 1985

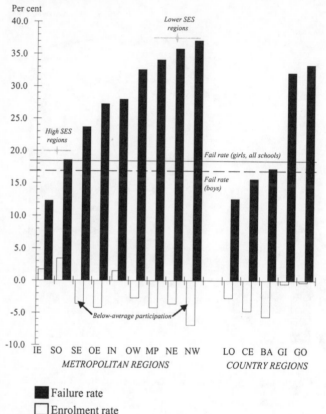

Failure rate

Enrolment rate

[1] Enrolment rates are expressed as deviations from the rate for all girls. Codes for regions:- IE (inner east), SO (southern), SE (south-east), OE (outer east), IN (inner Melb.), OW (outer west), MP (Mornington Peninsula), NE (north-east), NW (north-west); LO (Loddon–Campaspe–Mallee), CE (central Vic.), BA (Barwon–South Western), GI (Gippsland), GO (Goulburn).

Source: Unpublished HSC results, 1985.

Conference schools in most mathematics and physical science subjects in 1966 was greater than the honours rates in these subjects for all students in 1985, and by that time the results for these six schools were still further advanced (see Figure 21).[12]

Figure 21: Mathematics and physical science honours—six private schools compared with statewide levels, 1966–85

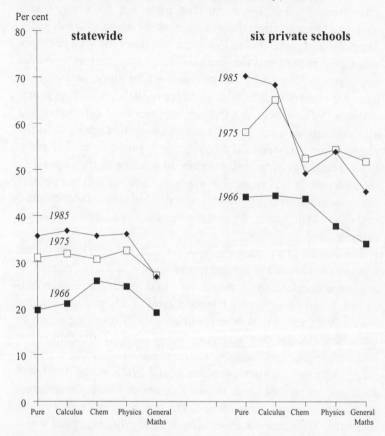

Source: For 1966, see I. V. Hansen, *Nor Free Nor Secular*, Melbourne, 1971, pp. 82–90; for 1975 and 1985, unpublished results of HSC exams.

School chemistry and strategic advantage

The social role of the syllabus in setting the most powerful students several decades ahead of their competitors in a mass secondary school system undermined the official pedagogical emphasis on relating chemistry to the real world of students. It focused attention on the theoretical and examinable content of the course, which was little changed from the past. If it was possible for some teachers—mindful of real-world relevance—to investigate salient properties of water before tackling molecular structure, others were free to launch into theory earlier, as the *Handbook* advised.[13] They could bypass issues of historical, social or industrial relevance —material that earned the scorn of examiners—and focus on the key concepts, principles and operations that alone provided the basis for statistical discrimination between students in the exam- inations.[14] Theirs was not the practical world of descriptive and applied chemistry, but the universe of conceptual entities and the physical and mathematical relationships between them. The peda- gogical task was not to relate theory to practice or the abstract to the concrete. It was to instil in students the ability to manipulate concepts at successively higher levels of abstraction through mas- tery of the symbolic codes and mathematical principles of chemi- cal relations.

The freedom to pursue theory—in the name of training future scientists—was also a licence to use theory as an instrument of academic domination. A decade of rapid growth in higher edu- cation, based on mounting retention rates in schools, accentuated the strategic role of chemistry and physics in reserving places in university courses that were gaining in career profitability, but had no intrinsic link with the sciences. Business studies attracted more and more high achievers during the 1980s as the Australian economy expanded and financial markets were deregulated, prompting a deluge of investment. The traditional training avenues to economic success, via the private-income professions and senior government and corporate appointments, were changing in their relative importance under the combined impact of glutted pro- fessional markets and business reorganization.

Girls from the most socially advantaged families continued to aim with confidence at medicine, despite shrinking quotas. Every third girl gaining top marks in chemistry from a private school in 1989 wanted to become a doctor.[15] Physiotherapy, occupational therapy, chiropractic and other paramedical courses drew much smaller numbers, but enough to make health sciences the largest single field of endeavour for the elite of science girls from private schools. But this group—the earliest of their sex to colonize the male domain of chemistry—was now also ready to take on the up-market business courses offered by universities. Around 16 per cent of private-school girls with first-class honours in chemistry aimed at commerce or law. The top girls in public high schools, on the other hand, were more modest in their medical ambitions—only 25 per cent wanted to be doctors or dentists, and 16 per cent would be content with paramedical training. They were also more traditional in the balance of their preferences between business (with its entrepreneurial tone and corporate orientation) and engineering (with its complexion of professional and government service). Private-school boys who had excelled in chemistry followed the market trend away from medicine into business. Against 27 per cent who planned to do medicine or dentistry, there were 21 per cent aiming at business, finance and accounting courses, mainly in the more prestigious universities. High-school boys with top marks in chemistry were only half as likely to strike out in this direction. Their faith remained with engineering, architecture, building and surveying, which together accounted for 42 per cent of their first preferences.

For young people receiving the most expensive and most socially segregated schooling, chemistry played a distinctive strategic role. It allowed girls to expand their share of medical places against contracting relative opportunities, and it ushered in business careers. Not an insignificant group (12 per cent) played the dilettante by enrolling in Arts courses, but always at the one university whose selectiveness made Arts especially acceptable. For boys, chemistry provided a continuing large share of medical places, while enabling them to shift increasingly into commerce. Chemistry training, as a form of educational capital, was thus used both to protect traditional professional markets and to expand into the new managerial markets.

General science courses at university lacked the clear economic rationale of medicine, physiotherapy, engineering and business, though they still attracted a large minority of the best chemistry candidates—around 16 per cent of girls (both in public and private schools) and 17 per cent of boys (marginally greater in high schools). To this extent, the chemistry syllabus implemented in 1979 succeeded in preparing new generations of potential research scientists, leaving aside those who might proceed from medicine to medical research. Science as a destination, however, had comparatively little weight among the range of other course preferences. If the hierarchy of conceptual demands in chemistry was meant to prepare for a hierarchy of intellectual operations, rising from those in technical support roles through to engineering and clinical sciences and on to fundamental research—the brighter the students, the greater their potential contribution to new knowledge —in practice this was not achieved. Instead the syllabus worked to translate successive grades of academic performance into an economic hierarchy, beginning with nursing and culminating in medicine. The average student seeking entry to general science courses was mediocre according to the scale of attainment applied by universities themselves (see Figure 22).

Revisions to the chemistry syllabus in 1966 and 1979 were made without reference to the nature of the students who would undertake the course. Why some succeeded and some failed and why the patterns were not socially random were viewed as irrelevant. So too was the range of employment and training destinations in which students might ultimately use their chemical knowledge. Homogeneity of client and homogeneity of purpose were the twin assumptions governing the revision of the examinable syllabus.

These matching assumptions point back to the fact that the changes were made from within the sphere of influence of the same institution. Dominating the hierarchy of tertiary institutions as measured by academic quality of students, level of social intakes and prestige of programmes, the University of Melbourne was sovereign over secondary schools and wore the mantle of real authority over the curriculum. The standpoint of this institution and the power that it exercised in its field accounted for the persistent failure to take the diversity of students and their variety of purpose into account in the process of curriculum change. The assumption that all students were alike—or at any rate *ought* to be if they wished to study chemistry—simply expressed that institution's demand that all students be compared on the same scale of merit. By offering better students the chance to assert their

Figure 22: Mean chemistry scores of applicants for university by intended field of study, 1990[1]

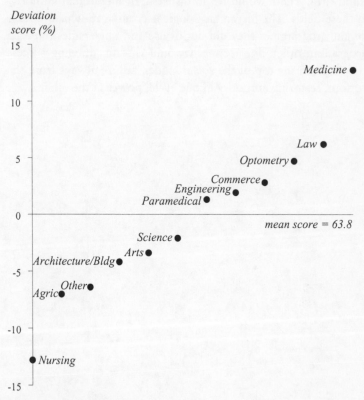

Deviation
score (%)

15

Medicine ●

10

Law ●
5   Optometry ●
            Commerce ●
        Engineering ●
    Paramedical ●

0   mean score = 63.8

        Science ●
    Arts ●
Architecture/Bldg ●
-5
    Other ●
Agric ●

-10

● Nursing

-15

[1] School leaver applicants only.

Source: Unpublished VTAC data, 1990. Chart relates to school-leaver applicants only.

superiority on a scale that applied to all, the University of Melbourne could assert its own pre-eminence: its students would come only from the top of the scale.

The integrity of chemistry as an academic discipline—there were not to be multiple subjects—enabled a conservative theory-based interpretation to prevail and in turn perpetuated a vertical scaling of intellectual quality on which the prestige of institutions could rest. While other disciplines, including mathematics, showed perilous signs of fragmentation when school-based programmes made their appearance in the 1980s, chemistry and physics would stand firm. There would be no dispersal of intellectual authority in these fields. The hierarchical logic according to which schools taught programmes they did not devise and universities imposed programmes they did not teach would run on, drawing success always from the top of the social ladder, failure always from the bottom, restoring authority in one cycle, power in the other.

8

Chemistry and the Victorian Certificate of Education

THAT THE BEST RESEARCHERS begin life as pupils with the best marks was an article of faith among scientists who had made university teaching their career in the 1960s. They owed their own advancement to the system of academic grades that began with Matriculation or Leaving Honours and culminated in a PhD, often awarded overseas. Research training funded by a scholarship followed on from their success as star pupils at school. So the potential to create new knowledge in the laboratory would tend to be seen to lie in the ability to reproduce old knowledge in exams. Having spurned the salaries and status of lucrative government and corporate jobs, university scientists were confirmed in their view that examinations were tests of nobility, and that it was from the highest ranks of the academic nobility in schools that new researchers came.

It was with alarm, then, that scientists and mathematicians in the 1980s observed a seemingly invariant pattern in which the pool of high-scoring students at school drained into courses for the high-income professions at university. Relatively few of the best candidates were left for research, and it was mainly average students who returned to teach science in schools. 'Many of our best mathematics and science students are going into medicine and law regardless of their aptitude for these careers', the federation of Australian scientific and technological societies complained in 1988. The better candidates who did enrol in science often completed an honours degree only to enter banking or finance or computing. They were lost to science.[1]

The drift from science began with the theoretical orientation of chemistry and physics and the construction of these subjects as conceptual systems whose structural integrity had to be guarded at all costs. One physics, one chemistry: only in the field of modern languages was there the same refusal to differentiate subjects, the same insistence on hierarchical order. It was the pursuit of fundamental principles that justified this monotonic view of physical science and demanded that all students take the one road leading to the ultimate hypothetical entities of physics and their logical concourse in mathematical space.

If a declining proportion of students took science, this was not only because it was a road of vanishing meaning. The tendency for physical science to condense into abstractions—essential for its theoretical progress—delivered the field over to strong students whose cognitive, linguistic and mathematical training, if not intellectual disposition or theoretical aptitude, prepared them to exploit it for career goals. Physics and chemistry, each elaborated as a hierarchy of concepts and principles, also functioned to grade learners in a cognitive hierarchy, making them ideal instruments for academic battle. Weaker students saw neither meaning nor economic value in these subjects and were quickly driven from the field. If the physical sciences were to grow—especially chemistry, the largest—they would have to draw increasingly from the newer populations completing school. But it was precisely these groups— the children of manual workers, many from non-English-speaking backgrounds, many from the country—who were most at risk of failure and whose low participation in reputedly hard subjects was a defence against failure.

The ideology of academic science was self-depleting. Indifferent to the real conditions under which students learnt and the barriers that different groups persistently encountered, the pursuit of excellence would continually diminish science. The drift from the sciences was neither more nor less than their contraction into the populations who, in an age of mass secondary schooling, most needed academic subjects for distinction and could best manage them. The senior academics responsible for interpreting the needs of science to the school system for much of the post-war period could no more question the links between academic excellence and social power or between discipline integrity and institutional dominance than they could doubt the standards entrusted to them by their own high marks in a bygone era. Faced with an image of ineluctable decline spanning the whole period of their stewardship as syllabus masters and examiners, they could only blame external forces—the lure of the market-place, the failure of government science policy (Figure 23).[2] And they would seek to cure the problem of declining interest by appealing to the very spirit of Olympian competition that had undermined the efforts of so many students in the first place.

The revisions to the chemistry syllabus in 1979 had done little to arrest the drift from science as retention rates crept up. The process of social regression continued: high-stakes subjects 'reverted' to the populations with the social power necessary to exploit them. The academic strength of chemistry students is reflected in the fact that in the mid-1980s nine out of ten candidates in chemistry also took university-preparatory mathematics, and half of these were awarded honours.[3] Economic dependence on school was growing, but the primary vehicles for access to professional and managerial training—including fields such as nursing, where entry levels were rising—were hardening against the newer social strata completing school.

If much of the energy to develop a democratic curriculum flowed into school-based subjects and full courses outside the jurisdiction of universities, there was also a growing recognition that this could only end in segregation. It was neither desirable nor possible to shield new populations from the cognitive and cultural demands of the academic curriculum. But, equally, to screen off the most theoretical and at the same time the most lucrative subjects from working-class, migrant and rural children could not be condoned. The reform movement of the 1980s would not be content with judging a subject's quality by the intrinsic rigour of concepts, vouched for by university academics in touch with only a fraction of the school population. It also demanded extrinsic or pedagogical rigour, the strengths of design and content that enabled a subject to be taught well and taught widely.

Figure 23: Decline of chemistry against the background of mass secondary schooling, 1947–96

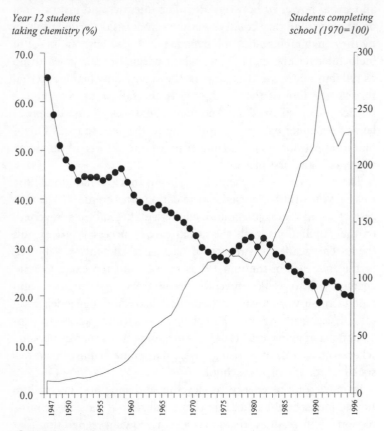

Year 12 students taking chemistry (%)

Students completing school (1970=100)

● Chemistry enrolment rate
– Students completing school

Source: Examination handbooks for successive years published by MU, Schools Board, VUSEB, VISE and VCAB.

Chemistry under the Victorian Certificate of Education (VCE)

In the 1950s and 1960s, the world-transforming powers of physical science had been proclaimed with an unbridled confidence. 'Physics . . . gives us the power to predict and to design, to understand and to adventure into the unknown'.[4] The 1970s and 1980s would see a reaction towards a more qualified view of science. Theoretical fundamentals were forced to concede space to analysis of how science was used or misused. The training of scientists, which began in school, could no longer be limited exclusively to inculcation of physical principles, quantitative concepts and operations, and experimental procedures. What mattered was the place of science in the world, not simply in the laboratory. The curriculum of schools should be made not only for the potential creators of science and for the engineers, chemists and technicians who applied scientific discoveries. The users of science, active or passive, had also to be considered: the 'consumers', the beneficiaries and potential casualties of scientific change, whether in diet, the environment, the workplace, the battlefield or the home. The writers of the revised chemistry syllabus introduced in Victoria in 1979 had already recognized the declining faith in science. But the impact of science on the quality of human and natural life merely supplied the context for reinvigorating a waning interest: there was no basic change in content. The challenge was to import into the examinable syllabus material that bore directly on how science changes life, for good or ill. But this was not taken up.

In the late 1980s, when the chemistry syllabus was again reformed, a more radical approach was taken, ending both the narrow theoretical conception of the discipline and the dominance of the University of Melbourne as the source of institutional authority behind this conception. In the senior year of the new Victorian Certificate of Education, the title of the first semester unit—Chemistry and the Market Place—announced the curriculum writers' intention to move the course into the real world of chemistry. Influenced by Selinger's *Chemistry in the Market Place* (1975, four editions to 1989), the first unit comprised consumer chemistry, industrial chemistry and surface chemistry.[5] Under these headings, students encountered qualitative and quantitative analysis, reactions and equations, stoichiometry, equilibrium, industrial processes and the physical and chemical properties of household products. The work programme took students into analytical procedures for commercial products, instruments in quantitative analysis, examples of equilibrium in living systems, the chemistry of extraction processes and the observation and explanation of the behaviour of surfactants.

The broad conceptual goals of 'market-place' chemistry were very similar to those of previous courses—mastery of fundamental chemical principles, ability to interpret experimental data, and understanding of experimental design and procedures. But there was greater emphasis on knowledge of how chemistry reacted on life, and on the scientific craft of chemistry as distinct from its theoretical foundations. This extended to the content on which students were assessed. Thus the multiple-choice tests on the first Common Assessment Task (CAT No. 1) in 1994 included topics from analytical chemistry (chromatography of food dyes) and industrial processes (cracking of crude oil fractions) as well as the more abundant tasks on reactions, equations and stoichiometry. Short-answer questions included iron in the blast furnace—reactions, energy and efficiencies (production and logistical)—and the manufacture of nitric acid (catalytic efficiency, recycling).

Physical chemistry occupied most of the course in the second half of the senior year. Energy—sources, conversion efficiencies, calorimetry, galvanic cells, the electrochemical series, electrolysis, and Faraday's Laws—and the periodic table as a framework for studying chemistry took the lion's share. This was supplemented by a smaller section on organic chemistry, studied under the rubric of food. The examinable content for this section of the course also represented a significant break from the past. While many of the short-answer questions comprising the third Common Assessment Task dealt with atomic structure, two of the seven questions were allocated to energy production in the human body and food chemistry. Knowledge of the historical growth of chemistry was also examined, and though this received only one question—covering Democritus, Meyer, Rutherford and Meitner—it represented an important pedagogical departure, taking context and history into the domain of assessment.

But continuities with the past were also strong. Most of the tasks demanded by the examiners for the two external examinations were quantitative problems. They tested comprehension of physical concepts (equilibrium, reaction, precipitation, energy), measurement concepts (volume, concentration, percentage, mass, mole), factual knowledge, chemical symbolism (empirical, molecular, and structural formulae, expressions of the state of compounds, symbols for substances), and mathematical aptitude (balancing equations, manipulating nomenclature, use of logarithms). Proficiency with the conceptual and quantitative language of chemistry represented the core set of skills and understanding, although the contexts in which this language was applied were broader than in the past and were brought into the range of examinable knowledge.

Participation and performance differences

Under the VCE, the curriculum offered a wider sampling of the world of chemistry. Market-place chemistry broadened the appeal of the subject among previously low-participating groups. Girls' enrolment rates rose between 1990 and 1994. Most of the regions that recorded growth had below-average participation in 1990 and were either depressed rural or provincial areas or low socio-economic status suburbs of Melbourne. Elsewhere, falls were only slight. In general, the new chemistry course supported greater participation among girls, especially in communities where this had been comparatively low.[6] On the other hand, interest in chemistry among boys continued to fall. The broadening of content areas to include food chemistry and surface chemistry in domestic life may have contributed to this trend, clashing with well-entrenched and gender-stereotyped views about the subject as simply a branch of physics.

Progress in extending access to chemistry did not imply that its strategic value for traditional clients had diminished or that standards had been lowered in favour of newer groups. Students whose fathers were in the professions or senior management were still only half as likely to fail as those from manual workers' homes, despite lower levels of participation among working-class students. Thus, while only 6 per cent of girls from tertiary-educated families failed chemistry in 1994, this rose to 15 per cent among girls whose fathers were in semi-skilled or skilled blue-collar jobs, even though participation fell from 29 per cent to only 19 per cent. Similarly, among boys the rate of failure soared as the social scale was descended, with the newest social strata to reach senior chemistry experiencing the greatest difficulty and being least likely to attempt the subject in the first place (see Figure 24).[7]

The tasks that made up the main examinable part of chemistry —numerical operations based on complex measurement concepts and on comprehension of physical principles—meant that students whose mathematical and language skills were weak were most vulnerable to failure. Students who were doing poorly in mathematics or English were likely to be turned away from the physical sciences before reaching the senior VCE year (Year 12), if they did not leave school altogether. Only 18 per cent of boys who reported coping 'poorly' or 'not well' in mathematics were admitted to chemistry in Year 11, compared to 31 per cent who claimed to be coping 'well' and 49 per cent who saw themselves as coping 'very well'. The same pattern occurred among girls. Likewise, the

Figure 24: Failure rates and enrolment rates in chemistry by occupational background and gender, 1994

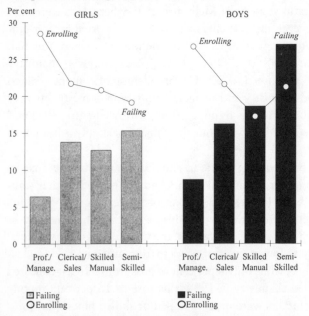

Source: Educational Outcomes Survey, 1994 (see source for Figure 7).

weaker the level of coping in English, the less likely were Year 11 students to be taking chemistry.[8] Poor communicative skills not only exposed students to problems in classroom learning—in both mathematics and chemistry—but also in reporting their learning. Short-answer questions required them to explain chemical reactions, processes or principles in accurate and unambiguous language, and carelessness or weakness were punished by the examiners as surely as arithmetical or algebraic errors.

Descending the scale of achievement in chemistry, there were more and more students who had been allocated to classes in terminal mathematics (Further Mathematics) and whose experience in mathematics learning was poor over many dimensions. Compared with the top achievers, those who were awarded the lowest grades in chemistry in 1994 were four times more likely to report trouble in coping with Year 11 mathematics. They were also much more likely not to see the purpose of their work in mathematics or the reasons for certain topics, and to view much of what they were learning as never likely to be used. Many reported that they were bored with mathematics, were in difficulties in Year 12 mathematics, did not understand the tasks set for them, and were receiving help from private tutors. By contrast, more than 80 per cent of the students with the highest grades in chemistry worked with confidence in their mathematics classes, were able to concentrate for long periods of time, could usually solve problems on their own, found mathematics enjoyable and challenging, and were taking it partly as a way of gaining bonus points for university selection.[9]

The flow of benefits undisturbed

The self-assurance with which the best chemistry students worked in their mathematics classes in 1994 contrasted with the fear and anxiety expressed when the new VCE was being phased in. Students in the cockpit of the school system, those who had most to lose by a perceived radical overhaul of curriculum and assessment, were caught between the secure and predictable world created by academic schools under the old Higher School Certificate and an unknown and widely criticized future of flawed standards and betrayed hopes. 'We are guinea pigs', a girl attending an up-market state high school complained in 1990. 'We're a mongrel year, basically', a boy from Wesley College confirmed.[10] But of all students, these were the best placed to weather the change. For the underlying continuities in content and emphasis in the curriculum, the concessions on assessment and grading wrung from a reluctant government by conservative universities, and the enlarged scope for school-assessed projects meant that the best-resourced schools would be quickest to adapt to the new regime.

Institutional resistance to change—including university threats to disqualify various subjects, impose special entrance tests and deal only with accredited schools—had been justified in the name of the brightest students, those with 'real ability from whatever background'.[11] The image of the heroic student, the outstanding individual, struggling to master the most difficult subjects, was the basic point of reference. There was no shortage of examples. Jane Paterson, who began viewing the night sky through a telescope when she was thirteen, gained 100 in Mathematics A, chemistry, physics and English, and 94 in German and Mathematics B in her HSC in 1988. Rising at six in the morning to complete mathematics exercises—'others wouldn't'—she expected university to be 'a lot of hard work' and sacrificed her summer holidays to get a head start in the chemistry department at Monash University. Other girls believed in balancing activities, but not Jane.[12]

Similarly, Karen Hall, who spent at least four hours a night studying for her HSC, easily exceeded the cut-off score for medicine at the University of Melbourne, where she would claim a place after a year 'looking around' while working in the genetics department.[13] Alex Sapozhnikov scored 100 for most of his mathematics and science subjects and for Russian and English as a Second Language in 1985. His HSC, under the old regime, meant 'committing facts and figures to memory, parrot fashion, rather than exploring concepts. But I don't see', he added philosophically, 'how that can be changed'. No time for sport, too lazy for the beach, he spent all his non-school hours in his bedroom on his computer.[14] Shelley Williams, whose father was a technical officer and mother a primary-school teacher, received six As and one B in her HSC in 1985. Violinist and captain of debating, she learnt

Japanese on a placement in Tokyo, where she planned to return for a working holiday before enrolling in medicine at Melbourne.[15] Year after year, journalists made much of such fine students who embodied a culture of scholarship. But it was not their achievements that demanded the most intense political intervention. No system would be proof against their efforts.

At risk was the merely average student in an academic school, the undistinguished student who yet must have distinction, the student who could not survive outside the all-sustaining and wholly organized world created by ambitious, insecure and powerful parents precisely to protect mediocrity from talent. Any radical departure in curriculum design in the high-stakes subjects used for strategic advantage—mathematics, physical sciences, languages— would react adversely on those students who were able enough to be permitted to study them, but needed instructional routine and predictable assessment to do well. It was this large group of middle-ranking students—those for whom bureaucratic–technical methods of testing, tracking and training had been evolved—who were most vulnerable to displacement during any major shift in curriculum. Worked as a group, they were most dependent on their schools' expertise to reduce the teaching programme to a set of exam-oriented routines and eliminate (or at any rate minimize) the appearance of unpredictable tasks in the exams. It was they who could afford to 'balance' schoolwork and personal interests, who could find time for sport and social diversions, because their academic programme was fully specified and their activities continually monitored. Organized by their schools rather than by themselves, they had room to manoeuvre. To the extent that their schools had perfected their systems of pupil management, these students' personal organization could fall well short of the religious devotion displayed by the complete swot. They would not work outside a system of finely graded assessment, because the intrinsic satisfactions of intellectual culture were too remote. 'Removing percentage assessments lowers the motivation of students to achieve outstanding results', observed the headmaster of a middle-ranking private school.[16] They needed a competitive milieu, because for them learning was a group enterprise and individual achievement a by-product of conformity to a collective goal. The joining of social pressures to organizational tactics kept them working, along with the realistic expectation that if they did work, they would succeed. That was why external exams and fine gradings of results were so important. Without them, there would be no place for the military training that went with the school uniform, the endless drilling that attached students firmly to the most abstract subjects studied without intrinsic commitment, the forced pace, all of which filled personal experience with the redeeming sense of collective purpose.

'Freedom is Exams!' pronounced the headmaster of Geelong Grammar School. 'No other form of assessment that I know of leaves pupils or teachers or schools so free to get on with the business of learning, teaching and (every bit as important) living'.[17] 'One reason why external examinations are anathema to the New [political] Class', opined the headmaster of Brighton Grammar School, 'is that they cannot control the outcome'.[18] But private schools could. It is a measure both of the continuity of the new certificate with the old HSC and of the adaptive capacity of the most academic schools that there was no interruption in the pattern of private school dominance in results. Almost all private schools enlisted higher proportions of their students in chemistry than average. They secured top grades for large numbers, often as many as a third of their classes and sometimes over 40 per cent. This placed their clients well outside the zones of participation and achievement represented by public high schools and Catholic schools. The small group of private schools that did fall within these overlapping zones consisted almost entirely of Christian fundamentalist or ethnic community schools serving poorer urban or rural-fringe communities (see Figure 25).[19]

In the unerring regularity that lies at the heart of private schooling itself, private schools continued to confer the same economic advantages as before the reform. Girls from these establishments were twice as likely as those from public high schools to be offered a place in medicine, dentistry, physiotherapy and other health sciences (excepting nursing). They were nearly three times as likely to be offered places in law courses. In medicine, private-school boys were just as advantaged relative to high-school boys, and were also twice as likely to receive an offer to study law. Chemistry was no less their servant for being reformed.

Figure 25: Top grades in chemistry and enrolment rates, private schools, 1994[1]

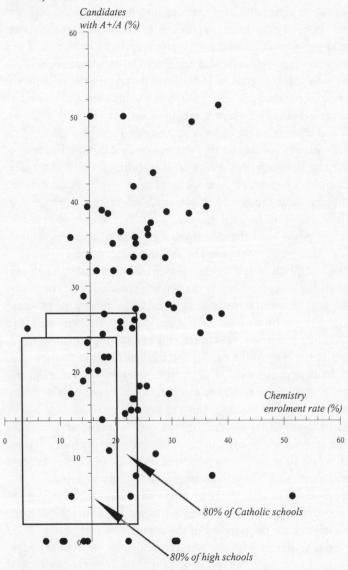

[1] The shaded zone at the lower left represents the area of performance into which 80 per cent of high schools fall. The lightly shaded area above it and to the right represents the zone for 80 per cent of Catholic schools.

Source: Unpublished VCE results, 1994.

Continuities and discontinuities

Up until the Victorian Certificate of Education, successive revisions to the chemistry curriculum made few concessions to the diversity of students who attempted it or who might have attempted it as a preparation for work or further training. The earliest major revision —the structural syllabus of 1966—translated into the syllabus the triumph of physical chemistry in the academic field and treated all students essentially as future missionaries imbued with this outlook and scornful of the older descriptive and practical sides. There was no question of the use that students would eventually make of chemistry. Rather it was a matter of instilling an attitude, a new philosophy of chemical science concerned with elucidating its theoretical foundations as a prelude, indefinitely extended, to worldly application. That inculcating a mental perspective was the main point—not the diffusion or growth of chemical knowledge as such—was emphasized by the dogmatic insistence that even students not bound for universities or technical institutes should be given the same teaching in the physical principles of chemistry.

Not only in social terms, but in pedagogical terms, the preoccupation with the 'inner logic' of the discipline was reactionary.[20] In 1979, when the structural course was revised and chemistry presented as the 'key to the earth', the recognition that students differed in their interests and capacities extended as far as giving contexts and cues to stimulate motivation, but not so far as examinable content. The real syllabus was little changed in the range of topics or their relative weight. The authorities appear never to have investigated why so many candidates failed under the old syllabus, nor the use to which successful learning was put once students entered university. Those who wrote the syllabus accepted it as a premise—not a problem to be tackled—that there might be systematic social and gender patterns in participation and achievement. These fell outside the purview of the curriculum authorities. Their concern was simply with the hierarchy of elements of knowledge, not with the hierarchy of learners, as if these cognitive and social scales were independent. If chemistry was made more attractive, the historical and applied aspects that made it more attractive were not to be examined and were contemptuously dismissed if discovered in the exams.

Only with the VCE was a broader view taken. It was recognized that the handful of idealists who would eventually train in chemistry departments to fourth year were not the only students. Physical chemistry was compelled to yield ground to more recent areas of academic growth, whose popularity represented a reaction to the unquestioning belief in the benefits of science characteristic of the 1950s and 1960s. Industrial chemistry, analytical chemistry, food chemistry, biochemistry, the mundane world of chemical substances and reactions—all intruded into examinations once reserved for abstract, higher-order concepts and numerical gymnastics. These changes promoted participation among groups whose real levels of access had been low, especially girls from lower-status backgrounds.

Broader and more sensitive to its student clientele, VCE chemistry still had to serve its institutional consumers, and this implied considerable continuity with the past, despite significant breaches in the examinable domain of the course. The key tests of student achievement remained tasks in which theoretical comprehension merged with mathematical dexterity. Students who were weak in conceptual development or mathematical skills—and to some extent language skills—would fail these tests. The examiners were aware of continuing problems in theoretical understanding, observing the failure of 'many students . . . to have developed any overview of the concepts of equilibrium'.[21] 'In particular,' they noted, 'the ability to undertake quantitative manipulation of the equations is a rare skill'. The most difficult question in the first Common Assessment Task of 1994 showed where candidates were typically undone—topics that combined 'quantitative demands with some difficult concepts'.[22] Given the weight of these compound tests in the examinations, VCE chemistry tended to gravitate back towards the previous course and to produce similar social effects in student achievement.

The promise of VCE chemistry to be more inclusive of the whole world of chemistry—and thus of a wider range of potential students—would be only half met if its impact on the students who did attempt it was to go unassessed. For if curriculum is a test of students, the nature of the students who succeed and fail is in turn a test of the curriculum. Systematic links between success and failure and the social characteristics of candidates are not simply a measure of relative pedagogical efficiency—as if teaching effort and classroom environment can be divorced from the organization and the demands of the curriculum itself. The test of curriculum reform is not whether all students are successful, whatever their backgrounds. It is whether design is sensitive to the whole range of students, does not presuppose uniformly advantageous teaching conditions, monitors quality of learning among different student groups, and tackles quality systematically where quality is systematically unequal. Failure to reform along these lines turns the curriculum from a path of intellectual ascent to a source of social power. Annexed to the economic needs of students in the most competitive schools, mastery of core conceptual and mathematical work will bear the same arbitrary relationship to future careers as mastery of Latin grammar once bore to medicine and law. If science has not followed Latin into complete eclipse, that is not due to fifty years of effort to widen its social basis, but to the unchecked impulse to make science do the work of Latin after Latin itself would no longer work.

9

Traditional Mathematics

Some people prefer to learn languages by the rules of grammar rather than by ear. This can be said to be true of mathematics—some learn it by 'grammar' and others 'from the air'. I learned mathematics from the air.

Stan Ulam, Adventures of a Mathematician (1976)

In December 1947, the Pure Mathematics examination conducted by the University of Melbourne attracted more than one thousand candidates from across Victoria. In ones and twos and threes, a good many—perhaps 40 per cent of the total—sallied forth from little private schools, Catholic schools and country high schools to meet the large classes assembled by the greater public schools, the senior state high schools and the Catholic congregational colleges.[1] Matriculation exams were a meeting place, and the subjects leading up to them were roads the candidates had taken many years earlier. For many, it was a shared pilgrimage, the road thick with like-minded travellers who bore each other along. For others, it was a lonely trek with inexperienced guides, a gamble based on stamina and inner conviction. Their different paths converged at one point, and this alone was important, not the paths along which they had come.

Of all the subjects in which candidates might choose to be considered alike by virtue of their training, mathematics makes the fullest claim. That it is indifferent to student origins follows from its very nature as a system of logic. Abstract and self-enclosed, its internal integrity—its rules of definition and proof—make it, at least potentially, the most universal and accessible of all disciplines. Yet the philosophy of mathematics—the general and necessarily abstracted form in which its propositions have to be formulated, the economy of its symbolic and notational devices, the deductive rigour that links its theorems and arguments—imposes an intellectual posture and habits of thought that are not easily instilled and, thanks to this, are too readily reduced to routines fit only for exams and short-term learning. The universality of mathematics —the formal character of its operations as an intellectual discipline —contrasts markedly with its particularity as a pedagogical discipline. Difficult to teach widely, mathematics at its higher levels is marked by sharp social contours in participation and achievement.

Syllabus content and examiners' expectations

The Pure Mathematics class of 1947 studied a traditional fare of algebra, co-ordinate geometry and trigonometry, and normally also calculus and dynamics as an additional subject (Calculus and Applied Mathematics).[2] With this foundation, they could continue with mathematics at university or technical college, either in professional courses (especially engineering and applied science) or in physics. Students who would not be required to continue with mathematics at university—future doctors, dentists, biological scientists, economists, humanities teachers—could choose to do General Mathematics instead. This 'comparatively wide elementary course' covered algebra, trigonometry, some calculus and statistics, including elementary probability theory and linear regression.[3] The division into a more intensive and at the same time more technically oriented stream of mathematics (Pure and Applied) and a generalist course (General Mathematics) was not specific to senior school mathematics in Victoria.[4] It reflected contemporary arrangements in England, where sixth-formers who stayed with mathematics fell into one of two groups—the 'mathematicians', who pursued their interests freely, and the 'physicists', who needed technical tools of trade for engineering careers. The choice, as in Victoria, was between a double mathematics and physics stream or mathematics, physics and chemistry.[5]

While the range of topics, the depth of their treatment and the overall time allocated to mathematics varied depending on whether students took the generalist or technical–applied option, in both cases the syllabus made extensive cognitive and cultural demands on students. In the three-hour papers attempted at the end of the year—two for General Mathematics, four for Pure and Applied—candidates were tested on their grasp of basic concepts (number, equality, power, factor, roots, function, variable, tangent, integral), laws and theorems, mathematical symbolism, manipulative skills, and the capacity to extend learning from one branch of mathematics to another (algebra to trigonometry, co-ordinate geometry to calculus).

Besides this technical competence—which comprised all the elements that could be methodically taught and repeatedly practised—the examiners demanded a freer intelligence. Students needed to be able to recognize when procedures they had learnt at particular points in the pedagogical sequence (for example, factorization, graphing of functions) could be applied in new contexts, outside this sequence. This synthetic skill—bringing concepts together independently of the context of their acquisition—as well as the analytical skills of dismembering a problem into partial problems to be attacked separately—represented the end point of training, loosely and characteristically summarized by the professors of mathematics as 'the power to think in generalities as well as particularities', 'the power, not merely to draw deductions, but . . . to keep one's wits about one'.[6] Seeing the whole picture—'the general lines of an investigation apart from its details'—involved either recognizing the characteristic form of a mathematical problem (a perception that could be trained) or intuition of potentially fruitful approaches (a matter of logical and mathematical culture, not easily formulated into 'system' or 'technique' and therefore not readily taught).[7]

It was here that students were expected to have achieved independence as mathematical thinkers, though very frequently they failed to display this. Questions in General Mathematics that were 'slightly off the beaten track' left candidates floundering, the examiner observed in 1948.[8] Since not much was new from the previous year's work, more flexibility was to be expected, based on a wider range of problems and examples. But the course did not work in this way. Students and their teachers fastened to routine. Instead of aiming at a growth of understanding in which mathematical reasoning became more fluent and versatile, they looked to the security of the well-worn path. 'Standard-type questions ... were usually fairly well done, but with all other questions many candidates were in trouble. This perhaps is natural', concluded the examiner, 'but rather contrary to the spirit of the General Mathematics course'.[9]

To reason independently in mathematics requires comprehension of the variety of forms that a problem might validly assume through successive algebraic or geometric transformations. From the stock of simpler procedures—such as transposition or simplification through elimination of terms—complex multi-stage operations can be applied, governed by formal assumptions or hypotheses that set boundaries around problems. These require experience and self-confidence, and involve a strategic rather than mechanical orientation. Students need to know what they are doing, or have at least a 'feel' for the direction of a solution. Learning is marshalled from a variety of phases in the developmental order, and thinking moves freely through these as so many dimensions of mathematical experience, in which 'concepts communicate' rather than being partitioned off in separate departments. The language of mathematics, built up from the requirements of generalizability and precision, works in the student's favour so long as the conceptual potential of each symbol, each term, each expression is recognized. Otherwise the stock of information contained in these codes cannot be exploited and the philosophy of mathematical expression is defeated.

At every stage in progress towards maturity as a mathematician, the student is exposed to failure and to the accumulation of unresolved conceptual problems and 'factual' ignorance, which will hinder progress at higher levels. Learning comes in fragments, and conceptual ligaments often fail to form between topics separately and imperfectly mastered. Where confidence is continually strained, the learner may take refuge in problems that are relatively simple, varying only within predictable bounds, and that are 'departmental' (bound to the pedagogical context). There is no question of taking risks. The task is always to find the pre-existing route through a problem that the examiner 'really' had in mind.

After six years of high-school mathematics—and sometimes an extra year at the end for those whose families could afford it—the matriculation candidates of the 1940s frequently presented a disappointing result to the examiners. Many had not matured beyond the classroom setting of rehearsed and staged learning, and too often they betrayed the tell-tale signs of concepts used but not understood, and knowledge poorly consolidated at the stages where rote and drill had been diligently applied.[10] Indices and logarithms had not been mastered—in the first Pure Mathematics paper for 1948, 'bad errors were common'—students were uncomfortable with log tables or could not use them, the graphing of functions was rarely done correctly, and many made basic and repeated errors in arithmetic, algebra and trigonometry.[11] Reasoning that involved leaps or risks—mathematical induction—was rarely displayed when the opportunity was given.[12] Complex problems, outside the predicted test zone, caught students unawares—'Very few showed that they really knew what they were doing'.[13]

The examiners' search for quality in student learning focused primarily on accuracy of work and basic knowledge. It was possible to obtain a pass in Pure Mathematics by meeting these requirements consistently on a minimum number of questions attempted, while showing no deeper grasp of concepts, reasoning ability or manipulative powers.[14] But candidates had to do more to get better marks and to demonstrate the effective (though not official) standard needed to continue with pure mathematics at university. They had to evince a broader knowledge of mathematics, to test themselves on more complex problems—productively and with control over the direction of a solution—and to display the conceptual, operational and stylistic strengths that were inherent in mathematics as a form of intellectual culture—perspicacity and strategic sense (detecting the general form of a problem and correct or appropriate lines of attack), logic (including induction and synthetic skills), methodical, economical and simple argument, and orderliness in overall presentation.

Poor candidates in mathematics made many elementary errors, which accumulated over their heads. They confused concepts, stumbled over indices and notation, struggled to find methods of approach—producing lengthy and unfruitful work or inventing 'new' solutions or proofs—they were ignorant of basic mathematical facts, applied formulae blindly, simplified expressions when they should have stopped, were stumped by unknown technical terms (tetrahedron, quartile), wrote badly and were untidy, and they worked in a 'clumsy' or 'amateurish' manner.

The implicit image of the good mathematics student

To judge by the failure rates in the late 1940s, there were almost as many poor candidates as good. Among girls sitting for Pure Mathematics at the first attempt, as many as 40 per cent failed in 1947, and among boys (whose participation was much greater) 45 per cent—with a further 2 per cent being absent. In General Mathematics, 38 per cent of both boys and girls failed, with another 1 per cent and 5 per cent respectively not showing for the examination.[15]

Although, in the main, candidates for matriculation mathematics had followed a sequenced course running for six years of secondary school, the majority—including those with bare passes—had not adjusted to the subject as an intellectual discipline. The system of selection used by schools to divide pupils into ability streams was based on grade results or IQ tests, and did not solve the problems of matching a diverse group of students to a hierarchical programme of mathematics. It was not only the weaker students who ended up in the terminal track, confined to arithmetic. Girls were frequently 'excused' from the trouble of taking algebra, geometry and trigonometry.[16] Where schools relied on IQ tests, low correlations with mathematics attainment risked mismatches in both directions. There was widespread frustration among teachers. Restless or bored classes were too often their lot. 'In its contact with the average child at the present time', the President of the New South Wales branch of the Mathematical Association concluded, 'mathematics teaching is often so negative in its benefits as to be unjustified'.[17]

It was not only the flaw in premature allocations to mathematics streams that resulted in pedagogical dissonance—unmotivated pupils, frustrated teachers. The problem was more fundamental. The syllabus, with its various deletions and modifications, had not been developed by teachers themselves, but by higher academic authority. It was assumed that there were identifiable layers of the school population corresponding to the formal and antique hierarchy of the branches of mathematics—arithmetic, algebra, geometry, trigonometry, calculus. Some would stay at the level of natural numbers, others could manage some work with rational numbers, still others could advance to the 'arbitrary numbers' of algebra, to the concept of equality, to roots and factors, and so on, confident that the ever-increasing depth of abstraction would all make sense in the end. But the framing of cognitive demands at each of these preconceived levels was based on historical experience from the era when the great majority of children went no further than elementary school. The syllabus was set, in other words, for an ideal pupil with an implicit historical referent—the child with educated parents, expected to attend university or to compete for civil service exams.

There was a profound disjuncture between curriculum power and pedagogical responsibility. The schoolmaster was lumbered with the task of interpreting and applying a cultural image of the 'good maths pupil' outside the historical context in which it had been fashioned. The university professor, by contrast, was free to conserve and enforce this image without regard to the quality of its contemporary realizations. Responding to the one in ten General Mathematics students who understood binomial distribution, the examiner wrote with an uncharacteristic flush of satisfaction:

> The maturity of expression and variety of presentation of pertinent comment by candidates were a great joy ... One cannot help feel that the eighty candidates who got full marks for this have really made their statistical knowledge part of their intellectual armoury.[18]

But the path they had traversed to reach this standpoint of equality with the examiner was unknown and unexamined. Why not the other 300? Was success at mathematics simply the sum of mathematical ability plus good teaching, the formula that established the professor's independence and control over the content of the course?[19] Or was mathematics a matter of cultural training? Perhaps it was so much an element of the personal culture of the mathematics professor that he was unable to reflect critically on the demands he made of students and why so few satisfied them.

The mathematics professor had ascended a path of learning that began with the decontextualization of numerical reasoning in the transition from arithmetic to algebra. Mathematics states problems in a general form in order to gain access to laws, rules and procedures that can be established through abstraction from all context and that provide for an unlimited field of application. Generalizability, the correlative of decontextualization, raises the plane at which problems are considered, but pedagogically this involves the assumption that the perceived gain in being able to deal with unknown contexts will compensate for the initial loss of meaning through the sacrifice of specific context. Entering this domain, the student submits to the grammar of mathematical form —the rules governing the formulation of problems, the formal statement of definitions, the laws authorizing procedures, the principles of logic, the use of symbol and sign, and the requirement of at least potential proof. Colonizing the internal world of mathematics not only gives the future professor access to the power of mathematical form as a generalized system for formulating and solving problems, but also introduces the mathematics of mathematicians, that is, the problems or entire fields of investigation that have no real-world correlative, but relate to mathematical structure as such. The self-standing problem in which mathematics is freed of its links with the external world and sets its own objectives—the autonomy of the discipline—is the end point implied in the first steps towards release from context and 'relevance' that began with elementary algebra.

The path that leads from the decontextualization of mathematical relationships to the autonomization of mathematics as the source of its own objectives is a process of cultural development rather than an immanent logical movement within mathematics itself. The historical limits within which algebra was explored by the Greeks and calculus by Babylon have their counterpart in the contemporary social limits on the diffusion of mathematical knowledge in societies where both these branches of mathematics are highly developed. Few individuals enter the higher reaches of the mathematical sciences, and those who do, do not theorize about the experiences that set them apart as exceptional individuals and at the same time link them together with other mathematical 'brains' to form a reference group (an artificial community).

Projection of personality through the intellectual medium of mathematics supposes not only logical skills—and the linguistic apparatus that supports and develops these, as in hypothetical and deductive reasoning—but sensitivity to form and pattern and a disposition to search for 'structure', for the regularities and relationships beneath the surface qualities of shape and movement. The interior of mathematics can only be occupied by suspension of extrinsic demands for relevance and application, by obedience to logic—including the logical implications of arguments reached intuitively—and by concentration (exclusion of other activities, intense and continuous focus on an abstract object). The mental navigation of the formal, constructed entities of mathematics— equations, sets, vectors, matrices—in turn implies an inner self-assurance about the value of the journey, and the creative energy needed to complete it. If, in the extreme case, mathematical talent appears to arise *sui generis*, self-produced—the theory preferred by mathematicians such as Weil, who thereby stake a claim to genius—too little would be manufactured by this means to account for the hundreds of thousands of theorems formulated by modern mathematicians as a routine part of their annual activity.[20]

The social distribution of success and failure

In the era before mass secondary education, the cognitive and attitudinal demands made on students by advanced mathematics were a major barrier to completing secondary school. Mathematics, which controlled access to the professions, was often seen as an indispensable study, particularly for boys, so that there was little point in continuing at school if one made heavy weather of this subject. Success in mathematics at progressively higher stages of the school programme intensified demands on the cultural resources of the students, as well as the training and skills of their teachers. Cognitive growth, confidence with numbers and numerical abstractions, aesthetic interest and appreciation of mathematical form (symbols and structure), manipulative dexterity, the power to concentrate and the pleasure of self-projection through mathematical accomplishment all pointed back to the intellectual milieu of the family and the schools that reinforced this or compensated for its inadequacies.

In the country, low survival rates to the end of school meant that the few students who did attempt matriculation would resemble metropolitan candidates in the main subjects that they took. There was little difference between country and city girls in the proportions taking Pure Mathematics (about 16 per cent). But despite the greater severity of selection for country girls, their achievements were often inferior. Failure was much more common in the country. While boys in rural or provincial Victoria were only marginally less likely than those in Melbourne to enrol in Pure Mathematics, they attempted matriculation less frequently in the first place and their failure rates were much higher (55 per cent of first-time candidates compared with 39 per cent in the city).[21]

It was in the larger private schools and the selective senior high schools (especially Melbourne Boys' High)—establishments that contained the highest concentrations of educated families—that students were least likely to fail Pure Mathematics and most likely to be awarded honours. At Scotch College, 35 per cent of boys who were full candidates for matriculation in 1947 enrolled in Pure Mathematics and every third obtained a first-class or second-class honour. At Melbourne High School, 40 per cent sat for Pure Mathematics and 31 per cent of these received honours. At Melbourne Grammar School and at Xavier—where 'engineering' mathematics was in much less favour (29 per cent and 16 per cent participation respectively)—the likelihood of honours was still greater (39 per cent and 43 per cent).

These large, mainly urban establishments differed sharply from the many small schools about their fringe or in provincial or rural

Victoria. They drew on the most economically or culturally advantaged families and in the senior forms were academically selective as well. As at Scotch, they devised streaming strategies to begin the cultivation of their mathematical elite from around the second year of the programme.[22] The most able students trained for longer hours and took more advanced work. Whole classes of such students could be formed because of the precocious mathematical and language development of children in educated homes and the competition among parents for admission to the school. Experienced and capable teachers could be retained in an era of growing shortages of specialist staff, because these schools could offer good salaries along with classes of high achievers. Even 'average' students by the standards of such schools benefited from this regime, because of the closer monitoring and supervision of their work and the pressure from parents to extract the full potential from their children in subjects leading to the professions. The setting created by the school—a hierarchy of streams led by an elite group—exerted competitive pressure on the students with 'prospects' to serve both the school and themselves in the struggle for honours.

While other schools might be academically selective and very competitive in orientation—notably the Catholic colleges that 'creamed' the most talented working-class or lower middle-class children from central schools—the pool of cultural resources available to them was much weaker, the economic insecurity of their charges much greater, and cultural aspirations more modest. In 1947 Parade College, in the inner northern suburbs of Melbourne, enrolled more than two-thirds of its boys in Pure Mathematics—the engineering and applied science stream—only to see nearly half of them fail and only 16 per cent receive honours. St Kevin's, located on the other side of the river, obtained somewhat higher honours rates (22 per cent) from the nearly six out of ten boys enrolled in the same stream, but it too experienced high failure rates (44 per cent). Similarly, University High School received punishing failure rates in Pure Mathematics (55 per cent) and only modest honours rates (15 per cent).

Failure in mathematics was due to conceptual weaknesses, to faulty logic and unimaginative reasoning, to poor manipulation and low accuracy, and to mistakes in reading and interpreting questions. But the roots of failure lay in the student's isolation—first from the cultural circles in which higher school mathematics was a family experience (as for the children of engineers, architects and surveyors, doctors and agricultural scientists, statisticians, secondary schoolteachers and public accountants); secondly, from age-peers with whom learning might be shared; and finally, from trained and experienced teachers. The young scholar, working in comparative isolation in a small country high school or a sub-urban private or Catholic school, risked displaying all the marks of immaturity—repeated inaccuracy and confusion (which might not have happened outside the exams), false starts and fruitless attempts, illegible handwriting and untidiness—which the examiners saw as symptomatic of a disordered mind.[23]

Marking practice and pass-rate policy

The examination papers in mathematics provided a multiplicity of specific points on which the behaviour of the candidates was marked. These ranged from the most menial operations in arithmetic to high-level conceptual work in calculus, so the candidate was exposed to the examiner on a wide front. This approach tested total conduct—the overall maturity of the student. Although a hierarchy of intellectual tasks was clearly recognized, all had to be performed accurately and appropriately. For mathematics was as much about process as result—about the work shown in scripts and the rough work so frequently concealed in separate, unsubmitted sheets.

Errors at one level produced other errors higher up the chain of reasoning. There was no shortage of evidence about the quality of a candidate, and the cumulative effect of errors and weaknesses often led to disaster. The examiner in Calculus and Applied Mathematics in 1949 noted the difference between the mature approach to the exam (which could be inculcated by experienced and confident teachers) and the immature response (which could be expected of students who had worked in greater isolation):

reasonably careful and complete answers to about half the number of questions on the paper would secure a safe pass, but ... even slight slips caused by a careless and hurried attempt to solve a greater number of questions usually spoil the solutions of questions completely, and thus ensure failure.[24]

The marking practice of the examiners in the late 1940s ensured high rates of failure and added to underlying problems of student learning arising from limited cultural training and pedagogical support. The approach to marking and the setting of high failure rates as a policy satisfied a view about the purpose of the exams, which was to identify the best candidates and to eliminate weaker ones on any combination of grounds. Elementary mistakes, commented the General Mathematics examiner in 1949, 'marred the majority of the answers and were, in many cases, the main causes of failure'.[25] The search for the brightest students—which was later to be officially described in the syllabus[26]—can be seen in the 1940s in the inclusion of questions that the examiners admitted were 'beyond the capacity of all but the best candidates' or 'beyond the power of most candidates'.[27] Both the Pure Mathematics and General Mathematics papers were bolstered with questions that only a minority proved able or willing to tackle.[28] There were numerous examples of a policy of testing students on questions known from experience to be pitched beyond what could reasonably be expected, but included on the grounds that abler students needed the opportunity to declare their strengths. How, on the pedagogical side, the average student was to be prepared to tackle these questions was evidently a problem to be solved by teachers, who would need all of their skills to compensate for the examiners' arbitrariness.

Prestige and influence

By operating a low-pass policy, the professors of mathematics—like those of science—raised the effective entry level to the professional faculties of the university. They demanded a standard of achievement that could be met by only about half of all candidates. Already a very small fraction of the total age group, the students who did reach the matriculation year and attempted either Pure Mathematics or General Mathematics were then further reduced to about three in 100 boys and fewer than one in 100 girls in their respective age cohorts.[29] Careers in medicine and dentistry, engineering, architecture and agricultural science, surveying and applied science were as a result made much more socially restricted in their intakes than would have been the case under a more rational pass-rate policy. Constructing examination papers around the needs of the ablest students entrenched the power and prestige of the independent schools and selective state high schools. For these alone offered a relatively high degree of security—thanks to the cultural, teaching and physical resources concentrated in them—and they dominated the high end of achievement in mathematics. Among this group, six schools alone— Melbourne High School, Scotch College, Geelong Grammar, Wesley, Melbourne Grammar and Xavier—accounted for more than three-quarters of all first-class honours in Pure Mathematics in 1947, which was more than double their share of candidates for the subject.[30]

Recruiting to the discipline of mathematics only those students who exhibited the intellectual maturity of the academic mathematician—those with a clear conceptual grasp, with a sense of direction and sureness of approach, who tackled the hard questions and worked with manipulative facility and accuracy—had the effect of protecting the high-income professions from the 'unrealistic' ambitions of individuals from socially modest backgrounds. Ignoring the conditions under which these students endeavoured to serve the cultural ideal of mathematics, the professors of mathematics placed themselves in the service of the families who commanded the optimum conditions for learning. To raise the bar to eliminate every second candidate was not socially neutral, nor was it disinterested. The setting of high fail rates in mathematics (and science) was a means of asserting relative prestige within the university community.

While matriculation mathematics subjects did not have the highest rates of failure—they were exceeded by economics (which began its institutional ascent in the 1930s) and by chemistry and physics—they were clustered with these subjects and involved the same groups of students (see Figure 26). Male-dominated and severe in marking standards, mathematics—like the sciences—based its prestige not only on practical applications (which were viewed with limited interest by the discipline) but on its relative

Figure 26: Relative prestige of Matriculation subjects in 1947: fail rates and males as a percentage of candidates

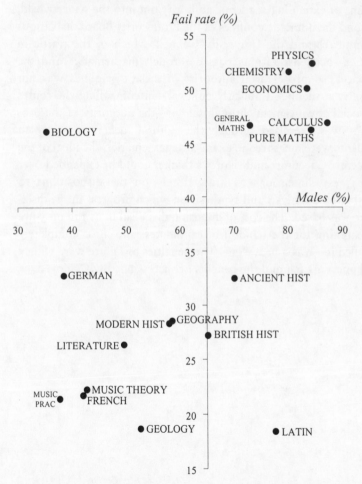

Source: MU, *Handbook of Public and Matriculation Examinations 1948*, Carlton, 1949.

level of difficulty and the implied quality of mind of its suppliants. The subjects in which boys were most highly represented—with the notable exception of Latin—were also the ones with the harshest standards. This was not because they happened to be 'boys' subjects', but because they were the keys to the professions—which were male-dominated—while the 'lenient' subjects (the humanities) led at best to teaching and could therefore be safely abandoned to low standards and the girls responsible for them.

At the same time, the high fail rates in mathematics were a means of extending academic authority out into the wider world, beyond the domestic confines of the Professorial Board, its various committees and the University Council. Much of the traffic in higher social aspirations passed through mathematics and the sciences, so professorial authority in these disciplines was not merely 'academic'. Implicitly political—in controlling the routes of social advancement through school—the authority of the professor was exercised through the cultural ideal against which students were measured in exams. In mathematics, the ideal of the perceptive, accurate and rigorous thinker could be expanded over many test dimensions to draw deeply on the dispositions to abstraction, analysis and synthesis on which progress in the discipline was based. The cost of imposing this ideal in its full measure —searching for the handful of candidates who most completely fulfilled it—was a heavy one. The penalties of failure were widely and unevenly felt and the benefits of success narrowly enjoyed.

10

Reforming in the Shadow of the New Maths

The coming of modern mathematics

Having failed more than 60 per cent of country candidates in 1950, the mathematics examiners launched an attack on the poor quality of teaching in schools.[1] It was not the students' fault: it was the teachers'. As if sensing that such dismal results would eventually call their own practice into question, the professors of mathematics demanded action. In the restricted pedagogical equation that they had formulated—mathematical ability plus good teaching equals success—there were few points available for intervention. With proper selection of students and adequate time and reinforcement—calculus students, for example, should have been doing Pure Mathematics at the same time—the only factor that was left to consider was teaching. Where there was evidence that student ability was *not* being translated into success—as in the country—teachers were to blame. There were no other terms in the equation. The selection of content for the curriculum, the choice of test items as a valid sampling of the taught syllabus, the comparative emphasis on different kinds of learning—factual knowledge, numerical facility, comprehension of principles, integrated conceptual application—the relative difficulty of questions and the style in which they were formulated, marking practice, and the setting of the pass rate, none of these elements was brought into the picture.

No blame could be assigned to the syllabus writers, the subject standing committees or the examiners themselves. Professorial authority was the guarantee of quality in curriculum design and in assessment methodology and behaviour. Failure was due to the inability of teachers to communicate the demands of a curriculum over which they had no control, not to professorial immunity from teaching and ignorance of the range of pupils, half of whom the professors of mathematics were determined never to meet, and half of whom they would deal with severely when meet with them they did.

The failure experienced by many country children in the early 1950s foreshadowed wider difficulties in both city and country once the population completing school began to grow. From the middle of the decade until 1964, the numbers of students attempting matriculation expanded at an average annual rate of 14 per cent.[2] The thousands of new students reaching this level were successful learners in a system of institutional segregation—the high-school population, saved from the technical schools or girls' schools—and of curriculum tracking within the high-school programme, and as such their numbers would often translate into new pupils in senior mathematics classes. As numbers of candidates spiralled, enrolments in the two mathematics options also tended to grow, especially in General Mathematics, at least until 1970. Given the key role of mathematics in selection to science-based courses in universities and technical institutes, this area of the curriculum was widely exposed to population growth and social aspirations, and the maintenance of participation levels from a rapidly augmenting population base bears this out (Figure 27).

Students newly completing school in the late 1950s and early 1960s did not face the same severe examining standards of the first post-war decade, but mortality was still very high. From 1955, the fail rate fluctuated around 33 per cent in General Mathematics and around 38 per cent in Pure Mathematics (the larger subject). Although the number of schools offering matriculation classes had multiplied since the end of the war, this expansion of opportunities was checked by the academic standard enforced by university authorities. In their view, the quality of learning was still often poor. Either students were frequently unrealistic in their aspirations for professional careers, or schools were failing to build on the talent available to them, as the examiners had alleged in 1950.

Figure 27: Growth in mathematics enrolments and in numbers of students completing school, 1947–75 (1970 = 100)

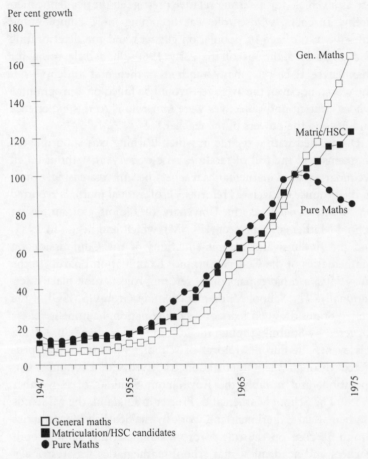

Per cent growth

□ General maths
■ Matriculation/HSC candidates
● Pure Maths

Source: Examination handbooks for successive years published by MU, Schools Board, VUSEB, VISE and VCAB.

The routine failure of as many as 40 per cent of Pure Mathematics candidates—at a time when only about one in four young people reached the matriculation year—gravely restricted teaching to preparation for exams. It also imposed on both teachers and their students defensive strategies that were incompatible with depth of understanding or pleasure in learning. Research in the mid-1960s showed that students in the mathematics–physics stream, though the most able of their age group, faced the greatest risks at the hands of the examiners.[3] Fail rates continued to operate as a vehicle for asserting relative prestige in the academic hierarchy. Teachers, whose role was becoming more complex and difficult in the face of population changes and the deteriorating pedagogical conditions of the early 1960s, had little room for manoeuvre. Each year, many hundreds of their best students—not the worst, not even the average—would be failed on a programme whose content and objectives were impervious to this experience and beyond the powers of the teacher.[4]

Dissatisfied with a regime in which learning was subordinated to exams and the toll of fatalities rose every year without relief, secondary-school mathematics teachers became increasingly open to the promise of overseas reforms.[5] Professional journals reported on initiatives such as the University of Illinois Committee on School Mathematics project (UICSM), which had begun in 1951, and the findings and recommendations of the Commission on Mathematics of the College Entrance Examination Board.[6] In the late 1950s, a rapid expansion of reform projects took place internationally. The School Mathematics Study Group (SMSG) in the United States drew on fears of declining national competitiveness triggered by Sputnik, though the inspiration for change pre-dated this event.[7] In Europe, reform of school mathematics was promoted through the Organization for European Economic Co-operation, and notably the Royaumont Seminar of November 1959.[8] The School Mathematics Project in England, the Midlands Mathematical Experiment and work by the Scottish Mathematics Group all rose on the tide of professional feeling, among both teachers and academics, that school mathematics was restrictive and outmoded.

While there was gathering support for fundamental change, there were also divergent perspectives on the directions that change should take. The curriculum reforms implemented in the early 1960s showed the influence both of 'formalists'—the abstract algebraists, especially French and American—and of applied mathematicians. The concerns of modern algebra were reflected in the official Victorian policy of shifting the pedagogical emphasis from 'the attainment of manipulative skills to that of a real understanding of . . . basic notions and an awareness of the underlying unity of mathematics'.[9]

The 'new maths' was intended to dissolve the traditional boundaries between branches of mathematics in favour of integrating concepts such as sets and functions, which captured the mathematician's basic concern for pattern and structure. Precise use of language and symbolism, grasp of underlying concepts, and systematic reasoning from axioms were to replace rote learning of rules and operations. The theoretical basis of mathematics was to be stressed over the procedural ('why?' over 'how?').[10] But more 'applied' concerns also gained expression in the curriculum reforms of the 1960s—or, more accurately, grew in recognition, considering progress before the Second World War, as in the case of probability and statistics.[11]

Reforms to matriculation mathematics in Victoria were not initiated by the University of Melbourne—the dominant partner in the Schools Board—but by the Mathematical Association of Victoria (MAV). This was a professional body covering schoolteachers and university and technical institute mathematicians. Leadership of the association had changed in 1959 and a stronger pedagogical orientation had developed, involving training activities for teachers and the establishment of a research committee.[12] It was in 1964, in the context of national discussions of school mathematics, that this committee submitted to the council of MAV a proposal for a six-year high-school programme in mathematics, which was subsequently adopted and put before the Schools Board for consideration.

The new matriculation course, first offered in 1967, reflected the influence of contemporary English projects—SMP materials appearing prominently among the course references—though it was not modelled on any particular experience. Set theory and matrix algebra made their appearance for the first time, Euclidean geometry was expelled, and there was some expansion in calculus (introduction of continuity and differential equations).[13] The Calculus and Applied Mathematics course, renamed Applied Mathematics, was substantially recast to cover probability and statistics, vectors, differential equations and mechanics.[14] Corresponding changes were made to junior secondary programmes, so that by

1969 students in the third year of secondary school were being introduced to deduction and mathematical proof, matrices and elementary probability theory.[15]

This attempt to revitalize mathematics through the language of modern algebra and the philosophy of axiomatic reasoning came at a time when the resources available to students had never been poorer. To implement reforms inspired by changes in mathematical research in universities, it was essential that teachers had either received undergraduate training in the more innovative areas or could be trained through in-service programmes. Neither of these conditions applied. Every fifth teacher in charge of a matriculation mathematics class in 1963 had 'never passed an examination in the subject at a university'.[16] Only 4 per cent held honours degrees. In Victoria, some 15,000 children in high schools received instruction from teachers who were either untrained for secondary-school work or had no mathematics background.[17] The conjuncture was thus extremely unfavourable. Furthermore, the reforms were implemented without any of the precautions urged by overseas experts—experimentation, monitoring and evaluation, extensive in-servicing of classroom teachers—and were poorly supported by textbooks and teachers' materials, especially at the junior level.[18]

But there were deeper problems behind the 'new maths'. Left unaddressed, these would distort and constrain the reform of institutionalized practice and the culture of secondary-school mathematics. The abstract algebraists who succeeded in channelling the broader current of reform in the direction of their own interests —as against the applied mathematicians who wanted industry-oriented change and the die-hard conservatives who opposed any change—were seeking programmes for able students.[19] Conceived at a time when secondary education was segmented into preparatory and terminal streams—usually in different types of schools— the 'new maths' failed to reckon with the burgeoning demand for academic schooling even from within the ranks of the educated middle classes, let alone from among working-class families.

The protagonists of reform opened themselves to the charge of substituting new barriers for old in the diffusion of mathematical knowledge. Formalization and abstraction, the search for underlying structure, the use of axioms as tools of logic, the insistence on relating mathematical procedure to theoretical principles—all implied an intellectual orientation to mathematics, a command of formal operational reasoning and advanced language skills. Protests against the loss of 'realism' in the United States and Canada, in England, France and Australia, highlighted the dangers of pursuing a reform based on intellectual rather than pedagogical impulse.[20]

While at least some overseas reforms were to target slower learners, taking advantage of new research on learning difficulties, in Victoria the reform process lacked a student perspective.[21] High failure rates, especially in the 'double mathematics' stream of the matriculation syllabus, frustrated teachers, regularly presenting them with the evidence of superficial learning. But there was little knowledge of the causes of failure—beyond the exam-driven framework and pace of instruction.[22] Who failed and why was unknown or merely surmised, even as major revisions were made to the syllabus. The risk was thus implicitly accepted that failure would be communicated from the old programme to the new, and the essential purpose of the reforms—improvement in the quality of mathematical learning—would be defeated.

Achievement under the revised syllabus

Courses in modern mathematics at matriculation level were phased in over the five-year period 1967–71, with the old courses running parallel. Not unexpectedly, students in the cohorts pioneering the new General Mathematics course fared less well in the first few years than their peers who stayed with the old programme, enjoying the advantages of routine over the hazards of innovation.[23] By 1969, however, there was a comparable standard of performance, measured over substantially overlapping courses. Teachers had succeeded in introducing the new courses, despite weaknesses in their own training, limited or even bad teaching materials and often poor pedagogical conditions.

Similarities of content smoothed the way to quick adaptation, but at the same time worked against any marked improvement in the overall standard of student mathematics. Indeed, with rapidly increasing numbers of candidates in the early 1970s, the standard seemed to be turning down. Many students, the General Mathematics examiners complained in 1970, were unable 'to relate their answers to reality'. They frequently omitted to explain 'how answers, often incorrect, were obtained', and the quality of their work in some areas (notably calculus) was 'generally poor'.[24] Pure Mathematics candidates—specifically those in the new course— were castigated for placing 'heavy reliance on rote learning of manipulative techniques without appropriate emphasis on understanding which would [have enabled] them to apply their techniques in new situations'.[25] These were the errors of old. Reviewing the quality of performance of General Mathematics students in 1971, the examiners noted some improvements here and there, but bemoaned 'the poor standard of calculus . . . a general inability to apply knowledge to practical situations, and a poor understanding of some of the basic statistical concepts'.[26] Faulty reasoning, poor expression and bad setting out of work bedevilled the Pure Mathematics group. Many had not mastered basic concepts that had been introduced much earlier in school, and they could not cope outside contexts that had been 'well-rehearsed'.[27]

If the inspiration for change during the 1960s had ultimately been the access of children to the foundations of modern mathematics, the reform process itself focused too narrowly on the selection and codification of examinable content rather than the capacities and experience, the attitudes and values of learners and teachers. While the protagonists of the 'new maths' had insisted on pedagogical reform,[28] it was a syllabus that was transformed, not professorial culture or academic values, and the point of reference remained the knowledge selected for transmission rather than the process of transmission itself. A better mathematics was made available, not a mathematics better taught. Quality of teaching was viewed exclusively in terms of the effectiveness of student preparation for examinations. The content of the syllabus was emptied of its original philosophical emphasis and reduced to a mass of rehearsable routine, to what Bishop calls the 'technique-oriented curriculum'[29] demanded by the culture of competitive advantage and enforced through examinations.

The fate of set theory in contemporary English reforms illustrated the code of interpretation that suppressed educational purpose in order to extract examinable materials. Meant to develop a unified understanding of mathematics, the language of sets was soon converted into 'a piece of syllabus content which was an end in itself'.[30] Similarly, the texts that were commercially commissioned and produced for the new courses in Victoria ignored the principles behind the reform and concentrated on boiling down the new content to a residue that could be transmitted according to pedagogical practices institutionalized long before. As one reviewer wrote of Lucas's *General Mathematics for Senior Students* (1968), 'the over-riding impression is that the book does no more than provide students with the means of thorough examination preparation'.[31]

The new ideas, flowing into an examination syllabus that acted to discriminate between candidates and select the best, would reproduce the same failings in students as the old syllabus. One Chief Examiner could find no relief from the mediocrity that flowed so abundantly into the old mathematics course over which he had charge, only to reappear in the new. He railed against the Calculus and Applied Mathematics class of 1971 with savage indignation:

> The simplest calculus was a cause of major problems . . . there was little evidence of even the basic ideas in mechanics . . . elementary arithmetic and algebra were careless, and there was little to suggest that candidates had thought about a question before attempting it . . . Geometrical and trigonometrical interpretations . . . were likewise poorly handled. In all, there were extremely few impressive scripts and very many bad ones.

He then turned his attention to the new Applied Mathematics students with unrestrained derision: 'Question 3—(a) Badly done. Reasons, if given, were usually ridiculous . . . However, this proved a good question to mark as the reasons given were often hilarious'.[32]

If the syllabus had shifted, the novel content or the extra emphasis on topics such as probability, functions and relations simply widened the terrain over which the expectations of the examiners could roam. Material that had been de-emphasized still lay in the rear, ready to come back into prominence through the choice of problems—as was the case with geometry[33]—or continuing to baffle candidates who now had to spread their efforts over an extended range of complex ideas. Less time on calculus only tended to make the examiners more sensitive to weaknesses in this area.

The growing sophistication of syllabus material enriched the model of the good mathematics student—the engineer was now more statistically oriented, the generalist had a wider concept of algebra—but the qualities of good scholarship had become no more accessible. To be awarded high marks, a candidate had to display conceptual depth—good understanding of basic concepts (vectors, complex numbers, probability, variance), recognition of their relevance in new or unfamiliar settings, ability to work from first principles (though sometimes *not* to), and integration of ideas learnt in different situations. Perception of form and structure in mathematical problems was vital for students crossing into the section of the examination paper designed specifically to challenge the more able. They needed strategic sense as well as inner confidence and resolution. Their operational skills must be of a high order and be exercised consistently and fruitfully, unmarred by petty and sometimes fatal errors, while the physical arrangement of their work had to mirror the clarity and logical purpose of their minds.

The examination regime produced various approximations to this ideal, while tending to undermine its fullest realization in the free and creative thinker. At the furthest remove were students whose grasp of concepts was poor and who had learnt manipulative skills from repeated trials within narrowly circumscribed contexts. They scanned questions in search of familiar form, rushed at them without thinking through their approach, made frequent errors in their arithmetic and algebra, confused concepts (variance, standard deviation) or had never encountered them, and produced volumes of misdirected mathematical prose, to their own and the markers' dismay. Academic mathematics appeared in these candidates' scripts like a language badly learnt, displaying systematic and therefore ineradicable errors that stopped it from ever being correct, with the speaker trapped and suspended in fundamental grammatical confusion.

The cultural externality of academic mathematics—as something learnt 'on the outside', not arising through the continuous, imperceptible influence of familiar others—was most evident among those populations who were newest to upper secondary education. In the west and north of Melbourne—working-class suburbs in the main, with large concentrations of non-English-speaking migrants —the chances of failing General Mathematics were nearly twice as high as in the middle-class inner east and south of the city.[34] This was despite the fact that enrolment in the subject was almost always lower, and from populations that reached the final years of school much less frequently. Girls from poor suburbs were especially vulnerable, with around 40 per cent failing General Mathematics. The trade-off that compensated reduced participation by at least average results no more operated at this end of the social spectrum than it did at the other extreme, where school completion and mathematics enrolment rates were much higher, but failure much lower (see Figure 28). In 1975, the magnitude of failure among those working-class students who did attempt General Mathematics placed them two decades behind—back in the mid-1950s—when the average student could expect to fail four times out of ten.[35]

At the closest remove to the ideal mathematics candidate were the students who did understand concepts, who were dexterous, careful and methodical in their work, who had learnt some strategic sense, could tackle problems independently, mobilize ideas from different stages of their learning, and were confident of their own powers. These were well-trained students, and their training by comparison with many others' had come easily.[36] From early in childhood, they had been taught the precise and accurate use of words and constantly shown how to use the resources of speech to differentiate meaning. Fuelled by this continual demand on personal exchanges in a formal medium, their cognitive growth had been precocious.[37] Success at school and pleasure in learning conditioned them to accept the logic of remote meaning that governs progress in mathematics and to convert the labour of abstraction

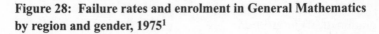

Figure 28: Failure rates and enrolment in General Mathematics by region and gender, 1975[1]

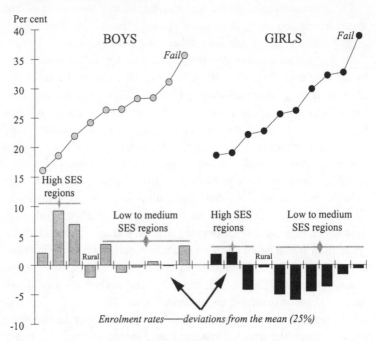

[1] Fail rates are shown in percentage terms; enrolment rates are shown as deviations from the average across all regions (i.e., 25 per cent)

Source: Unpublished HSC results, 1975.

into a game of pattern and structure. In them, the intellectual disposition that suspends claims of relevance and practicality could be cultivated earlier and more durably because the materials on which their personal transactions were based were more frequently ideas and arguments and because the community of opinion surrounding them was educated and intellectual.

Expected to do well in the world of learning, they more readily accepted academic success as a measure of their own maturity and acceptance by others. At school, in classes drawn largely from the same milieux as their own, the hierarchy of knowledge—elaborated into a regime of prestige and competition—imposed mathematics upon them with the force of a cult into which they might well have been born and from which they had little prospect of release. Cult-like, their practice of mathematics would be ruled by disciplined and focused teachers whose object was to produce whole classes of successful students rather than the select few for whom alone the too-exacting examiner had eyes.

If there was a geographical pattern in the spread of weak and strong candidates, the institutional pattern that partly underlay this was at least as striking. The likelihood of taking General Mathematics rose from around 23 per cent of boys in public high schools to 33 per cent in Catholic schools to nearly 40 per cent in private non-Catholic schools. General Mathematics was the option chosen by future doctors and other budding professionals planning private practice, and the rising gradient in participation from public to private schools reflected this bias. Girls too were more likely to attempt General Mathematics if they came from Catholic or private schools, though their levels of participation were somewhat lower (see Figure 29, upper panel).

Achievement in the higher bands showed almost the same slanted pattern as enrolment. Only about one in five boys from high schools were awarded honours in General Mathematics in 1975 (19 per cent) compared with 31 per cent of Catholic-school boys and 42 per cent of private-school boys. Rising from a progressively higher basis of participation came a progressively higher level of competitive performance. Much more likely to attempt General Mathematics (and to reach the end of school in the first place), boys in private non-Catholic establishments were more than twice as likely to receive first-class or second-class honours. Among girls, relativities in participation were not so steep, but performance in the top two bands was sharply differentiating. Private-school girls were twice as likely to be awarded honours as girls in public high schools. In Catholic schools, girls' participation rates were in an intermediate position between public and private, but their results placed them on a par with high-school girls. Though encouragement was there—and intelligent, devoted teachers[38]— the stress on competitive success was not widely ingrained and the teaching resources required were not widely available.

Pure Mathematics coupled with Applied Mathematics was the subject of preference for the boys from middle-class and upper

Figure 29: Honours rates and enrolment in mathematics by type of school and gender, 1975

(A) GENERAL MATHEMATICS

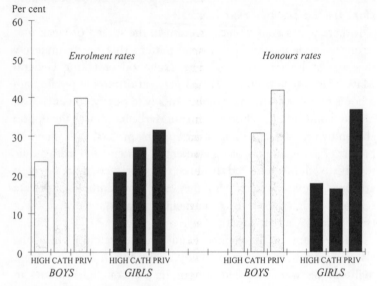

(B) PURE MATHEMATICS

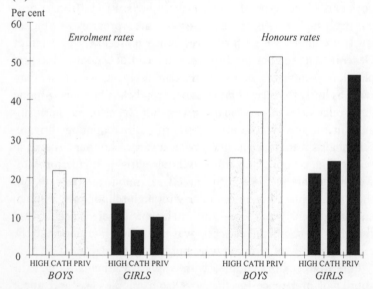

Source: Unpublished HSC results, 1975.

working-class homes who attended public high schools. They were aiming at engineering and applied science rather than medicine.[39] So the institutional pattern was reversed, with high schools dominating, both among boys and—at a much lower level—among girls (see Figure 29, lower panel). But in terms of competitive achievement, the gradient followed the same direction as in the case of General Mathematics, only sharper, reflecting the performance credentials of the more highly selected students tackling a double-mathematics option leading to university mathematics. In Pure Mathematics, every second boy attending a private non-Catholic school was given honours in 1975 (51 per cent)—again double the rate among boys from high schools (25 per cent). With girls, the relative advantage of attending a private school was even greater, though honours rates were marginally lower (46 per cent and 21 per cent for private schools and high schools respectively).

In the 1960s, 'new maths', with its emphasis on fundamental understanding and an integrated mathematical experience, had promised to break down the formalized divisions of school mathematics that had supplied the pedagogical framework for intensive competitive training on predictable, discrete tasks. The stability and productivity of the teaching effort in schools where high levels of global success were required was threatened with a philosophy that reasserted the individual learner and depth of comprehension as its goals. But the menace of radical change was averted, because teachers and academics interpreted the philosophy of the 'new maths' in light of expectations for a teachable and examinable syllabus.

The effectiveness of this domestication around the selection functions of the curriculum is evident in the fact that, five years after the full implementation of the new courses, the old patterns of relative social advantage were very much in evidence again.[40] The new content—set theory, matrix algebra, vectors, more probability and statistics—was quickly assimilated by those schools that already enjoyed major resource advantages in the form of pupil mix and highly trained and experienced teachers. While the persistence of examinations undermined the reform effort, the division of the school system into highly segregated and unequally powerful sectors ensured that the new courses would be exploited primarily as tests of corporate strength. The influence of exams is only as potent as the most powerful schools. Academic establishments, whether public or private, knew how to convert the courses into material likely to be tested and capable of being drilled—as in the case of the General Mathematics textbook written by Lucas of Wesley College[41]—and could thus meet the examiners on their own terms.

Schools serving working-class, migrant or rural communities often employed inexperienced and less well-trained teachers.[42] Nor could they draw on the wealth of family cultural and educational capital pooled in selective academic schools. Novel content, especially when justified as promoting individual learning, might appeal to young and committed teachers in charge of classes where achievement was modest and motivation mixed. But the task of making the new syllabus function pedagogically in this setting held a very different prospect from the business of making the new content work in a strategic way, as in the academic schools. As in other contexts, the power exerted through the expertise and cultural resources concentrated in selective public and private schools neutralized the philosophy of curriculum innovation, while transforming the content into new examination material with which to dominate other users.

11

Pedagogical Freedom and Institutional Power in Mathematics Reform

Preserving the old pedagogical order at university

Changes in the secondary mathematics curriculum in the early post-war decades are often seen as a result of discipline shift— with universities seeking to modernize programmes in schools—or pedagogical shift, with discovery methods replacing rote learning. It is less often recognized that demands for reform emanating from the discipline of mathematics arose at a time of major change in universities. By the time secondary schools came under pressure for reform, universities themselves had felt the winds of change. Academics were challenged to defend the economic relevance of their courses and especially the adequacy of their research output. But it was the changing nature of the student population that was crucial, because this had major implications for their teaching practice.

Reacting to the pressures of teaching ever greater numbers of undergraduates—using methods of instruction scarcely less ancient than the syllabus content of schools—academics demanded improvements in student quality. 'Already the universities are being adversely affected through their first-year students', wrote Bryan Thwaites, reporting from the Southampton Mathematics Conference of 1961. 'Despite the expansion of our universities, there has been no considerable increase in the number of really bright mathematical students, but there has been a large increase in the number of those [identified as] "second category of quality"'.[1]

He then went on to list the many intellectual failings of students arriving at university, though certified as mathematically competent by the examiners. An almost identical list could be prepared for Australia, based for example on the views of G. M. Kelly, examiner for the New South Wales Leaving Certificate in 1962.[2] As the nature of the undergraduate population changed, the cultural assumptions on which university teaching had been based began to break down and to act as obstacles to learning. Academics had to adapt. But they saw their first line of action, not in a radical reorganization of teaching and course design within their own province, but in a reform of the teaching of mathematics in schools.

Mathematics as an intellectual discipline had greatly expanded since 1800. But this fact—so often trumpeted by the champions of innovation—belied another fact, more fundamental to the process of reform. Mathematics as academic practice in universities had *not* changed. The lecture theatre was still the main vehicle of pedagogical transmission, and the hierarchy of ranks among staff was even more than ever a mechanism for distancing the producer of knowledge (the professor) from the receiver (the student).[3] All the adverse consequences that flowed from this broken relationship rolled before the eyes of the academic reformers of school mathematics—shallow learning, poor comprehension, transparent examination tactics, high failure rates and withdrawal from courses, generalized malaise among students and low morale among junior staff, whose heavy teaching loads freed the professors for research. Yet these manifestations of dysfunction formed an almost imperceptible part of the argument for reform of the curriculum. It was the historical obsolescence of the school syllabus, not the anachronism of university teaching practice, that supplied the rhetoric for change.

Undergraduates would more often survive the poor supervision, the lack of contact, the misunderstood and misused language of instruction, and above all the switch to 'free direction'—exhibited in the lack of prescription, the open choice of textbooks or even the absence of textbooks—if they had already developed intellectual tastes, were independent learners, and could appreciate mathematics on its own terms.[4] These were precisely the students whose precocious talents were to be liberated by abolishing Euclid.

The 'new maths' at school—or rather the changes made partly under its inspiration—would save the teaching of mathematics in universities from pedagogical collapse. Modern fields—number theory, topology, algebraic geometry, axiomatics and logic—would prosper with no change in university teaching practice, pedagogical roles or accountability. The 'new maths' was, in short, a means of saving the old maths.

It was not the subject content of the past that was at stake. It was the attitude, the emphasis, and the style of work—essentially the theoretical mathematician's pedagogical and economic liberty to work on topics of *mathematical* significance, to pursue research untrammelled by demands for relevance, application or meaning from the swelling ranks of post-war undergraduates. By privileging the kind of student who coped best with antique teaching practice and the kinds of topics that represented the free development of the discipline, pure mathematics made pedagogical tradition and the concomitant hierarchical order of institutions and roles the price for the dissemination of its modern content. The past would be kept in place against the extrinsic demands of applied mathematicians, of industry and commerce, and the instrumental career values of undergraduates and their parents. Those students who did reach university would be equipped with the theoretical disposition and a unified concept of mathematics that would bring to an end the tensions of meaning and purpose that were fracturing the intellectual life of the modern university. The 'new mathematics' was modern in content, reactionary in practice.

Dieudonné, addressing the Royaumont seminar in the winter of 1959, bemoaned the poor grasp of modern mathematical concepts among undergraduates:

> Under the new encyclopedic and overcrowded curriculum, most students simply emerge with the haziest notions of what it is all about. Not only have they not properly digested the modern parts, but they also have failed to acquire the technical proficiency in the old-fashioned 'epsilontics', which at least could be expected *occasionally* from their predecessors.[5]

But it was not a reform of higher education that he called for—not an attack on the 'encyclopedic and overcrowded curriculum', nor on the additional years spent in preparatory classes competing for entry to the *grandes écoles*, and least of all on the medieval teaching methods that underpinned professorial authority and ultimately social advantage as well. To extend the already long years passed in university would be intolerable. To reform teaching could only weaken research by diverting energy into remedial programmes. Quality of learning in higher education was instead laid at the feet of secondary schoolteachers as a problem for them to fix. That was the purpose of the 'new maths'.

To protect the pedagogical regime of the university—by filling lecture theatres only with students whose intellectual level and interests freed them from the need to attend lectures—was at the same time to conserve the narrow social basis of higher mathematical learning. To the reformers who had the upper hand, mathematics was an element of free culture to be appreciated in its own right. The task that fell to schools was to cultivate a mathematical consciousness in which the chief points of subjective interest were the internal hierarchy of concepts (for example, symmetry over the 'artificial plaything' of the triangle)[6], the detection of pattern or structure through abstraction, and the use of mathematical symbolism to stimulate interpretation and control the flow of thought. Turned in upon itself, mathematics exercised greater appeal to students from university-educated, professional families. They were more likely than the new populations to identify with its pure orientation as distinct from its applied temptations.[7]

Such students had enjoyed continuous progress in basic concepts during their years in primary school and in the academic streams of high school, but also the economically free and time-rich framework within which intellectual detachment could be fostered and mathematics pursued as a game of intrinsic or at any rate scholarly rewards. The standard of university teaching, relying for its success on this disposition rather than instructional efficiency, close supervision or the relevance of practical applications, thus perpetuated not only a 'pure' ideal of mathematical thought, but also an elevated standard of social intake. In the end, it was not to protect the teaching regime or professorial privileges as such that a reform of the secondary school curriculum was demanded. It was to preserve a way of doing mathematics at university and ultimately a way of life whose liberality was symbolized by this way of doing maths. For the liberal ideal of the disinterested mathematician would lose meaning outside the traditional setting of the university and the social patronage on which it rested.

Mathematical discovery demanded intense and sustained concentration, 'silence and solitude' for serious reflection. As Dieudonné put it:

> Above all the mathematician seeks to have enough time to devote himself to scholarly work, and this is why, since the nineteenth century, mathematicians have preferred the low teaching hours and long holidays that go with careers in university or higher technical school.[8]

But these conditions were being eroded, Dieudonné added in a note: 'Today this so-precious time is being increasingly nibbled away by a multiplicity of supplementary and exhausting tasks'. Teaching conditions—time on task, proliferation of duties, and the demands of students inspired by economic motives—were undermining the progress of mathematics, a discipline driven mainly by internal dynamics (not applications) and one whose disciples could not be treated as mere technicians without destroying their creativity.[9]

 Both the timing of the reform of school mathematics—during the first throes of the post-war expansion of universities—and the direction of reform in favour of pure mathematics show that the impulse behind the 'new maths' was a cultural, not a pedagogical ideal. But to demand the loyalty of schoolteachers to a historical image—the free practice of mathematics in socially exclusive institutions of higher learning—was to ask that they ignore the radical changes occurring simultaneously in their own classrooms. The displacement of pedagogical responsibility from university to secondary school invited teachers to perform two contradictory roles. On the one hand, they were to repair the conceptual shortcomings of the 'average intelligent' child bound for higher education.[10] This was to compensate for the pedagogical shortcomings of the nineteenth-century university, which wanted active and self-sufficient learners who did not depend on their teachers. But, on the other hand, teachers were to extend mathematical instruction to the much wider group of children who from the beginning of the 1950s were being offered places in comprehensive secondary schools.

The academic emphasis on conforming to an obsolete teaching culture in universities would eventually collide with the practical emphasis dictated by mixed-ability classes in secondary school. This is nowhere more apparent than in the increasing alarm expressed by teachers—and not a few academics—over the place of set theory in the curriculum. Pure mathematics had aimed to transform the mathematical consciousness of school pupils by changing the vocabulary in which they expressed their concepts. Set theory was to be the linguistic medium through which a radical shift was to occur in how concepts and principles were learnt. But teachers, untrained in modern algebra and logic and unclear about how the language of sets would facilitate comprehension of more advanced topics, could only see it as syllabus content to be mastered simply because it was on the examinations.[11] In the haste to adapt to the new philosophy, language and symbols were abused, mathematical concepts misused, new words proliferated and were badly defined, jargon and mathematical nonsense gathered over the heads of teachers and pupils alike.[12] Far from enhancing student understanding, the new language—with its stress on correctness in nomenclature and notation—put it at risk by hampering communication. 'It has discouraged the use of good English', complained E. R. Love, Professor of Mathematics at Melbourne University, 'instead of cultivating it'.

The tide of academic opinion was turning against the basic assumption of the 'new maths', that direct emphasis on underlying concepts through the grammar of set theory would produce superior learning. Formal attention to concepts and laws was denounced as excessive and unreal—'effective skills are being sacrificed on the altar of general concepts', argued G. B. Preston, Professor of Mathematics at Monash University. By shifting attention away from applications, the new courses had deprived mathematics of its intuitive strength, understated the role of interpretation and undermined creativity.[14]

These were very significant criticisms, given the inspiration of the new courses. Failure to relate mathematics to real-world problems had sapped the subject of its energy. What should always have been prominent in teaching was being treated as a mere by-product.[15] Teachers and mathematics educators were looking more and more closely at the impact of the curriculum on student learning outcomes, and were no longer content to rely on expectations of conceptual progress derived from Piagetian developmental psychology. As junior secondary classes became more diverse during the 1970s, the relative achievement of different subgroups began to be investigated and data disseminated through professional journals and conferences.[16] At the same time, the formal weakening of university control over the lower levels of the secondary-school curriculum enabled teachers to explore alternative approaches to mathematics for the groups described by the Schools Council in England as of 'average or less than average ability'.[17] The years of viewing secondary-school mathematics as a means of solving the cultural dissonance of the modern university were coming to an end.

Autonomy for schoolteachers in terminal subjects

In the mid-1970s, when teachers looked back over a decade of reform ending in frustration rather than fulfilment, they saw the freedom of the new concepts betrayed by examinations, and pedagogical principles by academic functions. 'We must no longer permit mathematics to be used as the yard-stick with which we measure and sort the "cans" from the "cannots"', concluded a passionate mathematics educator, who would not abandon the struggle. 'We need to think in terms of meaningful mathematical experiences which *all* children need in order to learn to move with confidence in the worlds of number and space'.[18] The universities were ready to cede some territory to teachers in exchange for immunity from the needs of 'non-academic' groups. This compromise allowed the universities to continue to ignore quality of instruction and learning in their own departments—by selecting only students with a high prediction of success—while on the other hand it allowed schools to run subjects focusing on mathematical comprehension and 'real-world' competence.

Curriculum development in schools was favoured by the division of Australian higher education into universities and colleges of advanced education, a division that had been consolidated in 1965. The technical institutes and teachers' colleges of the advanced-education sector competed with universities and were willing to recognize studies that were wholly school-assessed. Institutional diversity in higher education and competition for markets made it possible to create a space in the senior secondary curriculum that was under the control of teachers. Students, however, would have avoided this space if they could not use it to gain access to degree-bearing courses, even if these were not in universities. The designers of Mathematics at Work, for example, felt that most colleges of advanced education would welcome the subject—other than for 'heavily mathematical' courses in engineering and applied science. Employers too should have accepted the course, because it trained students to apply their knowledge to everyday problems,[19] but employers were also sensitive to status distinctions between university-approved and non-approved subjects. If there was more uncertainty here, the existence of an institutional 'shell' in the form of colleges of advanced education offered legitimacy to courses that were strongly practical in orientation.

Mathematics at Work was based on booklets prepared by the Australian Academy of Science. Themes of applicability were used to introduce concepts. Co-ordinate geometry, for example, was studied from the perspective of 'making the best of things' (optimization), while the theme of 'taking your chances' ushered in probability and statistics, queuing and simulation. This was a subject that could be taken by low achievers, including those who had abandoned mathematics at the first legal opportunity. 'The mathematical content is itself not demanding. Students who have completed a reasonable Year 9 or 10 mathematics course should have little difficulty with the [required] mathematical skills'.[20]

Business Mathematics, also school-assessed, contained computing strands, economic modelling, taxation, probability, queuing theory and a variety of projects and games. Begun on a trial basis in 1981, it was enjoyed by teachers, and students found it relevant and interesting.[21] Commercial Mathematics, introduced later, covered matrices, functions and graphs, and gave more detailed attention to probability and statistics (with the beginnings of inferential work).[22]

In the year that school-based subjects in mathematics became available, Australia entered the worst recession since World War Two. The sharp economic downturn in 1982–83 ended the decline in retention rates that had lasted for much of the 1970s and began a new phase in the long movement towards mass secondary schooling. Mathematics at Work, Business Mathematics and Commercial Mathematics followed this upward trend in school participation, so that by the end of the decade around 15 per cent of all candidates were enrolled in one of these wholly school-assessed subjects.[23] By contrast, the rapid increase in numbers completing school tended to depress participation in the university-approved Pure and Applied Mathematics and General Mathematics. Enrolment rates in Pure and General (or their equivalent from 1986) fell from a total of 62 per cent of boys and 41 per cent of girls in 1981 to 49 per cent and 33 per cent respectively in 1990.[24]

The new subjects played a larger role for girls than boys. They tended to compensate for the continuing gender gap in participation in mainstream mathematics (which barely changed over the decade). School-based subjects represented an increasing share of the total effort made by girls in final-year mathematics, rising from around 8 per cent in 1983 to 33 per cent in 1990. In other words, one in every three girls attempting mathematics in 1990 was in the 'terminal' stream not recognized by universities. A similar pattern occurred in boys' participation, but the contribution of the school-based subjects to total activity was lower, reaching only about 23 per cent at the end of the period.

The marked gender contrast in the role of school-assessed subjects was a reflection of differences in the career and training plans of boys and girls, though the perceived suitability of soft options for girls—whose self-esteem in mathematics was persistently lower—could only help shape more modest plans. This illustrates the dilemma of pursuing reform by working on only one side of a differentiated curriculum—the side rejected by academic authority. Teacher-controlled subjects enlarged opportunities for mathematical study by setting aside a field of work beyond the universities' jurisdiction. But the exploitation of this field also protected academic mathematics from having to respond to the needs of new populations, and the segmented curriculum tended to act as a translation of social structure. Relatively low participation in academic mathematics in working-class suburbs was balanced by higher enrolments in terminal mathematics. Opportunities were enlarged, but always on condition that terminal students did not raise their aspirations, and that academic mathematics remained deaf to their needs or potential.

Academic mathematics and economic manipulation

If the creation of terminal subjects for terminal students left academic mathematics undistracted by a changing population, its traditional users had so distorted its structure and rationale in the interim that reform of some kind could no longer be delayed. The credibility of traditional mathematics was sinking in the very schools that made the greatest use of it. The division of the mathematics curriculum into a cultural subject (General Mathematics) and a preparatory stream of two subjects (Pure and Applied Mathematics) had changed in function since the 1940s. Quite able students had come to exploit General Mathematics to gain the high marks needed to enter elite professional faculties at university.[25] Given the scarcity of places in medical and law schools, the less competitive of this high-aspiring group would be obliged to fall back on courses such as engineering, for which General Mathematics was inadequate. But many, on the other hand, did enter prestige courses, and indeed could dominate access to these because they enjoyed advantages of background that made top marks in General Mathematics a realistic objective.

By operating a subject of lower general standard, the universities in effect reduced the demands they made on the categories of students who were best placed to manage the curriculum, thanks to their economic and cultural resources. By contrast, the hard option of Pure and Applied Mathematics often fell to students who had far fewer advantages and whose professional aspirations were more limited. Academic mathematics thus offered two different facilities—on the one hand, less prestigious or lucrative careers, costing greater relative effort from students with modest family resources, and on the other, high-prestige, independent careers, costing less relative effort from students who enjoyed very considerable advantages.

It is not too much to say that a class system had become installed in academic mathematics. Those boys in public high schools who reached the end of school took the hard option of double mathematics somewhat more often than their peers in private establishments (29 per cent as against 25 per cent), but they were only half as likely to be rewarded with top marks. Struggling to meet the demands of the curriculum, they set their horizons on engineering and applied science, not the private-income professions. Boys in independent schools, on the other hand, took General Mathematics much more frequently than their counterparts in public education (44 per cent compared with 25 per cent), and they were given first-class honours three times as often. For here they were competing with the weakest mathematics students from the public system, mediocre candidates whom the high schools, still faithful to early post-war thinking, relegated to General Mathematics (see Figure 30).

The same broad pattern occurred among girls. Many of the best from private schools were aiming at medicine, so they entered for General Mathematics, where they could easily dispatch the less talented group deposited there by the high schools. The relative advantage of private-school girls in General Mathematics is evident from the fact that they triumphed *over all boys* in the subject, except those from the private system itself. General Mathematics was used, in other words, to trump gender with class.[26]

Academic mathematics was no less a social system at its interior than in its rejection of terminal students at the exterior. This was true not only in its structure of options—which eased demands on the best-placed students and intensified demands on the least advantaged—but in the scale of performance within each of its options, which doubled as a social scale. In 1985, the manipulative structure was abolished to protect the interests of high-achieving

Figure 30: First-class honours and enrolment in Pure Mathematics and General Mathematics by type of school and gender, 1985[1]

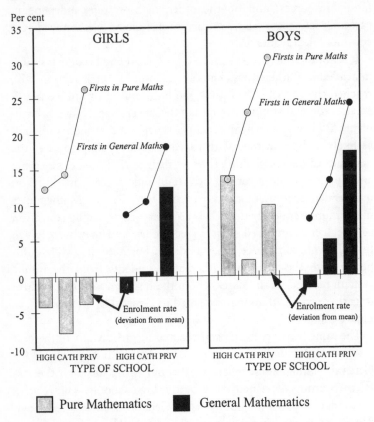

[1] First-class honours rates are shown in percentage terms; enrolment rates are shown as deviations from the average for all school students across all schools.

Source: Unpublished HSC results, 1985.

students whose access to traditional career options was being eroded. No similar concern was shown for low achievers. The revised subjects, coming into force in 1986, would merely communicate all the social rigidities of the past from one cohort to the next.

Academic autonomy and social inequality

To reconcile power over the curriculum with responsibility for teaching had been the guiding idea of reformers in the 1970s. But the principle that those with power should share the tasks of teaching—and that those who teach should have a share of power —would be interpreted one-sidedly. The hierarchy of mathematics subjects—from the ungraded Mathematics at Work through the graded but unrecognized Business Mathematics and Commercial Mathematics and on to the graded, recognized, but soft General Mathematics and thence to the graded, recognized and hard Pure and Applied Mathematics—was also marked by a progressive paring back of the role of teachers. Their authority was inversely proportional to the amount of university prescription; and the greater the prescription—of content, assessment, scaling and reporting practices—the higher the standing and prestige of the subject. Prescription removed the teachers' power to relate autonomously to their pupils and transferred it to university researchers.[27]

Academic freedom conferred the right to fill the syllabus with content and to dictate the pace of work—but to be absent from the classroom in which the syllabus was taught. It meant liberty to vary topics according to the drift of scholarly interests and tastes, to ignore or perhaps respond to shifts in student characteristics, to set examination questions that were easy or, at the other extreme, problems that at most a small fraction would find manageable.[28]

Above all, pedagogical freedom lay in the prescription of theoretical work. Although the syllabus for General Mathematics stressed the 'ability to formulate "real world" problems in mathematical terms', it was the conceptual sophistication and operational facility of the candidate that was being trained, not a sense of reality or knowledge of the 'real world' of applicable mathematics.[29] The question was whether a candidate could transcend the practical context in which a problem was cast—basically as a pretext—to express processes or relationships in mathematically fruitful language. From the examiner's perspective, the good student recognized the mathematical dimensions of a problem, developed lines of attack that were intuitively sound and logically controlled, mobilized conceptual resources acquired at different pedagogical stages, could detect and fix 'obviously' wrong answers, and was algebraically dexterous, accurate and self-composed.

What was needed in the syllabus, therefore, was not fully worked examples of 'mathematics at work'—case studies of the applicability of mathematics in the engineering workshop, the medical research laboratory, the insurance office, the broking house, the gaming house—but mathematics as 'theoretical practice'. Permutations and combinations, functions and graphs, matrix algebra, calculus and probability had to be studied on their own terms—as conceptual systems—before they could be applied, and it could not be assumed that they would ever be applied. Universities were there to develop this theoretical space and to expand it according to its own inner logic. That was the meaning of academic freedom, and that was why it brought with it the privileges of creating new knowledge but not applying it, of writing a syllabus but not teaching it, of assessing student achievement but not stimulating it.

Mathematics as theoretical practice demands a capacity for abstraction, interpretation and imagination. Success calls for language facility as well as ease with the dense text of algebraic symbolism. Sustained concentration and personal application are needed, self-confidence and the time-enhanced perspective that accepts an intellectual discipline for its own sake, not for everyday use.[30] The traditional pedagogical regime of the university was based on this model of the successful learner, even if real students often departed from it. In the post-war years, when universities increasingly adopted the tutorial system, this assumption of the independent learner with intrinsic motivation remained in force.[31]

It was the justification for selective admissions, for the magistral lecture as the primary instrument of communication, and for the pedagogical distance that dismayed undergraduates, but fortified academic authority.[32] Yet, however important 'maturity' was to academics, competition for places in the most selective courses at university dictated that the schools adopt a different emphasis. The cognitive and cultural demands of the curriculum would have reduced the ranks of students completing school to pre-war levels had academic secondary schools simply accepted the mandate from universities to select only the best. If public high schools proved more compliant, this was because they were part of a differentiated system in which junior technical schools and girls' domestic arts schools received weaker learners. But private schools and congregational Catholic schools served ambitious families intent on maintaining or advancing their social and economic position.

In the mid-1970s, high schools often over-corrected for the risk of failure by running stringent promotions policies,[33] but private schools were under pressure to act in reverse fashion. To reach the levels of competitive success demanded by their clients, they had to pursue strategies that fully utilized the cultural capital made available to them by educated families or compensated for its absence among less educated but economically well-off patrons. The reduction of the mathematics syllabus to rehearsable routines counteracted the culturally selective effects of the curriculum by unravelling the code of intellectual maturity on which it was based. Students learnt to anticipate the tasks that they would have to perform and practise the behaviours they were expected to display. Prior success in elementary mathematics and English, the integration of the student in a socially segregated setting with an academic ethos, and overt and attainable economic benefits made mathematical learning by copybook methods an effective reply to the aristocratic demands of university examiners.

If the tactics of schools aiming at global success did not produce independent learners—'any question that required interpretation was handled badly', the General Mathematics examiners groaned in 1983—the standard of achievement was enough to keep the traditional system of university teaching in place.[34] Only minimum concessions were made to students—maintenance of the tutorial system, streaming of students by mathematics background, continuous assessment as a supplement to exams, student counselling and study-skills programmes.

'Mass' teaching, however, remained. More than two-thirds of all instructional time prescribed for first-year mathematics at the University of Melbourne—including time on 'problem solving'—was taken up by lectures. In spite of its known inefficiency as a tool of teaching, the lecture was accepted in exchange for its low cost and the time saved for research.[35] In science-based courses, the overlap in content with senior school subjects and reliance on examinations ensured that students would apply the study techniques and philosophy they had learnt at school and that HSC marks would offer a good prediction of success.[36] University teaching did not have to become more efficient as long as the standard of student intake was kept up through minimum entry scores. Prediction of success rather than production of success was the key. By relying on high aggregate marks for selection, the leading universities could lower their teaching effort to release time for research, while maximizing their relative prestige as measured by cut-off scores.

But there were costs associated with this strategy. Performance in examinations was so closely linked with socio-economic status, and the standardization procedures used to produce additive marks were so weighted in favour of mathematics and physical sciences—these being the main instruments used to convert social resources into scholastic power—that the academically elite universities were of necessity also socially elite, despite protestations to the contrary.[37] While examinations supplied the statistical discrimination on which this system of social engineering was based, they did not produce the depth of student learning that was needed to defend it. Again and again, the examiners lashed at students— at the 'continuing poor standard of basic algebra and arithmetic', at ignorance of trigonometric functions, at simple conceptual errors in statistics and poor rudimentary geometry (such as not knowing the formula for the area of a circle).[38] In 1983, more than one-third of candidates attempting the fourth question of the General Mathematics paper could not solve a simple equation.[39] A common answer was, '$\sqrt{x} = .69, \therefore x = \sqrt{.69}$'.

Difficult to defend pedagogically, the mathematics curriculum produced major strategic advantages while severely punishing the newest populations to reach upper secondary school. In 1985, the last year in which General Mathematics was offered, only 9 per cent of boys living in the inner east of Melbourne and attending private non-Catholic schools could expect to fail.[40] But in the north-west of Melbourne, their peers attending public high schools —boys typically from non-English-speaking and working-class homes—failed more than five times as often (47 per cent). In the southern suburbs of Melbourne, somewhat more mixed than the inner east, 12 per cent of private-school boys failed, but in the industrial and high migrant density outer west, the high-school failure rate was 39 per cent. Among girls, those enrolled in private non-Catholic establishments and living in the inner east or south of the city failed 9 times in 100, while their high-school counterparts from the outer west or the north-west—where participation rates were lower—received E or F grades four times as often (36 per cent and 39 per cent respectively).

Relaxing the regulatory framework of the curriculum to make room for teachers bought time for the universities at the top of the institutional hierarchy. What teachers owned, universities abjured. Attempts to extend the influence of teachers within the academic curriculum by increasing the weight of school-assessed options were strenuously opposed.[41] Any widening of the role of teachers in *assessment* would tend to diminish the power of universities over *curriculum*. This could happen in different ways. But the result would be a potentially greater diversity in student achievement and a more problematic relative standard. The first would threaten the pedagogical freedom of the universities, because uneven preparation would require changes in course design and teaching strategies. The second threatened the credibility of selection by exam results. The leading universities therefore sought to stop any further expansion of school assessment within academic subjects. Too much of their own freedom was at stake to cede any additional liberty to schools.

More time spent in teaching would impede their research effort —the major source of their prestige. Selection other than by marks, besides taxing their teaching effort, would open the way to multiple scales of institutional worth instead of a single, easily manipulated, homogenizing scale that the public believed in. Guarding their pedagogical freedom and their system of prestige ranking, the universities enjoyed a minimum of accountability.[42] They opposed government efforts to make them more answerable for resource efficiency and student outcomes in the face of the rapidly increasing demand for higher education and escalating costs of the 1980s. Control over the curriculum and the mechanism of selection by score provided the leading universities with a refuge against accountability. They were able to divert weaker students into the colleges of advanced education , whose problems of teaching and learning would later be turned against them in the struggle for research funds when they were elevated to university status.

The positional behaviour of the top universities towards schools and other institutions within the graded system of higher education intensified the social manipulation of the curriculum. Machine for allocating individual chances, the curriculum also determined institutional rank as measured by relative student quality. In academic mathematics, the theoretical emphasis, the range of conceptual training and operational demands, the compression of content and pace of work dictated by examinations, and the scaling of questions to let better students 'identify themselves' called on the school system to prepare sites where these requirements could be exploited for competitive gain. At these sites, teachers would convert the pedagogical liabilities transferred to schools into academic notes payable at elite professional courses. At other sites, teachers received debt. They and their students carried this as the price of the institutional autonomy and social advantage accumulated in the traditional university.

12

Mathematics for the Majority: Reform and Counter-Reform

LONG AFTER IT HAD BROKEN with the notion that it was about the laws of matter and motion, earthly and heavenly, mathematics was returned to the world of human practice by the concept of problem solving. The sojourn, however, would have to be brief for the 1 per cent of the school population who became mathematicians. Unravelling mundane problems was not clever enough. In due course, to quote Polya, the mathematician had to solve 'significant mathematical problems'.[1] But problem solving, approached well by teachers, could nurture real mathematical talent that might otherwise be lost. It had the potential to generalize the social reach of mathematics and to place school curricula on a new basis. Once interpreted more widely than the traditional alternatives of scientific training or liberal culture, high-school mathematics could be offered to all school populations as a form of practical intellectual training, and could find a place in all school programmes, high and low. In the 1980s, problem solving became the dominant interpretation of school mathematics.[2]

Short-lived reforms and reaction

Like the 'new maths', which it pre-dated as a pedagogical concept, problem solving sought to reorient the teaching of mathematics so that it would become intellectually driven. This implied a freer view about the structure of mathematics as a school subject.

Training in mathematics did not necessarily mean a vertical ascent from arithmetic to analysis. Lateral growth along particular branches might be both practical and fruitful. A flexible curriculum would enable students to pursue a variety of interpretations, some following the old hierarchical model, others exploring a limited number of areas seen as more relevant or meaningful. On this approach, there would not be just one mathematics subject that alone enjoyed academic standing, or one reinforced by another involving more specialist work—the pattern that applied from 1986 in Victoria.

When the curriculum was first reformed for the new Victorian Certificate of Education, mathematics was developed as a set of alternative subjects having the same level of recognition, but drawing differently on the major areas of the discipline. Space and Number was concerned with number systems and spatial relations, and drew on the four core areas of arithmetic, geometry, trigonometry and algebra.[3] Change and Approximation dealt with functions and was based on co-ordinate geometry, calculus and algebra. Reasoning and Data tackled probability, inference, induction and proof, and included statistics, mathematical logic and algebra. Each of these studies could be taken in simple or extended mode, giving a total of six subjects. They could also be combined in different ways to increase breadth or depth of training. Rather than a fixed syllabus, there was a general design prescription for each study, so schools could impart a local emphasis to the curriculum. The transparency of the design concepts—objectives, areas of study, work requirements—broke sharply with the past, when syllabus content was specified as a legal codicil to an examination and learning expectations were phrased as vaguely as possible to give full rein to the examiner's judgement.

The philosophy of problem solving was combined with flexible structure and transparent design. The curriculum writers aimed for three kinds of learning—performing investigations, solving unfamiliar problems and mastery of routine practical skills.[4] The creative side of mathematics was accentuated. This carried risks. Although course content was meant to be adapted to who students were and how well their teachers were trained, the cognitive emphasis was historically remote, originating in attempts to deepen the learning of academic, mainly middle-class students. Pedagogical changes would have to reach deep into junior secondary and primary school to alter the mathematics experience and attitudes of working-class students and to lay the conceptual basis for the kinds of independent learning upon which the curriculum now insisted.[5] Sorry measure of the great distance to be covered, results for working-class girls on the investigative project in 1992 were catastrophic. Assessed by their teachers, as many as 43 per cent received the lowest possible grades or could not even meet the minimum criteria for the award of a grade. Girls in middle-class settings failed, for their part, only thirteen in 100 times.[6]

But it was not the fate of weaker learners that would spell the end of this first effort to reform the curriculum. It was the judgement by conservative academics that stronger students were not learning enough and were being penalized by the new framework. They had made up their minds before the mathematics programme was implemented at Year 12 level in 1991. Two years of preparation and consultation had elapsed in March 1990, when a committee of senior academic administrators who had remained aloof from the developmental process publicly attacked the new curriculum.[7] The VCE, in their view, had transferred the pedagogical burden from school to university. Tertiary institutions 'will need to re-teach the entire VCE mathematics syllabus to "minimum mathematics" students', they protested, 'so as to ensure that all students in the class are conversant with all of the material'. The reformers had departed from the hierarchical view of mathematics—'the most sequential and integrated of all subjects'—and had created a framework in which soft options would receive as much credit as hard options. There would be frustration and negative attitudes towards mathematics because some tests would not discriminate between strong students—whose relative strengths were not being recognized—while other tasks might be too hard for weak students.[8]

Before the full implementation of the new curriculum in schools, unofficial steps were being taken to assess its impact on the academic preparedness of students going on to mathematics at university. In 1989 a programme of annual 'diagnostic' testing was instituted by the mathematics department at Melbourne University.[9] This would benchmark the mathematics performance of students trained under the new VCE against the achievements of students under the old HSC. In 1993 the results were publicly aired. The poor standard of algebra—condemned by examiners throughout the 1980s—was even poorer under the VCE.[10] There had been a 'further fall-off in such basic skills as fractions, indices, surds, logarithms, factorization and the solution of simple equations'. Trigonometry was poor, though calculus, differentiation and graph sketching were 'satisfactory'. Monash University had already complained about the standard of student achievement. The emphasis of the new curriculum on process over content was rebounding on university teachers who expected greater routine facility.

'It seems the old grind of mathematics is just missing', the acting head of the mathematics department at Monash concluded. 'They are not doing the skills learning.'[11] There was a well-worn path for acquiring manipulative facility, and students had wandered from it. 'They are not doing enough of the traditional calculus skills which you acquire only by rather old-fashioned methods, I'm afraid.'

Melbourne University had accepted the need to compensate for student weaknesses by streaming its intake in 1992, but the longer-term solution to rebalance pedagogical roles was to compel a rewriting of the syllabus.[12] This had begun in 1992. 'We are moving slowly back to a more hierarchical system', observed the director of first-year mathematics at Melbourne University, 'which will allow those [students] who want to do particular things with their mathematics training to do them'. The bright students— including the 'super-bright'—were not being identified by the VCE.[13]

Taking charge of the mathematics curriculum in 1992 were the two oldest-established universities in Victoria—Melbourne and Monash. They drew, respectively, from the top 15 per cent and the top 25 per cent of students completing school.[14] Under the stewardship of these sought-after institutions, mathematics was returned to a simple hierarchy. At the bottom was Further Mathematics, a general and comparatively accessible course designed for students in Year 12 who were planning to leave school for work or who would not be taking mathematics if they did go to university. Mathematical Methods was a prerequisite for undergraduate science, clinical and economics courses. Specialist Mathematics—which had to be taken with Mathematical Methods—deepened preparation for future engineers and applied scientists.[15]

Each of these new subjects was more tightly controlled in terms of content and assessment than the previous array of mathematics studies. Choice was curtailed and was restricted to pre-defined options. Mathematical Methods—the main preparatory subject—was written as a 'closely sequenced development of material'. Its content—co-ordinate geometry, trigonometrical functions, calculus, algebra, and probability and statistics—was 'fully prescribed'.[16] Specialist Mathematics extended on the same areas, but included additional work with vectors. In this subject, students could choose one optional module from a group of four—statistics and probability, geometry, mechanics or logic. Later the options would be narrowed down to two by deleting the probability and logic modules.[17]

Some flexibility was allowed in Further Mathematics, the subject geared for work or 'general tertiary purposes'. After a compulsory core of probability and statistics, students selected three modules from a group of six—arithmetic and applications, more probability and statistics, geometry and trigonometry, graphs and relations, business-related mathematics, and networks and decision mathematics. But in each case the content was prescribed in detail.

School autonomy was further reduced in 1993, when the number of teacher-assessed tasks was halved. Examinations now carried about the same weight as under the old Higher School Certificate (66 per cent compared with 70 per cent). The hierarchical effect of greater prescription of content and greater reliance on formal examinations would later be reinforced by the reintroduction of scaling. Students tackling 'hard options' such as Specialist Mathematics and Mathematical Methods would be rewarded with more generous grades, while the grades of students who took 'soft options' such as Further Mathematics would be lowered.[18]

With the hierarchical syllabus restored, universities could continue to transfer the pedagogical burden from lecture theatre and tutorial to high-school classroom.[29] By specifying the content of senior secondary mathematics, the leading universities spared themselves the efforts made by lesser tertiary institutions to correct uneven preparation among students through remedial programmes and bridging classes. The higher up the prestige scale, the duller the impulse to change. To the most powerful institutions, there could be no question of relying less on selection mechanisms and raising their own standards of instructional efficiency to accommodate greater student diversity, nor of enlarging pedagogical freedom in schools—the key to reducing failure—at the expense of academic freedom in higher education. On the contrary, the deteriorating political conditions of the late 1980s and early 1990s had presented ample scope for conservative dons and vice-chancellors to reassert their rights. By manipulating public uncertainty over the reforms, they extracted from a dying Labor government concessions that would bend the new curriculum back upon its past. Mathematics was a key element in this campaign. For it was through mathematics that aspirations for social improvement had to be asserted, and it was through mathematics, of all subjects, that family economic and cultural resources were converted into scholastic power.

Transformed into a vertical structure, the revised curriculum made sharper distinctions between students, while offering fewer opportunities for choice. The least able took Further Mathematics (if they took anything). The more able took Mathematical Methods. The most able also took Mathematical Methods, but extended it through Specialist Mathematics, making a double option.[20] Under this arrangement, competition for scarce university places became concentrated at one site in the curriculum—Mathematical Methods. The contraction of the domain of preparatory mathematics into a single extendible subject with fully prescribed content could only magnify the culturally selective effects of the cognitive demands of the curriculum by reducing the areas in which differences in student learning were assessed.

The mathematics hierarchy and cultural attributes

If mathematical prowess had to be demonstrated at one highly defined site in the curriculum—Mathematical Methods—this could be approached along different roads. Double servings of mathematics in Year 11 and—for the most capable—the additional work of Specialist Mathematics in Year 12 supplied the extra preparation needed to be competitive. The long route to Mathematical Methods represented by these additional classes raised the bar for the average student, whose thinner preparation would tell in comparative results. Boys who attempted Mathematical Methods in 1994 without taking Specialist Mathematics at the same time were more than five times as likely to receive low grades—and girls six times as likely—as those who had tackled Specialist Mathematics.[21]

But the long route was not open to all and sundry. To carry a heavy load of mathematics over the two years of the VCE, it was essential for students to have developed the right attitudes towards schoolwork and towards mathematics itself. The syllabus was packed, choice had been truncated, and the pace of teaching in Mathematical Methods could not be greatly varied to suit a wide range of abilities. Much depended on the qualities of the students themselves—not only their prior success in mathematics, but also their personal organization, study habits, concentration, self-reliance in the face of difficulties, and more generally the intellectual disposition enabling them to attempt the most theoretical and abstract subjects in the curriculum. The structure of the new mathematics programme looked for students with these sustaining characteristics.

Promotion up the scale of the mathematics curriculum was associated with an ever-richer personal experience—as a survey of student attitudes in 1994 showed—while relegation down the scale of opportunities was linked with a progressive impoverishment of experience.[22] At the null position in the hierarchy—no mathematics —were students whose confidence, ability to concentrate and ability to solve problems on their own were all low. At the intermediate positions—the 'soft option' of Further Mathematics and the 'hard option' of Mathematical Methods taken without Specialist Mathematics—the quality of student learning experience was much higher. There was little to separate these two groups, though their confidence and learning facility differed according to the different levels of mathematics they were attempting. At the highest position —the double option of Mathematical Methods plus Specialist

Mathematics—came students who, in the great majority of cases, were confident and independent learners.

This broad pattern confirmed that access to progressively more demanding work in the redesigned mathematics programme depended on the cultivation of positive attitudes, on depth of positive experience and on prior success—as well as the more intensive training to which these held the key. But the full extent to which the raising of cognitive demands over successive levels of the mathematics hierarchy called more and more on embedded scholastic attitudes and behaviours only becomes apparent when student learning facility is analysed *by level of achievement* at each step of the subject hierarchy (see Figure 31).

If the average student in Further Mathematics was no less confident and no less independent a learner than the average student in the more academic Mathematical Methods, this was a poor guide to the range of facility and attitudes in the two subjects. In Further Mathematics only 37 per cent of the lowest achievers were confident when doing mathematics, compared with 67 per cent of the highest achievers, and an even sharper gradient operated in Mathematical Methods (30 per cent at the base compared with 80 per cent at the top). Similarly, the strongest performers in Mathematical Methods were twice as likely to claim that they could usually 'solve problems by myself' (77 per cent, compared with 39 per cent of the weakest students).

Success within each subject was closely linked with academic self-esteem, favourable study habits, such as the ability to concentrate for sustained periods, and degree of training. The layers of the mathematics curriculum—from the 'abandoned' level of no mathematics through to the specialist double option—allowed students to be grouped on broad lines of academic potential, motivation and interest. Then, within each layer, a further sorting out occurred in which high marks went to self-confident, persistent and self-directed learners. Over these two phases of selection, an extremely wide gulf emerged between the lowest-achieving candidate at the lowest level of the subject hierarchy and the top performers at the top of the edifice. Only about 8 per cent of students who had given up mathematics and who placed themselves at the bottom of the previous year's class had confidence in their math-

Figure 31: Independent learning, confidence and concentration by type of mathematics and level of achievement, VCE 1994[1]

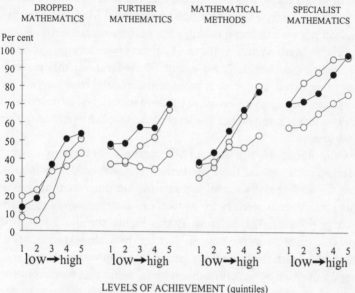

LEVELS OF ACHIEVEMENT (quintiles)

● 'I can usually solve maths problems by myself'
○ 'I am confident when I do maths'
○ 'I can concentrate on maths problems for a long time'

[1] For the 'no mathematics' group, the scale of achievement is derived from self-reported position in class during the previous year (Year 11). For the other groups, the scale is based on quintiles of achievement in final VCE assessment.

Source: Educational Outcomes Survey, 1994 (see source for Figure 7); unpublished analysis.

ematical abilities compared with 98 per cent of the Specialist Mathematics students in the highest band of achievement.

That the cognitive demands of mathematics as a generalized system of modelling and quantifying relations were culturally selective—favouring an 'academic' disposition—is borne out by the images students used to represent the subject.[23] The image of mathematics as a 'scientific' discipline—either natural or social sciences—became stronger and stronger among students as the hierarchy of general and preparatory options was ascended. The image of the mathematics classroom as a 'laboratory where you learn to use tools' was endorsed by 22 per cent of Further Mathematics students, 33 per cent of Mathematical Methods students, and 50 per cent of those taking both Mathematical Methods and Specialist Mathematics. Since these subjects were arranged in order of scientific orientation and extent of preparation, this result is not unexpected. But what is more striking is the tendency for the dominant pedagogical image of mathematics to be embraced with greater fervour, the higher the level of student achievement *within each stream*.

Only about 15 per cent of the weakest students in Further Mathematics viewed their mathematics classrooms as a laboratory for honing skills in problem solving, but the top candidates in this same stream were twice as likely to see themselves in a lab-coat (see Figure 32). Starting at this higher threshold were the weakest students in the next subject up the scale—Mathematical Methods—with the laboratory image then climbing to 45 per cent among the high achievers in this subject. Again this was about the level of agreement with the laboratory image on the part of the poorest students in the next highest stream—the double option of Mathematical Methods and Specialist Mathematics. From there, endorsement rose to between 50 per cent and 55 per cent in the middle ranks, and would have grown still higher except for the behaviour of the elite male students in this stream. For 13 per cent of them deserted the laboratory in favour of a truly aristocratic image. Their mathematics classroom was a 'studio in which you learn to be an artist'.

If a sense of purpose in mathematics, as in the laboratory and its conceptual tools, grew with each increment in achievement, rising up the hierarchy of the curriculum—till arrested by a comfortable sense of the irrelevance of purpose at the pinnacle—falling achievement and the descent down the slope of grades and subjects were expressed by images of empty purpose. No research setting, the mathematics classroom was to many a place of work where repetitive operations were performed on instruction from superiors. Specialist Mathematics, the most demanding subject, had its share of students—every fifth—who saw their class as an 'office where you learn to follow routine' or a 'factory where you're there to work'. The feeling of carrying out tasks that were imposed from without rather than inspired from within grew as learning weakened—from 21 per cent of the top candidates in this top subject to 29 per cent of the weakest (see Figure 32).

This high point of discontent in Specialist Mathematics—among students who were struggling with the heaviest load of mathematics —corresponded to the lowest level of discontent at the next layer down in the subject hierarchy. The best performers in Mathematical Methods (taken alone) were almost as likely as the worst performers in Specialist Mathematics to point to routine, not discovery,

Figure 32: Laboratory, factory and office images of the mathematics class by type of mathematics and level of achievement, VCE 1994

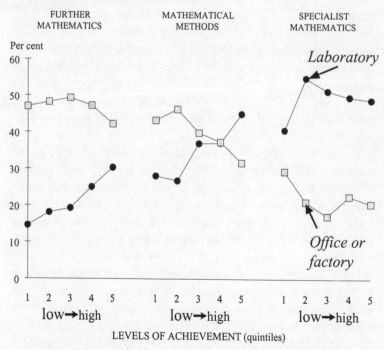

Source: Educational Outcomes Survey, 1994 (see source for Figure 7); unpublished analysis.

as the instructional object. Within Mathematical Methods, this experience then widened from the upper grades of achievement (32 per cent) to the lowest grade (43 per cent). And here, once again, the threshold of discontent was established that represented the *least* negative feeling at the next lowest level of the mathematics hierarchy—Further Mathematics. For the best candidates in this subject were just as likely as the worst candidates in Mathematical Methods to declare themselves office workers or factory hands, not scientists (42 per cent compared with 43 per cent). Finally, as achievement fell within Further Mathematics—the least taxing subject—the images of routine increased only marginally. Here, in a subject leading to work or to vocational training, the 'office' and the 'factory' predominated.

That so many students should view mathematics merely as work routine was not so very far from being imposed on them. After all, the subject in which this was the modal image—Further Mathematics—gathered in students who in earlier days would have been considered too weak 'to think for themselves'. They had not succeeded in taking possession of mathematics at its interior. Like consumers, they could only handle the products of mathematical thought—the algorithms—not drive the processes. But was this due to their intellectual deficiencies, or was it due to the grafting of an intellectual pedagogy on to a mass system of upper secondary education?

Certainly the prevailing pedagogical view—as embodied in the vertical syllabus, the completely prescribed content, the stipulated classroom hours, the official assessment criteria—was that mathematics was a mass of conceptual material to be mastered by *immersion*. True, there was a pre-determined sequence of graduated difficulty ('depth'). But in the end it was only by 'doing mathematics' that the student learnt mathematics. There was no way that the learner could impose preconditions on the teacher—clear explanations of purpose, engaging illustrations, convincing links with job needs. These were matters of good teaching that the syllabus merely hoped would be addressed, and were often sacrificed to the pace of instruction and the pressures of competitive performance. The real object was to learn the properties of the materials that made up mathematics by intensive familiarization, by habitual practice and rehearsal, by testing in contrived situations that represented pedagogical device rather than real-world simulation. Teaching mathematics as *scholarly practice*—as a form of theoretical work—would alienate the many students whose intellectual disposition was poorly developed and whose modest achievements turned them away from abstract and complex subjects. To them, too often, immersion in mathematics had been an ordeal. They had paid with the shame and humiliation of failure.[24] If they persisted, why would they not view mathematics as mere unfulfilling work?

Descending the hierarchy of mathematics subjects, the quality of students' instructional experience deteriorated. Of the students attempting the most advanced level in 1994—Mathematical Methods plus Specialist Mathematics—only one in three complained that their teachers went 'too fast' (Figure 33). This rose to more than half of those tackling Mathematical Methods without Specialist Mathematics, and to two out of three of those at the bottom of the hierarchy in Further Mathematics. In other words, even after successive reductions in content and difficulty, the pace of instruction was experienced as steadily more oppressive. In Specialist Mathematics, the number of students reporting frequent difficulties with their work was not inconsiderable—every fourth candidate. But this more than doubled in Mathematical Methods and was marginally higher again in Further Mathematics (55 per cent rising to 60 per cent).

Poor comprehension of tasks showed the same trend. Only 29 per cent of Specialist Mathematics candidates reported that they did not 'always understand what we're asked to do' compared with 56 per cent in Mathematical Methods and 61 per cent in Further Mathematics. To move up the ladder of mathematical training required adaptation to the dominant teaching practice with its emphasis on 'doing mathematics', its assumed rather than demonstrated purpose, its pace driven by the syllabus, and its 'skills' orientation driven by exams. The pattern of deteriorating instructional experience operated not only across the subject hierarchy, but emerged *within each stream of mathematics* as well (see

Figure 33). Grades tumbled as teachers pressed forward, conceptual difficulties went unresolved, and tasks poorly understood were saved up for the examinations. The philosophy of immersion, applied to a population two-thirds of whom believed that they would never use much of what they learnt, was academically discriminating but pedagogically unproductive.

Figure 33: Bad instructional experience of mathematics by type of mathematics and level of achievement, VCE 1994

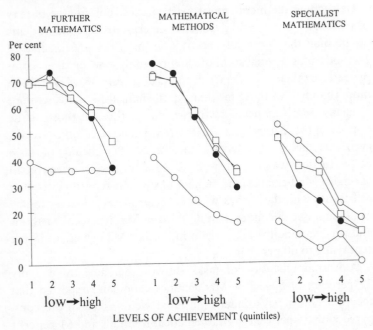

○   'Teachers go too fast in maths'
○   'I found the material too abstract [in previous year]'
●   'I often have difficulties with maths'
□   'I don't always understand what we're asked to do in maths'

Source: Educational Outcomes Survey, 1994 (see source for Figure 7); unpublished analysis.

Participation and attainment

Self-confident, persistent, independent, the best students enjoyed the challenge of mathematics and related to it as theoretical science. If most students, whatever their level, believed in the contemporary promotional slogan, 'Maths widens your options', it was only the top stream who could match this slogan with high intrinsic satisfaction and strong teacher encouragement. The mathematics curriculum had brought them to the top, as its conservative critics had demanded, and this meant an inner mirroring of contentment against an outward recognition of merit and strong objective career prospects. The structure of the curriculum was indeed a machine for harmonizing private interest and public good. The scholarly effort extracted from the most talented and ambitious students ensured that advanced mathematics was preserved as a branch of knowledge and developed over generations.

But this machine, like the eighteenth-century economic clockwork on which it was modelled, was also a social translator.[25] The cultural attributes that underlay progression up successive grades of achievement and over successive levels of the mathematics hierarchy were not equally well developed in all individuals. The vertical structure of the curriculum was a means of intensifying cognitive demands on students by increasing the mass and complexity of content and the required pace of assimilation. This in turn augmented the discriminating potential of the cultural demands that were implicit in the curriculum—appreciation of the intrinsic meaning of mathematical activity, sensitivity to form and pattern, willingness to explore and to test intuition ('risk taking'), power to concentrate for sustained periods of time, and confidence in personal ability. The cultivation of the mental disposition and the behaviours to match these demands was more likely to occur among families who could anticipate academic pressures and whose life-styles reinforced school values and interests— through early reading, intellectual stimulation, structured leisure time, supervised homework and friendships and choice of school.

The influence of family educational, cultural and economic capital over relative access to mathematics is apparent both in the average social level of students enrolled in the different streams of VCE mathematics in 1994 and in the different bands of performance within each stream. Students of lower socio-economic status were more likely to drop mathematics. Attempting Mathematical Methods rose in line with family educational levels, from 27 per cent of working-class girls to 38 per cent of their upper-middle-class peers, and from 34 per cent to 47 per cent among boys.[26]

Achievement in Mathematical Methods displays even more forcefully how the mathematics curriculum operated as an engine of social advantage. With all academic ambitions converging on this subject, from whatever family background, the possibilities of lateral discrimination based on achievement were amplified, and it is striking how each increment in achievement was accompanied by an increase in the average socio-economic status of students (see Figure 34). It is a measure of the implicit cultural homogeneity of the mathematics curriculum as a whole—based on sequenced and overlapping content and a shared conceptual emphasis—that the average social level of students rose at each level of performance, not only in the one preparatory subject, but in each mathematics subject.

Institutional segregation and mathematics achievement

If social gradients in learning match the contours of cultural adherence to mathematics as an intellectual discipline, this is because the further up the hierarchy of cognitive demands, the greater the call made by the curriculum on cultural resources and the narrower the social base from which these are available. The curriculum of strategic subjects reaches well beyond the classroom for the aptitudes and dispositions needed to compete successfully. This is why academically ambitious families seek, in return, to augment the resources that are available in the classroom in the form of pupil-mix and pedagogical expertise and to redouble efforts at home. Segregated schooling—whether institutional or geographic, whether private, Catholic or public—acts as a relay for transmitting and amplifying cultural capital, and thus for in-

Figure 34: Mean social level of students at each band of achievement in each strand of mathematics, VCE 1994[1]

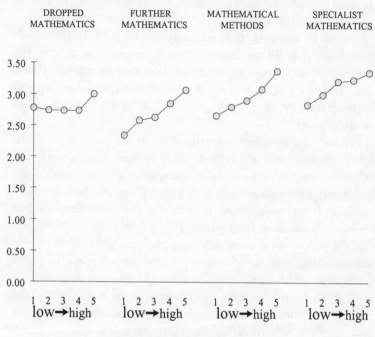

LEVELS OF ACHIEVEMENT (quintiles)

[1] The socio-economic status scale is based on father's occupation, but adjusted for the relative status of mother's occupation: '1' = lower blue-collar, '4' = upper white-collar. The scale of achievement for the 'dropped maths' group is based on reported levels of coping in Year 11.

Source: Educational Outcomes Survey, 1994 (see source for Figure 7); unpublished analysis.

creasing the productivity of teaching and the instructional effort more broadly. The more discriminating the curriculum, the more this response is encouraged, so that the curriculum philosophy of seeking the brightest students ends up by discovering the richest.

In Australia, private schooling is the most important (though not the only) vehicle for combining the cultural and economic capital of educated middle-class families. The social distance between private non-Catholic establishments and public high schools in Victoria is wide, with little overlap at the high end of the occupational or educational structure. In most private schools at least half of all Year 12 students have one or both parents in professional or managerial careers and at least one who is tertiary-educated. By contrast, the great majority of public high schools have fewer than 40 per cent of their students with professional or managerial backgrounds and tertiary-educated parents (see Figure 35). The few private schools that lie within the social range of high schools are almost all Christian fundamentalist colleges or ethnic schools.[27]

Private establishments—legally free to choose their clients, whose private costs are in turn offset by substantial public subsidies—lower the dependence of individuals on their own talents and present a common front to the hazards of selection by examinations. It is these schools, in particular, that are able to exploit the socially discriminating potential of school subjects to the full. For the potency of the cognitive and implicit cultural demands of the curriculum lies in the isolation of individuals from the social settings in which intellectual acculturation occurs. Schools save individuals from near-certain destruction at the hands of the curriculum by interpreting and formalizing its cognitive demands into a programme of group work in which concepts and operations are mastered pragmatically, that is, as a set of practices that represent ends in themselves, the 'business' of the classroom and the exam. Reduced to a series of staged and rehearsed routines—of which the manuals of 'questions and worked solutions' that appeared so quickly after the launch of the VCE are the mere tip of the pedagogical iceberg—the syllabus is converted into a source of group integration.[28]

This is all the more necessary in subjects that are abstract and complex and are frequently taken for competitive reasons rather than intellectual interest. But it is just in these subjects—mathematics and physical sciences especially—that the social basis of group work becomes critical. For it is not pass results that are needed here, but high marks, and these are required globally—that is, for the *majority* of students—not merely occasionally, for outstanding individuals. Starting from an elevated social intake, academic selection in schools further concentrates the cultural

Figure 35: Recruiting from the high end of the social structure: high schools and private schools, Victoria, 1996[1]

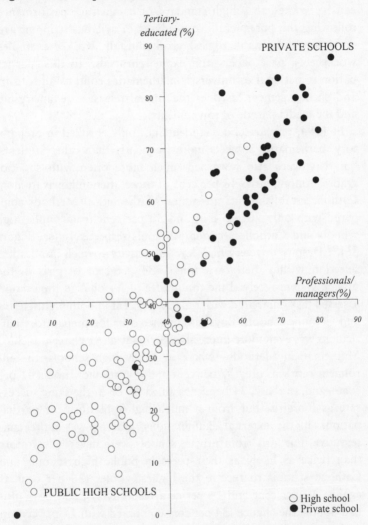

[1] Percentage of Year 12 students with at least one parent in a professional or managerial job (horizontal axis) and percentage of students with at least one tertiary-educated parent (vertical axis). Schools are included if they had at least twenty students in Year 12.

Source: Educational Outcomes Survey, 1996, unpublished analysis of a weighted sample of 8056 high-school students and 4220 private non-Catholic school students.

reserves of students into classes of high average ability, matching the compression of intellectual content in the syllabus. These classes can be worked to a high standard of competitive performance, following the bureaucratic procedures of syllabus-stripping (reduction to examinable topics), chalk and talk, worked examples, worksheets, past papers and exam rehearsals. To this, participation in national or university mathematics contests adds lustre and encouragement, as does the annual release of exam results and the media parade of top students.

In 1994, private-school students not only enrolled in preparatory mathematics subjects more frequently than other students, but they were also rewarded much more often with superior grades. Among girls, 48 per cent of those attending private non-Catholic establishments attempted Mathematical Methods compared with only 26 per cent and 30 per cent from public high schools and Catholic secondary schools respectively (see Figure 36).[29] Despite this very high level of activity—which implies less selection within their own ranks—34 per cent of girls in the private system received the top grades of A+ or A in the school-assessed task compared with only 22 per cent in both high schools and Catholic schools. Boys' dominance over the preparatory curriculum was even more impressive. As many as 61 per cent tackled Mathematical Methods—where in public high schools, the enrolment rate was only 37 per cent and in Catholic schools 41 per cent—and, of these, 34 per cent gained A+ or A (the same success rate as for girls, but from a much higher platform of participation). In the external examinations, grading was more conservative, but girls from private schools were nevertheless more than twice as likely as their peers in public high schools and Catholic schools to receive the highest grades (26 per cent as against 10 per cent and 11 per cent respectively), and boys also had double the chance (34 per cent compared with 17 per cent in each of the other sectors).

In school environments that are denuded of the pooled scholastic and cultural capital needed to manage the formal and latent demands of the curriculum at a globally high level of performance, students are thrown back on individual talent. They work in generally smaller classes, where greater self-selection has occurred,

Figure 36: Mathematical Methods: high grades and enrolment rates by type of school and gender, 1994[1]

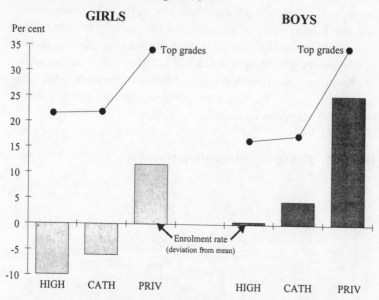

[1] Candidates receiving A+ or A grades in the school-assessed 'project' (CAT No. 1) in 1994 are reported in the line chart. The columns show enrolment rates in Mathematical Methods, expressed as deviations from the statewide level (36 per cent).

Source: Unpublished VCE results, 1994.

and they are vulnerable to inexperience (more common in high schools) and also to any professional or personal weaknesses among teachers. Success is much more dependent on individual effort, personal organization and talent. In comprehensive high schools, residential segregation brings together many students with multiple disadvantages—low self-esteem, poor basic learning, language handicaps, poverty and family breakdown. Instead of a mass of cultural and economic resources being concentrated on one advantageous site and applied to the high end of the curriculum—as happens in private schools—there is an accumulation of liabilities at the one site. This weakens the instructional effort and risks severe retribution against those students who stray into the more academic subjects.

But even at the bottom of the hierarchy of the mathematics curriculum, the risks of failure are high, testifying to the essential conceptual continuity of high and low options in mathematics and the homogeneity of the demand they place on cultural resources. As many as half of all boys in the working-class north-east of Melbourne attending high schools failed terminal mathematics in 1994, more than double the rate of their counterparts in the educated inner east of the city. Residential segregation performed the work otherwise done by institutional separation (see Figure 37).[30]

Figure 37: Failing terminal mathematics: boys in high schools by region, 1994[1]

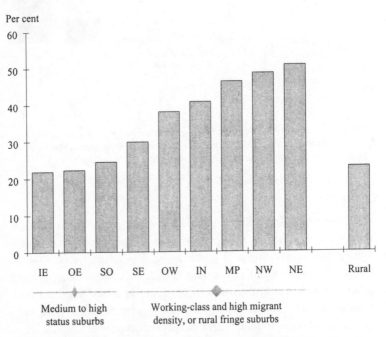

[1] 'Terminal mathematics' = Further Mathematics in the Victorian Certificate of Education. The vertical axis measures the percentage of candidates receiving E+, E or UG (ungraded) results in the external examination (Common Assessment Task No. 3). Codes for regions: IE (inner east), OE (outer east), SO (southern), SE (south-east), OW (outer west), IN (inner Melb.), MP (Mornington Peninsula), NW (north-west), NE (north-east).

Source: Unpublished VCE results, 1994.

Design logic and the logic of outcomes

It is a tribute to the deeply conservative nature of mathematics as a school subject that working-class boys in the lowest stream of the curriculum in 1994 were dealt with as harshly as the average candidate for matriculation in 1947. There was, in other words, no relaxation of 'standards' over the fifty years, only a displacement of their severity on to the newest and most vulnerable groups. Such continuity of function was based in part on pedagogical adherence to the cultural values that invested mathematics with its 'free' purpose. But the authoritative or binding quality of these values rested in turn on the maintenance of a hierarchy of institutions and on the transmission of prerogatives across generations of academics through this structure of intellectual subordination.

Wielding power over the school curriculum were no longer the Chief Examiners, the professorial potentates who were the scourge of the 1940s and 1950s. But the lower ranks through which the seigneurial rights of old had been relayed into the 1980s and 1990s were no less influential, if less visible.[31] Like their predecessors, they exercised curriculum controls unconstrained by pedagogical responsibilities. For they too only ever met the survivors of the courses that they ran but did not teach. Even in the case of 'vegie maths' for vocational students (Further Mathematics), they took as their point of reference, not the intellectual tasks that school leavers would perform at work or in their daily lives, but the conceptual hierarchies of mathematics as a theoretical system.

Reducing cognitive demands on the terminal group of students in the VCE did not diverge from the basic organizing principle— selection from the cupboard of concepts, choice of topics of merely *potential* application, teaching mathematics as a generative grammar, but without regard to the functional value of the outputs, and above all with no regard to quality of learning.[32] Characteristically, the syllabus of Further Mathematics, in which failure reached such high levels, was filled with material imported from first-year university courses—even though the programme was meant for students who would go into the workforce or training.[33]

Universities export syllabus content into schools to free their own programmes for more advanced material—often chosen on the basis of discipline interests and tastes—and to free their classes of weaker students defeated by the lower-level content deposited in schools. Importing material from universities, schools on the other hand are prevented from developing lateral curriculum links with the 'world of work' into which the majority of their students often enter.[34] Instead, programmes are integrated within a graded system of education whose logic is vertical and whose content is determined by hierarchical authority.

The rise of probability and statistics to the status of the only compulsory module in Further Mathematics illustrates the practice of vertical displacement—in this case from elementary statistics courses in economics and psychology—as the basic mechanism for designing the curriculum of senior secondary school. Exposed to intellectual demands for which they often lack the necessary capital, working-class students frequently experience mathematics at its worst and are shattered at the exams. Deflected into the workforce, they carry with them elements of academic knowledge dictated to them by the universities that have refused to receive them.

The restoration of mathematics as a hierarchy of studies weakened the vocational value of the subject for students in the lowest stream, but strengthened it for those in the highest stream. The fact that every second boy from a high school in the north-east or north-west of Melbourne received low grades in Further Mathematics did not help relieve unemployment, which in these regions was among the highest in the state. But the syllabus of Specialist Mathematics, designed for engineers, functioned admirably for the 41 per cent of boys and 59 per cent of girls in private schools who used the subject to become doctors, dentists, occupational therapists, pharmacists, optometrists, podiatrists, lawyers, financial planners, investment advisers and accountants. The new mathematics syllabus, with its high-level cognitive demands and intensive procedural training, provided them with the machinery of academic discrimination needed to achieve these goals. But was this what higher mathematics had been designed for?

Viewed from the perspective of the destinations of students, the new mathematics curriculum was not inclusive. Propensity to failure led simply to demotion down the academic ladder, not integration into programmes with an industry or occupational focus or with more intensive pedagogical supervision. Abstraction from the external world was not simply a characteristic of mathematics, but of the writers of mathematics programmes. The study designs they produced for the later VCE programme were self-enclosed units of academic planning. They did not reflect how mathematics is actually used in the workplace or serves other theoretical studies. As a result, the consequences of poor or successful learning in the subject could only be expressed in internal terms—formal assessment criteria, firmly pasted at the top of all exam papers, and the letter grades themselves.

Curriculum reform that fails to consider the real uses to which learning is put and the consequences, both economic and psychological, of failure to learn, risks simply reproducing the content of the subject and the kinds of learners to whom it has been historically adapted and thereby subordinated. If, at first, the VCE menaced the stability of the framework within which competitive advantage had annually been generated, reversion to a vertical structure with fully prescribed content removed this threat. The dominant cultural orientation towards mathematics and the exam-oriented expertise accumulated in schools would continue to support the strongest students. They could ground their personal efforts, keen or meagre, in the collective enterprise of academic mathematics. The weakest learners would be left to themselves to find or forge the links between mathematics and the real world lying beyond.

13

Curriculum Hierarchy, Monopoly Access and the Export of Failure

THE HISTORY OF curriculum reform and counter-reform shows that even major changes in systems of subjects, thorough revision of content and varied assessment methodologies produce little discernible impact on social patterns of results. This is in part because the specific content of subjects—which may shift a lot over fifty years—is always subordinated to deeper and more continuous demands on the qualities of the learner. Powers of abstraction and concentration, sensitivity to form and structure, logical and retentive abilities, language and communicative skills, personal organization, intrinsic motivation, self-confidence and maturity of perspective and argument are the characteristics of the ideal student that the academic curriculum has sought to inculcate through all the surface changes in material, whether mathematical, linguistic, textual or empirical. Examiners have unfailingly demanded these qualities, whatever the circumstances under which real students have learnt. Fidelity to this model—which spans the disciplines and controverts the divisions between sciences and humanities—underlies the great stability in social patterns of student learning.

Yet it is not only this image—and its pedagogical implications—that accounts for the seeming imperviousness of the curriculum as a cultural system to wave upon wave of new populations in upper secondary school. If social advantages in student outcomes are so constantly restored after each major revision of school programmes, this is because the curriculum belongs to a structure and cannot be manipulated independently of this structure.

Structural inequality exists when the locations in the school system typically occupied by different social groups yield advantages or disadvantages that are large, persistent and predictable. Inequality does not arise from the attributes of individuals considered in isolation, but from the ways in which individuals are brought together at particular sites within the school system. Differences in the social complexion of schools, however, are not enough in themselves to explain how achievement comes to be sharply differentiated. Student learning is relative to the nature of the demands contained in school programmes. Just as an analysis of the differential value of positions within the school system is needed to understand the origins of inequality, so too is an analysis of the differential value of positions within the curriculum.

If the value of a school is to be conceived in terms of organizational and teaching efficiency, quality of pupil mix, the cohesiveness of its academic culture and the magnitude of its technical and specialist resources, the value of a school subject lies in the discriminating nature of its cognitive and implicit cultural demands and its legal or quasi-legal status as a required body of knowledge. Subjects gain in value, the harder it is to satisfy the demands they make on intellectual disposition, prior learning, capacity for abstraction, conceptual and operational fluency, memory and concentration, and interest in topics of remote vocational relevance. These difficulties may represent assets or liabilities, depending on the more or less advantageous position of the school charged with managing them. Structural inequality results from the interaction between these two domains—the differential organization of the school system and the differential organization of the curriculum.[1]

The architectural principle of the academic curriculum

Dependence on structure and stability in the curriculum grows with academic success. It is the most proficient users of secondary education—and the institutions that depend on these groups for their prestige and influence—who display the greatest resistance to change. For this may threaten years of investment and accumulated expertise. A framework of curriculum that distinguishes between students—according to the subjects they take and their results in these subjects—is also in the long run a framework for harnessing and accumulating resources and for compounding learning advantages, derived initially from family background. If the curriculum imposes on each new cohort of students the need to compete among each other, the consolidation of expertise over time also tends to reserve certain spaces within the curriculum for competition between selected groups of students and to marginalize, if not exclude, others. The needs of the strongest students come to prevail—in how the curriculum is organized (as a structure of progressive difficulty), in the discriminating power of assessment instruments, and in the refinement of reporting grades.

This historical bias reflects the unequal capacity of different social groups to influence the content of the curriculum and to exploit the scale of opportunities that it contains. Historical infrastructure, the curriculum grows in strategic importance as the range of the population dependent on school and university widens. Its hierarchy of streams multiplies the value of family educational and cultural assets and acts as the symbolic structure that schools exploit to translate economic and cultural capital into scholastic power.[2] For any given individual at any given point in time, the curriculum provides no relief from work or stress—even the most talented are at risk. But over time the accumulation of latent advantages in the hierarchy of subject options and intellectual tasks increases security and reduces exposure to competition for whole classes of individuals. Even as the mechanisms of competition give discriminating structure to the curriculum and expose individuals acting in relative isolation to risk, they ultimately undermine competition and lower the risk experienced by the most advantaged groups acting in unison. From this results the paradox that a curriculum defended *in the name of the individual* as maximizing fairness and unpredictability also delivers great inequality and *predictability of social outcomes*.[3]

The social beneficiaries of secondary education protect their collective interests by assuring the capacity of the strongest individuals to compete among themselves. The requirement that talented students be free to demonstrate their strengths in open competition imposes on the curriculum a series of academic mechanisms—specialized subjects, a hierarchical order of options within subject areas, external examinations, homogeneous, reliable assessment measures and finely scaled grading of results.

The stress on the virtues of competition among individuals, however, overlooks the mechanisms whereby stability and transparency in the curriculum are used to build up scholastic advantages over generations of students and to undermine real competition between social groups. The elaboration of scales of intellectual worth across and within subjects—the creation of the academic divisions that are fundamental to selection—enables schools to structure their efforts and to target those points on the scales amenable to the greatest investment and yielding the highest returns. It is at these points that the strongest students assemble. The subjects in which the most intense competition occurs are distinguished not simply by their use in university selection, but by the scholastic and cultural attributes of the students who take them. The further up the academic hierarchy of subjects, the more young people from professional and managerial families dominate enrolments, so that the curriculum draws more and more completely on these students' prior scholastic success, cultural capital and cultural dispositions. Competition becomes progressively restricted in social terms, with the bar being raised high against groups new to upper secondary education.

Curriculum hierarchy

It is not just any subjects that occupy the top levels of the curriculum, but those that give the greatest play to the economic power, cultural outlook and life-styles of the most educated populations. Located at the top of the hierarchy are languages, advanced mathematics and the physical sciences (see Figure 38).[4] These have a strong cognitive architecture. That is, each is a system of concepts in an ordered relationship that is pedagogically well defined. Attached to these theoretical structures are masses of data—lexical, chemical, physical, mathematical—samples of which enter the syllabus as the growth media for the conceptual elements with

Figure 38: Social and academic hierarchy of the curriculum, 1996[1]

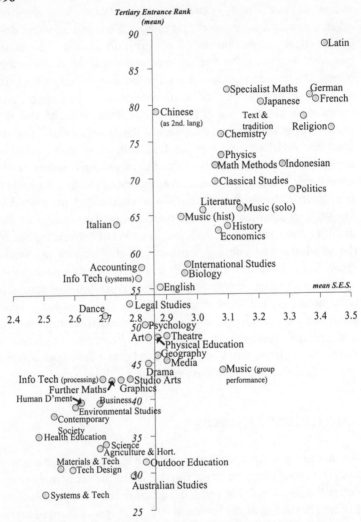

[1] Tertiary Entrance Rank is the relative order of merit of students, based on aggregation of scaled marks in VCE subjects. It is the score used by universities and TAFE institutes to selected students. *SES*—socio-economic status of father's occupation (where 1 = lower blue-collar and 4 = professional/managerial). Arabic, Greek and Turkish language studies are not shown because their extremely low SES values (2.23, 1.93, 1.74 respectively) compress the horizontal scale and obscure differences between other subjects.

Source: Educational Outcomes Survey, 1996 (see source for Figure 35).

which teaching is really concerned. In each case, the pedagogical aim is to master this interior space of fundamental ideas, arguments, laws, principles and rules, or at least to be proficient in the operations that depend upon them, such as using algorithms, writing chemical equations, producing correct sounds and sentences.

The theoretical emphasis of these subjects places a high value on quality of early learning at home and school, in both language and number. Precocious and continuous success enables children to master the formal operations involved in intellectual abstraction—the perception of relationships between phenomena, the detection of underlying order or pattern, the discrimination of form, the processes of analysis, simplification, classification and so on. Success also builds self-confidence, openness to new challenges, risk-taking and creativity, helping to establish school learning as a source of interest gratification and social identity. Continued success demands concentration, personal organization and the growth of suitable attitudes and dispositions that sustain intellectual effort and convert school goals into internal goals. Languages, mathematics, chemistry and physics expect these attributes, so families must cultivate them. If they cannot or will not, success comes to rely wholly on schools.

The traditional humanities are found somewhat lower down the curriculum hierarchy. History subjects—though not Australian History—Political Studies, International Studies and especially English Literature recruit from about the sixtieth percentile of student achievement, compared with the seventieth for the main preparatory mathematics subject (Mathematical Methods), Physics and Chemistry, and the eightieth for advanced mathematics (Specialist Mathematics) and European and Asian languages. Not all the older humanities occupy this band—Geography is the notable exception—but those that do have intellectually discriminating features that attract academically able students, especially girls. They are language-rich and also culturally rich domains. Writing in the traditional humanities—and writing is exactly what they are about—demands insight, judgement, argument, interpretation, order, sense of direction, vocabulary, style, colour, feeling, conviction, poise, sensibility and good sense. These characteristics in turn require early literacy, intellectual stimulation, structured leisure activities aimed at cognitive growth, wide and continuous reading, access to educated 'speech models' (parents and family network), to say nothing of extra-curricular activities in school—debating, public speaking, drama, media workshops, writing competitions, school magazines and culture clubs.

Though no less intellectually rigorous than mathematics, chemistry, physics, or French, German or Japanese, the subjects that make up the most 'academic' humanities are not as highly structured and methodically codified as mathematics and the physical sciences. Because of this, they attract a somewhat broader range of students—some who see them as more accessible (but who struggle to get results), others who relate to them with ease and enthusiasm (but who could have coped just as well with chemistry or preparatory mathematics and often do). Yet differences in conceptual architecture and pedagogical refinement between languages, mathematics and sciences, on the one hand, and traditional humanities, on the other, also imply differences in the likely 'academic return' on investment of effort. For the capacity to reduce teaching to methodical routine and to saturate the instructional environment with resources—laboratories, first-language tutors, libraries, computer databases, specialist teachers—is much greater among the first group of subjects than among the second. So too is reliability of assessment. And so too is the examiners' ability to drive up the level of difficulty in a controlled way in search of the best candidates. It is for these reasons, and not only for relevant preparation, that the more prestigious universities recommend languages, mathematics and sciences over other subjects, that they operate scaling systems that favour them or offer bonuses for them in tertiary selection. The most talented and ambitious students are thus drawn to them, much more so than to the traditional humanities, though the latter still play a large role—much larger than languages—for students of above-average ability.

To cross the space of the curriculum from the fields cultivated by more able candidates to the fields worked by the less able is to cross a historical divide. Languages of culture, advanced mathematics, physics, chemistry, Shakespeare, Chaucer, Renaissance and Reformation are the ancient sites of the academic curriculum, and the only sites occupied by the elite troupe of students who survived to matriculate fifty years ago. But the space of the curriculum has expanded, and the sites occupied mainly by students of average ability or below-average ability are usually new subjects. Business subjects—long offered at lower levels of the curriculum —belong to the middle or lower reaches of the hierarchy. So do the newer humanities—Drama, Psychology, Human Development, Australian Studies. Some old-established subjects have given purchase to the new populations completing school in the 1980s and 1990s—Geography, Art. At the lowest level of the curriculum hierarchy are technology, general science and craft subjects— Technological Design and Development, Systems and Technology, Materials and Technology, Graphic Communication, Environmental Studies and Science. These represent the most recent intrusions into the academic curriculum, generally developed from the programmes of the old technical schools or from school-assessed subjects under the old Higher School Certificate.

To cross the historical space of the curriculum is also to traverse its social space. And it is also to move along an institutionally constructed scale of achievement, represented by Tertiary Entrance Rank (TER). To go forward in curriculum time—from old to new subjects—is simultaneously to descend the social structure and the axis of relative academic merit (that is, the scale of institutional worth). To go back in curriculum time—to recede to the oldest subjects—is to climb the social ladder and ascend the scale of institutional esteem. Curriculum structure, as captured by the photography of the sociologist, is not a mere moment in time. It is time suspended by social power, the future delayed by the past, the past leading the future.

Officially a scale to allow the ascent of the best students into the most elevated disciplines, the curriculum is at the same time a vehicle for asserting social distance and ultimately social domination. To climb the axis of academic achievement is to rise up a social scale—in other words, to convert social position into academic rank. As subjects become more academically rich in terms of the density of talent attracted to them, they also become richer in socio-economic terms. Curriculum structure is a translation of social structure.

It is not only the hierarchical differences between subjects that permit the exercise of academic power. Few subjects are so academically exclusive that they admit only the narrowest competition, waged between the most advantaged groups. Most subjects have a mix of populations, and thus a second principle of differentiation comes into operation—horizontal distance based on achievement. This provides insurance for students whose family origins would normally imply a superior position in the curriculum hierarchy, but whose talents or commitment are unequal to the task. Descending the structure, they occupy inferior positions —subjects of lower prestige and less tradeable value. But their family and school advantages enable them to turn these more modest opportunities to good account. They are more than competitive at these levels, fending off the claims of students from less socially advantaged backgrounds. There is no subject in which economic and cultural resources do not play a discriminating role.

The horizontal divisions that occur at every level of the curriculum hierarchy lead inexorably to one conclusion. For students from socially advantaged families, the curriculum offers a range of options enabling them to distinguish themselves, *regardless of the relative level of their achievement within their own group*. If they are very bright, they will take languages, mathematics and physical sciences. If above-average, they will manage preparatory mathematics, chemistry and biology very well, but will increasingly migrate to the traditional humanities. The merely average and the below-average may find themselves still lower down the subject hierarchy. But wherever they find themselves, they will tend to outclass the opposition.

This is not the experience of working-class and many migrant students. Their descent down the curriculum hierarchy is not redeemed by competitive advantage in lower-prestige subjects vacated by stronger students. On the contrary, here they encounter the middle and upper middle-class students who are weaker relative to their own group, but who retain sufficient advantages of family and school to gain discrimination in the newer humanities and business subjects. Thus, for the socially most advantaged students, the curriculum operates as a structure for *generalizing competitive achievement across all levels of ability*. Both the strong and the weak find valuable opportunities for personal distinction, and relative weakness is offset by absolute strengths. But for the socially disadvantaged, the curriculum is a system for *limiting the assertion of academic merit to the most able*. Weaker students from lower blue-collar families who take refuge in subjects lower down in the prestige hierarchy cannot turn these into sources of academic distinction, because even here the cognitive and cultural demands embedded in the syllabus favour students from educated family backgrounds who have been relegated from the top streams of the curriculum. There is, in other words, no safety net for working-class students. Failure to evince the attitudinal and behavioural characteristics that alone can enforce a claim on strategic subjects leads to a free fall down the curriculum. No position is safe. If subjects are not sources of discrimination for the most able or sources of compensation for the socially advantaged but less able, they have poor links with tertiary education, generally poor vocational potential and no prestige.[5]

Monopoly access to the academic curriculum

The hierarchy of the curriculum cannot be exploited as a system of social advantage without a hierarchy of schools in which to deposit the 'reserves of talent' created by educated middle-class families. Though there are different ways of segregating populations to concentrate these reserves at particular sites—residency rules or scholastic tests for high schools, confessional allegiance for Catholic congregational schools—the Australian approach of a government-sponsored market for private schooling offers the convenience of public subsidies to reduce family costs, balanced by fees to maintain social exclusion. Economic power is used to raise the average *cultural* level of families patronizing these establishments by fixing fees at a suitably high level and also by cross-subsidizing 'poor but meritorious' pupils on scholarships. Academic controls are used to screen out the 'rich but thick' pupil and to preserve the ability mix of classes in the subjects on which a school's reputation depends. Liberally applied, this formula eventually stratifies the entire secondary-school system along the jointly varying dimensions of socio-economic status and scholastic achievement.

Private schools, operating on an assured platform of public grants, drain secondary education of the cultural resources represented by family education, life-style and know-how and pump these into the most profitable locations of the curriculum. The school system becomes polarized. The population of academically successful students from culturally and economically advantaged families is largely monopolized by private schools, while the population of average or below-average students from modest or poor backgrounds is consigned to public high schools and regional Catholic colleges. A comparison of schools according to the average social level of their final-year intakes and the average results of their students (as condensed in Tertiary Entrance Rank) captures this polarization of private and public schooling (see Figure 39).[6]

Private schools act to concentrate and enrich student attainment, attitudes and aptitudes formed in individual families and to turn these into a collective force with which to excel over other schools in a corporate enterprise. Honours results bear out their success, not simply as individual establishments, but as a system of provision, underwritten by government and based on academic and social segregation. In the areas of the curriculum that count most—mathematics and sciences, languages, traditional humanities —high marks invariably advantage the private system by a large margin. In Chemistry, some 30 per cent of private-school students are placed in the top fifth band of achievement, compared with only 15 per cent of public high-school candidates. In Physics, the margin is 29 per cent against 16 per cent; in Biology, 44 per cent as against 15 per cent; in Mathematical Methods, 28 per cent compared with 15 per cent; and in Specialist Mathematics, 28 per cent compared with 15 per cent.[7] These high rates of success rise from higher rates of participation than in the public system, as also happens in the traditional humanities and to a lesser extent in languages, where the private schools again dominate. The more culturally selective nature of the students taking history, social sciences and literature in private schools is generally associated with even larger relative advantages in performance. In Australian History, English Literature and other history subjects, private-

Figure 39: Mean academic ranking and mean socio-economic status of private schools and high schools, 1996[1]

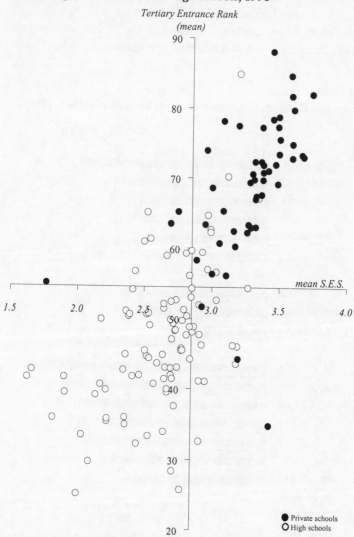

[1] Tertiary Entrance Rank is the relative order of merit of students, based on aggregation of scaled marks in VCE subjects. It is the score used by universities and TAFE institutes to select students. *SES*—socio-economic status of father's occupation (where 1 = lower blue-collar and 4 = professional/managerial).

Source: Educational Outcomes Survey, 1996 (see source for Figure 35).

school students are three times as likely as high-school students to receive high grades, with every second candidate or more being placed in the top fifth band (see Figure 40).

In almost every 'academic' subject in the curriculum, private schools bring to bear a much higher average social level of candi-

Figure 40: Honours in selected subjects by type of school, 1996[1]

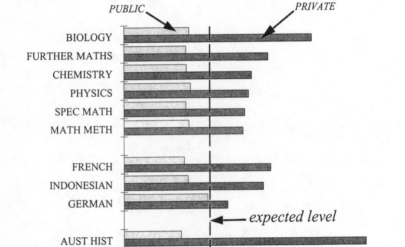

[1] The term 'honours' is used arbitrarily here to denote achievement within the top 20 per cent of students. For each subject, the 80th percentile of the distribution of scaled marks was chosen as the threshold for gaining 'honours'. The chart shows the percentage of students at or above this percentile.

Source: Educational Outcomes Survey, 1996 (see source for Figure 35).

date than do high schools. The exceptions occur in subjects with narrow enrolments, such as Political Studies, or those taught mainly in selective state high schools, such as German. If elevated social intake is not a sufficient condition for academic success, the cultural homogeneity of private schools is at any rate necessary to achieve *globally high* success rates in key subjects and at the same time to deplete the cultural reserves available to other schools (see Figure 41).

Figure 41: Mean social level of students in selected subjects by type of school, 1996[1]

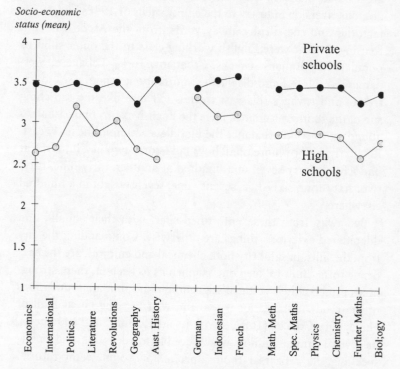

[1] *SES*—socio-economic status of father's occupation, where 1 = lower blue-collar and 4 = professional/managerial.

Source: Educational Outcomes Survey, 1996 (see source for Figure 35).

Exporting failure

One strategic objective in an age of mass secondary education is monopoly access to the subjects that count, monopoly implying higher participation and superior results on a recurring basis. Another is the elimination of failure. A school system differentiated into strong and weak sectors allows success to be concentrated in one and failure to be driven into the other. At the core of the school system are secure sites, scarcely touched by failure. On the periphery are exposed sites whose inhabitants defend themselves against the demands of the curriculum only with difficulty, and often with heavy losses. In the outer reaches of Melbourne, on the great basalt plains to the west, extending from the old quarter of noxious riverside industry to the empty shells of 1940s and 1950s factories and the silent railway yards, from the Ascot Vale and Kensington that were English working-class to the outer suburbs populated by Italians, Greeks, Croatians, Turks, Lebanese, Vietnamese, displaced and displacing, mortality at school rises to extremes and ravages this vast treeless expanse like the scorching sun of the southern summer. Here the English exams find casualties abundant to counterbalance the bloodless action in the leafy east. Regularly, half or more of all boys fail—forty-two in a hundred at one school, forty-seven in a hundred at another, forty-nine, fifty-two, sixty-four, sixty-five, seventy-one, seventy-eight in a hundred elsewhere.[8]

But away from these unfortified sites, with their squalid and dilapidated exteriors, things are otherwise. Commanding the city from the hills, in salubrity both chemical and cultural, are the academic forts. Built to keep out as much as to keep in, these strongholds preserve their vestigial seigneurial rights, but are foundations of the modern state, not feudal throwbacks. The Great Hall of Haileybury College (1982)—with its auditorium for 1200 guests, its several drama studios, which double for debating and public speaking, its rehearsal rooms, percussion room, eight tutorial rooms and so on—the College Chapel (1987), approached through the lichgate, colonnade and entablature, with its peal of bells, exceptional height, its Romanesque forms and its castle keep—for all their medieval yearnings, the one the 'heart', the other the 'soul', are but the armature of a modern business enterprise, state-subsidized to secure its capital base and limit its exposure to the market.[9] In such private academic compounds (for ultimately they are no more than this), failure comes in decimal points or zeros— 1.2 in 100, 2.0 in 100, 1.8, 0.9, 2.1, 1.6, 0, 0, 0, 0, 0, 0, 0—and this among boys, among whom it is worst (see Figure 42).

The elimination of failure from 'secure sites' within the school system—private schools and other selective schools—can only be accomplished by intensifying the incidence of failure at other sites. What appears as an entirely plausible and valid aim for one or two types of school to pursue—the total elimination of failure from among their own ranks—becomes unfeasible or completely illegitimate when stated as an objective for the school system as a whole or indeed for the weakest sections of it, among the populations who can least afford to fail.[10] The burden of failure, which once lay heavily on the mainly upper-status and middle-class students who aimed for university, is shifted to newcomers. They must pay the price for the progress of the traditional users of secondary education, for whom the total impact of public policy over the past half-century, both in the funding of schools and in the reform of curricula, has been an unqualified success.

Structural inequality arises from the vertical integration of schools with universities through the medium of the curriculum and the elaboration of an institutional hierarchy among universities, from the peak of which power is exercised over the curriculum in favour of the strongest users. While this creates the need for academic compounds to exploit the most profitable sites in the curriculum, how well these compounds operate depends on the quality of the resources put at their disposal at any given time, not simply the historical resources contained in the curriculum as a regime of intellectual demands.

The system of structural inequality is not self-sustaining. It depends on continual political action. It has taken more than three decades of state and federal government subsidies to modernize hundreds of private schools, which were once small, inefficient and unlikely to recommend themselves as objects of any public

Figure 42: Zones of security and zones of academic insecurity: boys in English and mathematics, 1994 (comparing private schools and western suburban high schools)[1]

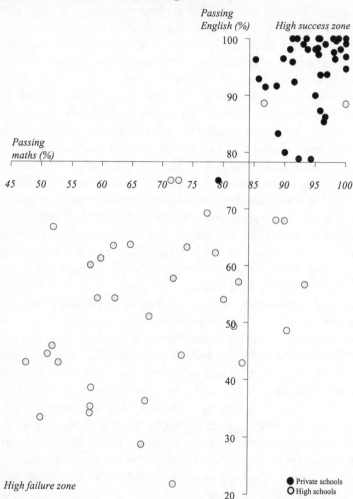

[1] Schools are plotted according to the percentage of boys above the lowest fifth of English (vertical axis) and percentage of boys above the lowest fifth of Further Mathematics or of Mathematical Methods (horizontal axis). Failure is arbitrarily defined as achievement in the lowest fifth of performance. Small schools have been omitted.

Source: Unpublished VCE results, 1994.

policy aimed at improving the quality of learning of the average child. Transformed into large and usually efficient establishments, private schools have seen no loss of their autonomy or had their accountability broadened in line with their changed funding base. On the contrary, their capacity to be socially selective has actually been increased thanks to an enhanced academic emphasis. So too has their ability to weaken other schools through predatory recruitment and selective dumping practices. Fortified sites within the school system, most draw from the top third of the achievement spectrum as measured by tertiary entrance rank. Their success in abolishing failure—or, to be precise, exporting it—and monopolizing access to the strategic heights of the academic curriculum is now so complete that almost all of their students are offered places in university. When offers from TAFE institutes are included, only 7 per cent of private-school students do not receive any tertiary offer (see Figure 43).[11]

This contrasts sharply with the insecurity experienced by students in the sites most vulnerable to the cultural action of the curriculum and the discriminatory funding policies of government. In high schools serving the western suburbs of Melbourne, students are most commonly drawn from the bottom 40 per cent of the achievement distribution. It is rare for any individual school to have more than about half its students receive an offer of a place in university (the range is usually between 30 per cent and 40 per cent) and many of the offers that are made come from local or provincial universities that present no threat to the quality end of the market dominated by private schools. If students in the western suburbs have comparatively low chances of selection for university, they compensate for this by comparatively high offers of places in TAFE (34 per cent compared with 25 per cent across the state).

Despite this, students from these schools are still vulnerable to the loss of recognized training avenues at the end of their school careers. They are three times more likely than private-school students to receive no offer of a tertiary place (24 per cent compared with 7 per cent). Completing their schooling in a region of high unemployment, they have fewer—not more—educational opportunities available to them. Academic insecurity is here added to economic insecurity. Elsewhere, through the system of structural inequality, economic and cultural advantages are converted into academic power and thence again to economic position and educated life-style, from which again the cycle is renewed.

Figure 43: University offers and mean tertiary rank of students: all private schools and western suburban high schools, 1995

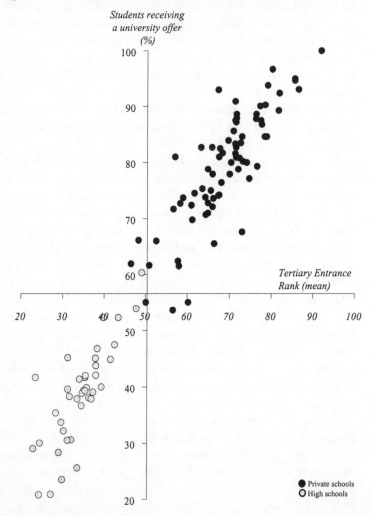

Source: Unpublished VTAC data, 1995.

14

Power over the Curriculum, Historical Progress and Structural Reform

Power over the curriculum

To exercise power through the curriculum and through the selective schools that specialize in the most lucrative subjects rests on long-term academic control *over* the curriculum. While families can generate scholastic power through choice of school, choice of subjects and competitive performance, this assumes that the curriculum is held in place over time as a coercive, authoritative structure. Yet so great and so persistent are the differences in student achievement that they constantly threaten to undermine the legitimacy of the system. The curriculum that produces these inequalities can only survive as long as public information is limited and, above all, the system of subjects and student assessment is regarded as fair and reasonable and as the best available. Such a view will be the more widely shared when it is promulgated by the most prestigious universities, on which social aspirations are most highly focused.

Control over the curriculum hinges on the ability of the top universities to dominate their field and as a consequence to expand both their institutional and their academic autonomy. Relative prestige gives them access to bureaucratic and political power, while at the same time limiting the direct involvement of government in academic affairs. It enables them to enforce the authority they claim on academic grounds against contending claims from schools, teacher unions, subject associations or other universities lower down in the hierarchy—or indeed by all of these forces together.

Universities form themselves into a pecking order by commanding the channels of professional and managerial training and recruitment, by drawing on the most successful students—and, therefore, aligning themselves to the socially most advantaged strata of the population—and by exercising intellectual pre-eminence in the most highly ranked fields of knowledge. Autonomy—freedom of action—grows in proportion as an institution achieves distance from others on these multiple dimensions of worth. The greater the prestige, the weightier the claim to direct the statutory agencies responsible for the school curriculum, the fuller the public authority to speak out on 'standards' and the 'knowledge base', and the more palpable the threats to defy government-initiated reforms of examinations and selection.

University power over school curricula is more intense where an intellectual discipline is a major source of institutional control and status—as with science and mathematics in particular—and where the universities' technical expertise is viewed as beyond question. Subjects such as history and geography are not so crucial to the universities' strategic concerns to dominate professional training markets or to monopolize the 'quality' end of the feeder school system or to gain notoriety in research grants and scientific or technical breakthroughs. So the teaching of cultural subjects in schools—and still more so, vocational subjects—attracts much less interest from university authorities, while science, mathematics and languages are regarded more acutely. Strategic subjects are given professorial chairs and teaching departments and represent points of competitive development from which to ascend the institutional slope or to dominate it, once ascended. While cultural subjects enjoy sufficient esteem to be retained by elite universities as 'filling out' their profiles, no wars will be fought for the right to determine what schools will teach under this rubric or how, within certain limits, student learning will be assessed. But it is another matter when school subjects are also the major arms through which institutional distinction is achieved.

Specialist subjects in mathematics and science act as a conduit of academic authority. Formal and abstract disciplines, they are more hierarchically ordered than the humanities and lend themselves more readily to authoritarian closure as intellectual fields. The greatly expanded frontiers of science and mathematics narrow rapidly at the point where intensive intellectual training begins in senior secondary school and where knowledge is consolidated into the traditional divisions of physics, chemistry and biology. Here there is far less movement and little adventure, far less diversity and more uniformity, and more authority than creativity. The theoretical systems of science and mathematics are vehicles for asserting discipline authority at the base—however fluid and expanding their horizons may be—while fields such as history or geography, literature or politics are relatively open. Science and mathematics tend to resist fragmentation into multiple subjects at school (the reverse of what happens in research institutions), while the humanities and social sciences are prone to it. Thus the 'hard options' of the school curriculum tend also to be the major vehicles through which universities exercise power over the curriculum, independently of the technical rationale of essential sequenced preparation. If the consequences are pedagogical conservatism, programme narrowness, declining student interest and strategic manipulation rather than intrinsic satisfaction, the elite universities receive in exchange the scales of student quality on which to base their prestige.

Social and institutional beneficiaries of curriculum power

Achievement in science and mathematics acts as a generalized basis of access to higher education. This occurs partly through the legal prescription of preparatory studies, partly through the complex scaling practices that inflate the relative performance of physical science and advanced mathematics students, and partly through the internal features of these disciplines, which provide the greatest scope for generating marks. The top students gravitate towards these subjects, whatever their real interests, and their adherence in turn fortifies the academic authority of the departments that enrol them and the positional authority of the institutions in which these departments are housed. The power exercised by the leading universities over the curriculum secures the routes along which the most competitive students travel, enabling them to convert the social advantages of home and school into scholastic power and reserving to these universities the students of the highest calibre. A cycle is created in which academic authority is used to impose competitive and selective programmes on schools and to monopolize access to the most successful students, whose values, as shaped by the prestige and economic hierarchy of professional courses, convey them to the doors of the elite institutions, thereby reinforcing their academic authority.

Such a cycle relies on close mutual dependence between the universities that dominate professional and managerial training routes and the secondary schools that dominate the market of economically advantaged or culturally rich families. The top universities need elite feeder schools to ensure that the specialist academic demands they make on students can be satisfied globally—not simply by a handful of brilliant students, scattered across the school system. Their academic authority and prestige depend on large numbers of students qualifying at a high level and competing very successfully for distinction. In turn, private schools, congregational Catholic schools and selective public high schools need the top universities and the power over the curriculum that they exercise in order to assure their markets. Positional conflict between universities, which effectively segments higher education into relatively closed and relatively open sectors, compels families whose children can realistically aspire to high-demand courses to organize themselves in the most effective fashion. Whether this takes the form of private schools, selective high schools or independent Catholic schools, the underlying impulse toward a collective mobilization of energies leads to segregated systems in which high-value resources are combined and trained on the most discriminating parts of the curriculum.

The hierarchical structure of university education requires a counterpart in the school system to serve it and to underpin it as the game of competition between school students is elevated to the plane of a battle for paramountcy among institutions. The elaboration of a scale of establishments within higher education and the positional behaviour of the institutions at its peak supply the mechanisms for individual families to congregate in selected schools, pool their advantages, and convert financial and cultural capital into academic capital. Acting in isolation in separate open-access schools, these families could not demand the only possible guarantee of individual success—that is, the global success of the group. They could not demand the seemingly self-destructive, coercive grading of curriculum opportunities to measure this success and to establish pre-eminent claims on the most profitable courses in university.

The more universities draw only from the most successful students, the greater is their proximity to the dominant sector of academic schooling in Victoria—private non-Catholic schools. In other words, the attempt by the top universities to distinguish themselves on the basis of the academic quality of their student intakes leads them ever more closely into the arms of private schools. Through this institutional relationship, the social clients of the private schools and other selective establishments are able to enforce on the whole school system their requirements for a competitive curriculum, thereby compelling the majority of students to take up lesser positions within the structure of higher education—or none at all.

The use of private schools as a mechanism for combining family advantages, focusing these on strategic subjects and dominating access to the most lucrative tertiary courses can be seen in the tendency for the academic rank of universities to rise in line with their exposure to private non-Catholic schools (see Figure 44).[1] At the foot of the institutional hierarchy—somewhat displaced from the diagonal linking these dimensions—are the institutes of technical and further education (TAFE). These draw from the weakest third of students leaving school (though this population is not in fact their primary market). Further up the scale are most of the provincial universities. These are former teachers' colleges and technical institutes. They draw from the lower half of the achievement distribution (with the exception of the campus of Deakin serving the great provincial centre of Geelong). Both TAFE institutes and provincial universities are remote from private schools, only enrolling between 10 and 15 per cent of their school-leaver

Figure 44: The university hierarchy: mean academic rank of students and proximity to private schools, 1995[1]

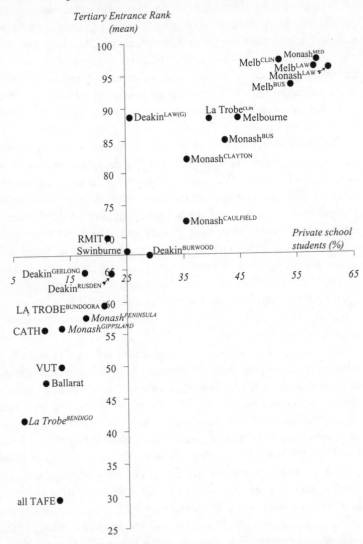

[1] Vertical axis—mean Tertiary Entrance Rank of school students offered places in the relevant institution; horizontal axis—percentage of school students offered places who were attending private non-Catholic schools. Labels in superscript indicate either a particular discipline (*BUS* = business, *CLIN* = clinical sciences, *LAW* = law, *MED* = medicine) or a regional campus of a multi-campus institution (e.g., *BENDIGO*).

Source: Unpublished VTAC data, 1995.

entrants from this sector at most. This is partly because of the comparatively thin implantation of private schools in the country and partly because the users of private schools aim for professional courses at prestige institutions.

In the middle bands of achievement are the newer metropolitan universities. These too are former teachers' colleges and technical institutes. Their geographical location and the reputation of their courses—especially in engineering and applied science—bring them closer to private schools, which supply around one in four of their students on average. Finally, the oldest metropolitan universities—furnished with medical and law schools—draw from the top 20 per cent of students, as do health science courses at La Trobe (formerly the Lincoln Institute). Here the exposure to private schools is greatest, with between 36 and 45 per cent of all tertiary offers being made to students in this sector—students representing only about 21 per cent of all school-leaver applicants.

Within these universities, and at the extreme end of the scales, are the health and clinical science courses, law and the most reputed business courses. Up to 61 per cent of offers to enrol in these programmes are made to private-school students—about three times the expected rate. If the definition of 'private' is extended to include schools maintained by Catholic teaching congregations, then the private system controls almost all access to medical training, most legal training and the elite courses in business in Victoria.[2] Public high schools have only a minor share of these training markets, and this is mainly through selective-entry establishments that emulate private schools. For example, in 1995 just three high schools received nearly half of all offers made to high-school students from the Medicine faculty at Monash, and seven received half of all high-school offers from Melbourne clinical sciences.[3]

Universities assert pre-eminence in their field by monopolizing the training routes that the most competitive students seek to occupy and by superior research performance in the disciplines on which professional training is based. Distinguished on these key criteria, the leading universities enjoy positional authority and the prestige and influence that goes with it. They can extend their control of professional training back into the curriculum of schools by requiring specialist subjects that express their academic authority and a discriminating system of exams that enables the best students to compete for places in their professional courses. Striving to excel over other institutions, the elite universities find willing allies in the schools set up to deliver group excellence to their clients. Protest though they may that they are academically but not socially elitist, the leading universities cannot fail to be both. For the assertion of power *over* the curriculum as an instrument of institutional domination enables the socially most advantaged families to assert economic and cultural dominance by exercising power *through* the curriculum put thus at their disposal.

Continuity and change

Though the struggle for economic dominance through the curriculum is one-sided, the evolving context in which this occurs requires the social beneficiaries of school to build and rebuild their advantages anew. Methods of transmission of status across generations become impaired because of changes in occupational structure, business organization and the relative value of different kinds of economic, cultural and scholastic capital.[4] Doctors can no longer bequeath a medical practice with any certainty of its future value, and access to medical training is increasingly complex; engineers are outflanked by managers, accountants gravitate to multinational firms, and few talented students now aim for teaching.

If there is continuity in the relative social outcomes of school, this is because a robust institutional structure and a cultural system absorb pressures, but always through continual and imperfect adjustment, with unforeseen results, new menaces, new demands, new groups. The school system grows under tension, exposed to pressures that are irresistible and whose consequences cannot be managed by any single mechanism of social power. The most obvious examples in the 1990s have been the doubling of school retention rates in a decade, the inflation of credentials, sustained high levels of youth unemployment, and vocational training problems among university graduates.

Structural inequality is a system under continual stress and change. In the early post-war decades, the curriculum acted as a vehicle of social advantage primarily because of its remote, academic character, the equally remote professions to which it led, and the opportunity costs of staying on at school to tackle this curriculum instead of taking the bountiful jobs then available for early school leavers. In the 1990s, the curriculum retains much of its culturally distant quality—despite the intrusion of mass subjects—but the economic imperatives on its exploitation are far stronger and weigh on the whole of the population, not simply the more educated strata. If far greater use must be made of the curriculum to gain advantages—rank achievement is much more important than in the past—the subjects in which this effort is concentrated are not so culturally impervious as to exclude new populations. Indeed the effectiveness of private schools in reducing preparatory mathematics, chemistry and physics to factory routine shows that these subjects cannot escape vulgarization, precisely because it is only for exams that they are so often learnt.

Structural inequality does not work by the exclusion of newcomers from profitable subjects—though deterrence, based on subject image and relative difficulty, is the first line of defence—but by cognitive architecture on the design side and intensification of effort on the user side to achieve competitive results. So, for example, as the social space of the mathematics curriculum has enlarged, the traditional consumers of secondary education have had to work harder to improve their relative performance in order to dominate this field. But they have not succeeded in locking the field against outsiders.

Structural inequality is also a system that does not work simply for the rich. The social inequalities that are such a habitual and institutionalized part of secondary education are by no means incompatible with rising educational levels over the long term and with a widening exposure of the population to higher forms of learning. Today only 10 per cent of lower working-class girls study chemistry in their final year of school, 9 per cent preparatory mathematics and 8 per cent physics. Yet only a small minority of girls from these backgrounds would have completed school two decades ago, let alone attempted these very selective subjects.[5]

Structural inequality creates the illusion of permanence because a cross-section of social differences in achievement taken at any given point in time conveys the same impression of unequal outcomes as another cross-section taken at an earlier or later point in time. The illusion that no change has occurred arises from the failure to relate these several different snapshots to underlying movement in the school system over the whole period. Thus there were striking regional disparities in mathematics participation in 1975, as there were again in 1985, but the proportions of the age group reaching the final year of school rose steeply over this decade. Stability or even modest falls in mathematics participation mask a wider diffusion of benefits.

Similarly, the growth in the number of girls studying preparatory mathematics has kept pace with the growth in the numbers reaching the final year of school over the period from 1947 to 1990 (see Figure 45).[6] For every increase in numbers completing school, teachers have enrolled a proportionate increase in numbers in their preparatory mathematics classes. They have successfully extended opportunities in a demanding subject to an increasingly diverse population, rather than simply accommodating students in devalued streams. If at every step of the way they have been daunted by student failure, it is also true that in this time the cognitive demands in preparatory mathematics have grown rather than diminished.[7] In other words, against a rising standard of tasks, an ever more mixed population has been given access to preparatory mathematics, and many students without family advantages have succeeded. If to this is added the many more students who today undertake terminal mathematics in the final year of school—a university-designed subject that shows no lack of academic bias, as the annual wave of casualties testifies—it is evident from this field alone that teachers have been remarkably successful in a project on which the majority of the population now depends.

But if the growth of mass secondary schooling has achieved more than is often recognized, much remains to be done. The magnitude of differences in student learning outcomes is great as between rich and poor, and shows no sign of diminishing. These differences are unacceptably large, not only because of mass econ-

Figure 45: Long-term trends in preparatory mathematics enrolments for girls and numbers reaching final year of school, 1947–90[1]

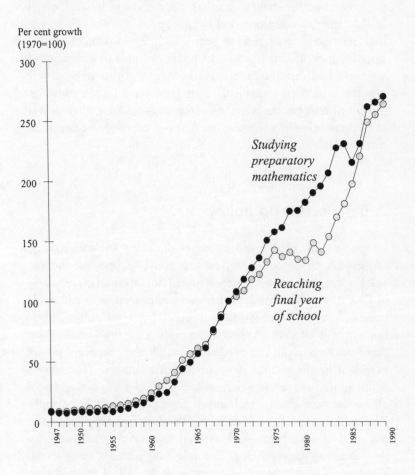

[1] Full candidates for Matriculation (later HSC) and enrolments in preparatory mathematics subjects (Pure Mathematics and General Mathematics until 1985 and Mathematics A from 1986) are expressed as indexed growth (1970 = 100). Participation in mathematics beyond 1990 cannot be represented as part of the mathematics series because of changes in the structure of the programme.

Source: Examination handbooks for successive years published by MU, Schools Board, VUSEB, VISE and VCAB.

omic dependence on school—which withdraws the choice of whether to stay in the system or leave, and stiffens the penalties for failure—but because systematic social differences in participation and achievement mean that it is not the individual who is at the centre of education, but the group.[8] If it is possible to predict accurately from year to year which sections of the school population will succeed and which will fail, this implies that advantages and disadvantages have become institutionalized. It is not the efforts of individuals acting on their own merits that govern results, but the extent to which students are sheltered from real competition by collective resources or exposed to destruction through lack of support.

A perspective on policy

To improve the quality of learning of the many students who do fail cannot be made to rely on the poorly supported and unacknowledged work of teachers acting in isolation and essentially—in view of the deep divisions that they are powerless to address in isolation—as itinerant workers. Progress rests on public policy, not invisible efforts. A collective response on behalf of the most disadvantaged groups is needed to match the corporate power exercised by the socially most advantaged families. This implies an integrated approach, based on a theoretical grasp of the system of inequality, without which improvements are likely to be negligible and initiatives contradictory. Measures that are confined to one level of education—such as early literacy programmes—run the risk of exhausting their effects unless supported at other levels. The fate of compensatory programmes in the United States during the 'War against Poverty' is a reminder that policies aimed at individuals can offer no long-term relief if they leave untouched the structures that shape outcomes for groups.

It is notable that throughout the post-war period in Victoria, the reform of secondary education—ranging from the abolition of public examinations in Years 10 and 11 in the early 1960s and 1970s to the complete reconstruction of the senior levels in the late 1980s—has never extended beyond schools to universities. The autonomy of universities has been taken as a premise and a fixed constraint on the nature of the reforms that might be effected within the school system. This has protected the universities' pedagogical freedom, enabling them to continue with antiquated methods of teaching that are known to be ineffective and methods of assessment that are unreliable and pedagogically senseless. The problem of instructional efficiency is transferred to schools, leaving universities free to select those students most likely to survive under conditions of instruction that were condemned forty years ago. It falls to schools to produce success, while universities merely presuppose it. On the other hand, schools have little control over the programmes in which success is to be produced. Control remains firmly in the hands of academic authority, so that the pedagogical motto of the university becomes a simple inversion of the schools': 'all responsibility, no power'.

If government has felt too weak to take reform up to universities, it has also failed to use the vocational training system as a source of renewal for schools. TAFE institutes have been viewed with suspicion or outright contempt, stemming from the same adulation of academic culture that has so effectively shielded the universities from public scrutiny and intervention. When the upper secondary curriculum in Victoria was reformed in the late 1980s, the curriculum routes that had been developed from within the vocational training system to link technical schools, TAFE institutes and colleges of advanced education were terminated. It was argued that a single, comprehensive certificate would do better than these initiatives by raising the level of general education contained in school programmes and by improving public esteem. But government did not take the necessary, complementary step of diversifying the system of tertiary education to compensate for the homogeneity imposed on secondary education by the new all-purpose certificate and the abolition of the technical schools. The way was thus opened for universities to impose their values and priorities over the whole field of activity in secondary education. The leading institutions eventually asserted pre-eminence through their positional authority and their involvement, in the case of one institution, in the downfall of the reforming political party.

Only by building up the vocational training system as a mass, viable alternative to universities—recruiting across the whole range of ability—could government have hoped to protect the new curriculum of schools from reverting to the search for the best students on behalf of the best universities. But this was not done. Banned from poaching school students under the Pathways Policy (1988), TAFE institutes were compelled to operate at a vertical distance from schools—that is, according to the academic model of graded education—and thus to take their chances under the imperium of the universities. The potential for diversification represented by short-cycle programmes (two years instead of three or four), smaller classes, vocational emphasis, industry practicum and flexible admissions was not exploited.[9] Instead TAFE institutes gravitated more and more towards universities, unable to find a clear basis for market differentiation or to develop their own distinctive relationship to schools. It was only a short step to view the complete assimilation of TAFE institutes into universities as a positive policy, failing to see the effects this would have on the curriculum of schools and on student learning outcomes.[10]

The policies of successive federal governments have had the same effect. By converting colleges of advanced education—former teachers' colleges and technical institutes—into universities, the federal government has spread the influence of academic culture, narrowed the relationship between schools and tertiary education and between tertiary education and industry, and fortified the power of the top universities. If at the same time government demanded greater equity of intakes, broader admissions policies and improved teaching practice, this only shows how a compartmentalized approach to education policy ends in defeating itself. The reforms proposed by the conservative government in 1998 were scarcely more consistent. The introduction of 'student-centred funding' (vouchers)—officially as a mechanism of consumer-driven quality and competitiveness—would throw open to price signals a market already structured by prestige indicators.[11] The employers of university graduates have only to interpret quality according to the relative private cost of tuition to entrench a hierarchy that is already scaled by the relative academic merit of incoming students.

In providing even more scope for the elite universities to discriminate in selecting their clientele, the conservative government could claim consistency on at least one point: it has transferred ever greater funds to private schools, thus easing the cost burden on the families who patronize the top institutions. But then why bother to improve the basic literacy standards of working-class students, as the government has also proposed? Any cognitive growth in primary school will be undermined by the frustration and relegation experienced in senior high school when students are forced into artificial competition with private-school students, literate before they begin school and using the curriculum as an instrument, not of intellectual growth, but of social domination.

The reform of school curricula cannot succeed without corresponding changes in the structure of tertiary education. Nor can an approach that deals with programmes in secondary education, but not outcomes. This is basically for the same reason. Quality of learning for all students depends on pedagogical freedom. This is curtailed both by excessive prescription of content (loss of curriculum control) and by inadequate resources. To write a recipe for mass scholastic failure, it is only necessary to narrow programmes and cut staff widely. To put it another way, to reserve success to a social minority, keep programmes narrow and augment the resources available to them. This approach deprives teachers of the freedom of action they require if they are to relate to the individuals who most depend on good teaching. Equally, it ensures that the students with the greatest family advantages have more teaching than they can ever use: the surplus is applied to exploit the weaknesses of students disabled by lack of resources. For, thanks to the narrowness of the curriculum, they all must meet in the same lists, if the weakest have not already been driven out. If teachers are denied pedagogical freedom, governments must compensate by putting much greater resources at their disposal. Without this, outcomes for different groups of students will grow apart.

When the upper secondary curriculum in Victoria was consolidated into a single certificate, it was intended that the study designs for generating particular programmes would provide this freedom. When, in turn, assessment requirements were introduced to make learning tasks comparable across schools, the freedom of teachers was reduced, both in design and in assessment. Later changes, especially in mathematics, brought teachers back to the subordinate position they had occupied before the reforms, or even before 1981. Each step backwards made the quality of teaching increasingly critical, for there was less and less space to manoeuvre within the curriculum.

Teaching must be better, not worse, when programmes are more fully prescribed. All programmes make assumptions about the average cognitive level and the cultural attributes of students, and teaching is the major instrument that corrects for these assumptions in the widely varying contexts of the school system. But with a change of government after 1992, large-scale cuts were made to the teaching service and class sizes rose. Simultaneously, the curriculum was narrowed to meet university demands *and* teaching resources were withdrawn. A more effective vice to crush the average-ability student completing school could not be imagined. Directing this pincer action was a minister declaring, with great consistency of purpose, that 'Outcomes are rubbish!', a minister entranced by the magic of freeing schools to spend budgets they did not have and freeing students of teachers they did not need.[12] But the same minister approved increases in funding to private schools to further strengthen the academic compounds whose inhabitants stood to gain by capitulation to the top universities and fiscal austerity in the government sector.

An integrated approach to the problem of structural inequality would involve tackling the multiple points at which scholastic failure is generated or reinforced. Schools representing the 'exposed sites' in the education system need targeted support—to reduce class sizes in line with the greater dependence of lower working-class and migrant children on individual attention, to provide more continuous global supervision of the work of senior students (who are merely supposed to be self-directed learners), to run tutorials in the subjects where failure is rife, and to develop integrated programmes that base cognitive growth on vocational benefits, not illusory academic advantages.

TAFE institutes must play a much larger role for school students —through jointly constructed and delivered programmes, through flexible admissions policies (ending reliance on 'selection by score'), by guaranteeing training places for school students, by generalizing industry placements for students who are unemployed or not in the workforce, and by joint award courses that facilitate movement into higher education. Where a curriculum fails to gather in every fourth girl and every third boy, despite high unemployment, it is time to develop structured alternatives with a focus on the economic benefits that early school leavers, punished by academic expectations, so urgently need. An integrated programme that spans the final years of secondary school and the vocational certificates leading to middle-level technical awards and in which progression is by internal promotion (not selection by score) would provide the security that is currently the preserve of a minority of students at the top of the curriculum.

Universities serving the most vulnerable sectors of the population have nothing to lose by breaking with the traditional model of a university education debased in the 1960s and thriving in the 1990s under the impact of budget cuts—selection by score, mass teaching methods, traditional assessment, research before teaching, poor industry links. But they need targeted support from government—and no small dose of courage—to make key changes to this model. These would involve open admissions (as at Victoria University), small-group teaching, closer supervision of student work, greater accessibility of staff, short-cycle awards through TAFE departments or alliances, industry placements, and industry input to course design to reverse corporate prejudice against their graduates.

Universities that recruit almost wholly from high achievers have a double relationship with the schools from which they draw practically no recruits. Dominating the curriculum, they also train many of the teachers who accept posts in poorer high schools and Catholic schools. But they do not train them to work specifically in these settings. Large cohorts of generalists are released on to the market each year by the leading research universities, using programmes that in structure and emphasis pre-date World War II. Although these institutions are distinguished by their research capability—and are therefore best placed to fashion training programmes to have specific effects—the practice of recruiting the 'better graduate' and staff preference for research all work against targeting programmes to particular populations and applying the pedagogical effort needed to develop them.

No field of professional training has been subjected to more desultory official inquiries than teaching. It is remarkable that the more the population depends on successful learning, the more the leading institutions of teacher training withdraw into the shell of academic culture, unwilling to develop training models that might threaten to cut them off from this culture and its system of discipline-bound accountability (publications, research grants and so on). Were universities to compensate for their control over the curriculum by targeting programmes of teacher training to the populations most damaged by the curriculum, rights might be seen to be more balanced by duties.

If the overriding objective of education policy is to raise the quality of learning of the average student—and therefore to reduce the incidence of failure among the less able—all levels of education must share responsibility for this task. No sector can claim exemption. For the institutions that enrol only the brightest students drive the curriculum that also produces the weakest. Viewed against the severe disadvantages produced annually in the school system, the universities' claims to selective responsibility—to ensure 'excellence', to protect 'academic freedom' and university autonomy, to nurture the 'gifted'—represent indefensible immunities. No such indemnities are enjoyed by the thousands of young people who every year fail English or mathematics, biology, chemistry, accounting or business management—except that they are no longer classed as failures, only graded and treated as such. With no protected compounds from which to sally forth, no refuges to retire into, they are simply the dark grey backcloth of mediocrity against which success is crowned. And if, to be enjoyed, success must be inscrutable, failure borne in silence will be its close companion.

Notes

1 The Age of Curriculum

1. On poverty in Australia, see B. Gregory and P. Sheehan, 'Poverty and the collapse of full employment'. For students held in a state of suspension in school, see P. Bourdieu and P. Champagne, 'Les exclus de l'intérieur', pp. 71–5. On multiple institutional failure in depressed urban zones, see P. Bourdieu, 'La démission de l'État', pp. 219–28.
2. Educational Outcomes Survey (hereafter EOS), unpublished data.
3. VUSEB, *Handbook of Directions and Prescriptions, Public and Matriculation Examinations 1961* (hereafter *Handbook 1961*).
4. The symbol 'UG' (ungraded) is applied to student work too poor to be given a grade.
5. For the role of school in the consecration of culture, see P. Bourdieu, 'Intellectual field and creative project', p. 178; on cultural transmission and implicit cultural demands, see P. Bourdieu, 'Cultural reproduction and social reproduction', pp. 494–5; on the importance of curriculum streams as the main vehicle for transmitting advantage and disadvantage, see P. Bourdieu and J-C. Passeron, *The Inheritors. French Students and their Relation to Culture*, pp. 13–14 and p. 152, n. 10, and P. Bourdieu and J-C. Passeron, *Reproduction in Education, Society and Culture*, p. 83; on cultural distance, see P. Bourdieu, *The State Nobility*, part 1, chapter 1. For the social construction of school subjects, see I. F. Goodson, *School Subjects and Curriculum Change*. For Australian research on cultural selection through school, see Stephen Lamb, 'Cultural selection in Australian secondary schools' and 'Cultural consumption and the educational plans of Australian secondary school students'. For a detailed analysis of cultural demands through school examinations, following Bourdieu, see Uldis Ozolins, 'Victorian HSC examiner's reports: a study of cultural capital'.
6. On social characteristics of students in Australian tertiary education, see D. S. Anderson and A. E. Vervoorn, *Access to Privilege: Patterns of Participation in Australian Post-Secondary Education*; C. Power, F. Robertson and D. Beswick, *Access to Higher Education: Participation, Equity and Policy*; R. D. Linke, *Regional Analysis of Socioeconomic Trends in Educational Participation*; DEET, *National Report on Australia's Higher Education Sector*, chapter 9.
7. Bourdieu, *The State Nobility*, pp. 116–23.
8. The reasons for choosing these subjects can be stated briefly. English has been the only compulsory subjects for final-year secondary students in Victoria since 1944, mathematics is virtually compulsory for entry to professional and business courses, and chemistry is the physical science with the highest participation.

[9] Emile Durkheim, _L'Évolution pédagogique en France_, p. 13.

[10] On the education of future managers and politicians, see Antonio Gramsci, 'On Education', p. 28.

[11] For city–country differences, see _University of Melbourne, Reports of Examiners. Public and Matriculation Examinations 1950_ (hereafter _Reports 1950_), pp. 103–4.

[12] On the symbiotic relationship between elite schooling and elite universities and the consequent dynamic to conformity in higher education, see R. Teese, 'The traditional structure of the university market in Australia', pp. 17–21 and 'Le conservatisme social du marché universitaire australien', pp. 83–6, and S. Marginson, _Markets in Education_, p. 251.

[13] Schools Inquiry Commission (Taunton Report), vol. 1, p. 596.

[14] For the career of Leonie Kramer, see Leigh Dale, _The English Men. Professing Literature in Australian Universities_, pp. 132–42.

2 English in the 1940s: A Service Course for the Professions

[1] A. M. Badcock, 'The Secondary Division', pp. 516–17, 597 n. 83; for the introduction of the new matriculation certificate, see P. W. Musgrave, _From Humanity to Utility: Melbourne University and Public Examinations 1856–1964_, pp. 255–62, and _Whose Knowledge? A Case-Study of the Victorian Universities and Schools Examinations Board, 1964–79_, pp. 30–1.

[2] D. J. Palmer, _The Rise of English Studies_, pp. 13, 10–11.

[3] For English in the nineteenth-century curriculum in Australian secondary schools, see R. Fogarty, _Catholic Education in Australia, 1806–1950_, vol. 2, pp. 360–1, 363, 376ff; A. Barcan, _A History of Australian Education_, pp. 164–5, 166–7; Badcock, 'The Secondary Division', p. 461; N. Kyle, _Her Natural Destiny: The Education of Women in New South Wales_, pp. 117, 109.

[4] On teaching literature, see _Curriculum and Examinations in Secondary Schools_ (Norwood Report), pp. 91–8; Scottish Education Department, _Secondary Education_, pp. 68–70.

[5] _Reports 1949_, p. 365.

[6] Norwood Report, p. 93; Scottish Education Department, _Secondary Education_, p. 69; P. J. Hartog, _Examinations and their relation to culture and efficiency_, pp. 73, xv, 9.

[7] _The Training of Secondary School Teachers_ (Spaulding/Morrison Report), pp. 82–3, 119–20.

[8] Durkheim, _L'Évolution pédagogique en France_, pp. 360–7.

[9] Cf. P. Bourdieu, J-C. Passeron and M. de Saint Martin, _Academic Discourse_, pp. 14–15, and Bourdieu, _The State Nobility_, pp. 35ff.

[10] _Reports 1944_, p. 88.

[11] _Reports 1944_, p. 89.

[12] _Reports 1944_, p. 90.

[13] _Reports 1948_, p. 85, original emphasis in capitals.

[14] _Reports 1948_, p. 86.

[15] For examinations and personal culture, see P. Bourdieu, 'Systems of education and systems of thought', pp. 195–7.

16 *Reports 1948*, p. 89; *Reports 1946*, p. 86; *Reports 1949*, p. 111.
17 *Reports 1944*, p. 88.
18 *Reports 1948*, p. 85.
19 *Reports 1944*, p. 88.
20 For reading habits, see W. F. Connell, E. P. Francis and E. E. Skilbeck, *Growing up in an Australian City*, pp. 189, 185; see also *15 to 18*. (Crowther Report), London, 1959, vol. 1, p. 112.
21 *Reports 1948*, p. 83; B. Bernstein, 'Social class, language and socialization'.
22 Spaulding/Morrison Report, p. 81.
23 P. B. Ballard, *Teaching and Testing English*, p. 71.
24 Spaulding/Morrison Report, p. 77.
25 On separating intellectual training from art, see Spaulding/Morrison Report, p. 84.
26 On assessment methods in English, see H. A. Greene, A. N. Jorgensen and J. R. Gerberich, *Measurement and Evaluation in the Secondary School*, pp. 133–49.
27 P. Hartog and E. C. Rhodes, *The Marks of Examiners*, p. xviii; Ballard, *Teaching and Testing English*, p. 142.
28 J. G. Coates, Reading Habits and Interests of Victorian Boys and Girls.
29 Unpublished results of the matriculation examinations, 1947; see Teese, 'Curriculum hierarchy, private schooling and the segmentation of Australian secondary education', p. 406.
30 J. J. Findlay, *The School: an Introduction to the Study of Education*, p. 146.
31 Weston Bate, *Light Blue Down Under. The History of Geelong Grammar School*, p. 212.
32 Bate, *Light Blue Down Under*, p. 212.
33 Bate, *Light Blue Down Under*, pp. 186, 212, 278–311, 305–7; M. C. Persse, *Well-Ordered Liberty. A Portrait of Geelong Grammar School 1855–1995*, pp. 24–5, 27–8, 31, 34–5.
34 See the contemporary survey by E. G. Biaggini, *English in Australia. Taste and Training in a Modern Community*, pp. 117, 119–20.
35 Alice Hoy, *A City Built to Music: The History of University High School, 1910–1960*.

3 Cultural Ideal and School Systems: English in the 1970s

1 'Pauper' is from Ian Baker, *Age*, 12 March 1970, quoted in T. Roper, *The Myth of Equality*, p. 41.
2 J. English, 'BGHS: a personal view', p. 128.
3 The first edition is given as 1934 by O. S. Green and L. J. Blake, 'The teacher and the community', p. 1277.
4 Demands on English in technical schools increased in the late 1950s; see J. Docherty, 'The Technical Division', p. 709.
5 Biaggini, *English in Australia*, pp. 117, 119–20.
6 This is the theme of the influential study by John Dixon, *Growth through English*. For trends in teaching and in pedagogical values, see the fine contemporary study by Tony Delves, *Issues in Teaching English*. Few areas of English

were spared searching reviews in the professional journal *Idiom*; see, for example, J. Sargent and B. W. Carozzi, 'Evaluation and English'; W. Hannan, L. M. Hannan and G. M. Dow, 'Literature in the secondary school'; and W. G. Tickell, 'How can schools develop the ability of critical thinking?'. For the evolving scene in books, see I. V. Hansen, *Young People Reading*.

7 For the scandalous condition of schools, see David Holbrook, *English in Australia Now*, p. xiii.

8 From a contemporary survey led by Diana Davis, reported in UNESCO, *The Teaching of English*, pp. 81–5. For the growth of English, its increasing complexity as a school subject and the widening role of the teacher, see Margaret Mathieson, *The Preachers of Culture*, pp. 163–71.

9 For syllabus changes, see VUSEB, *Circular to Schools*, no. 14, 1967; nos 29 and 31, 1969; no. 41, 1970; no. 49, 1971; W. F. Callander and S. B. Heywood, 'Matriculation Expression: the course and the examination'; V. Volk, 'The place of the prescribed books in the H.S.C. English Expression course'; H. Schoenheimer, 'Henry Schoenheimer criticizes H.S.C. English'; and the astute analysis in D. M. Murison, 'H.S.C. English—where is it going?'.

10 Tickell, 'How can schools develop the ability of critical thinking?', pp. 7, 9.

11 The socio-linguistic research of Bernstein was beginning to circulate in Australia; see his 'Social class, language and socialization', pp. 157–79; the writings of Bourdieu were appearing in English translation in collections such as Michael F. D. Young (ed.), *Knowledge and Control* and J. Eggleston (ed.), *Contemporary Research in the Sociology of Education*. For the technical schools, see Jacqueline Lublin, 'Where angels fear to tread', p. 10; further details in *Idiom*, vol. 7, no. 4, 1972, p. 15.

12 VUSEB, *Circular to Schools*, no. 29, 1969, p. 3. The underlying confusion in aims was evident to teachers; see D. M. Murison, 'H.S.C. English—where is it going?'.

13 VUSEB, *Reports of Examiners 1971* (hereafter *Reports 1971*), p. 160.

14 *Reports 1977*, p. 114.

15 *Reports 1971*, p. 165.

16 *Reports 1971*, pp. 165–6.

17 Ministry of Education, *The Road to the Sixth Form*, p. 56.

18 *Reports 1971*, p. 161.

19 *Reports 1971*, p. 162.

20 *Reports 1977*, p. 123.

21 F. De Dainville, *L'Éducation des Jésuites (XVIe—XVIIIe siècles)*, p. 223.

22 Unpublished HSC data, 1975.

23 House of Representatives, Budget Debate, *Hansard*, 20 August 1969, p. 485 (reference is to Andrew Peacock).

24 *Schools in Australia* (Karmel Report), pp. 69–70.

25 P. Davey, 'Financing of Education', p. 42.

26 Karmel Report, pp. 38–42.

27 F. Fomin and R. Teese, 'Public finance to private schools: the argument of the Karmel Report and later policy', p. 186. For concessional deductions for school fees from 1952, see House of Representatives, 6 August 1952 to 16 September 1952, *Hansard*, vol. 218, pp. 73, 199, 759–60; the government rejected the advice of the Royal Commission on Taxation (1932–34).

28 R. Teese, 'Australian private schools, specialization and curriculum conservation'.

29 Association of Independent Schools of Victoria, 'Report on the survey of parents', p. 22.

30 'Report on the survey of parents', p. 9.
31 R. Teese and R. Fawns, 'Social and attitudinal differences amongst high school students', p. 75.
32 Based on unpublished HSC data, 1975.
33 *Girls, School and Society.*

4 English under the Victorian Certificate of Education

1 Unpublished HSC 1975 data.
2 Based on R. F. Henderson (ed.), *Youth Unemployment*, Appendix, Table 1, and Australian Bureau of Statistics, *The Labour Force Australia. Historical Summary, 1966 to 1984.*
3 VUSEB, *Special Circular to Schools*, May 1969.
4 *Report of the Ministerial Review of Postcompulsory Schooling* (Blackburn Report), vol. 1, p. 21.
5 Blackburn Report, vol. 1, p. 25.
6 Blackburn Report, vol. 2, p. 64.
7 Blackburn Report, vol. 1, p. 30.
8 VBOS, *English Study Design*, pp. 12–14.
9 VBOS, *Reports to Teachers*, p. 76.
10 *Reports to Teachers*, p. 74.
11 Robert Doyle (ed.), *New Perspectives 87*, p. 131.
12 Unpublished VCE 1994 data.
13 Subsequently school assessments would be checked against a General Achievement Test; later still, the 'take-home' tasks would be abandoned altogether.
14 VBOS, *Enhancing their Futures*, pp. 36–9.
15 VBOS, *Reports to Teachers*, p. 80.
16 VBOS, *Official Sample CATs: VCE English*, p. 49.
17 VBOS, *Reports to Teachers*, p. 80.
18 VBOS, *Reports to Teachers*, p. 81.
19 VBOS, *Official Sample CATs*, p. 62.
20 VBOS, *Official Sample CATs*, p. 44.
21 VBOS, *Official Sample CATs*, p. 37.
22 VBOS, *Official Sample CATs*, p. 36.
23 VBOS, *Official Sample CATs*, p. 62 (emphasis added).
24 Based on unpublished tables of estimated income of non-government schools as at December 1984 prepared by the Commonwealth (May 1986); for recurrent costs in government schools, see Commonwealth Schools Commission, *Commonwealth Standards for Australian Schools. Recurrent Resource Goals*, pp. 11–14.
25 Unpublished VCE data.

5 Searching for the Scientist: Post-war Chemical Reform

1 J. Gani, *The Condition of Science in Australian Universities*, pp. 19, 73.
2 Gani, *The Condition of Science*, p. 75; J. Radford, *The Chemistry Department of the University of Melbourne. Its Contribution to Australian Science, 1854–1959*, pp. 236–8.

3 Radford, *The Chemistry Department*, pp. 237–9.
4 Oliphant cited in A. E. Alexander, 'Some reflections on the teaching of chemistry in Australian universities', p. 37; *Tertiary Education in Australia* (Martin Report), vol. 3, p. 25.
5 Radford, *The Chemistry Department*, p. 154.
6 Radford, *The Chemistry Department*, p. 208.
7 A. R. Blance, Senior school chemistry in Victoria—syllabus prescription and pressure for change, p. 48. The author is especially indebted to this invaluable study.
8 E. W. Jenkins, *From Armstrong to Nuffield. Studies in Twentieth-Century Science Education in England and Wales*, p. 293; VUSEB, *Handbook [1948]*, pp. 348–9.
9 Blance, Senior school chemistry, p. 105.
10 R. T. Fitzgerald, *The Secondary School at Sixes and Sevens*, p. 141; K. Lee Dow, *Teaching Science in Australian Schools*, p. 66.
11 *Reports 1944*, p. 86; *Reports 1946*, p. 80; *Reports 1948*, p. 80; *Reports 1949*, p. 103.
12 Blance, Senior school chemistry, pp. 10, 110.
13 *Reports 1946*, pp. 79–80.
14 *Reports 1946*, pp. 79–80.
15 University of Melbourne, *Public and Matriculation Examination Papers 1946–7*, Chemistry Examination (December 1947).
16 *Reports 1946*, p. 79.
17 *Reports 1949*, pp. 103–4; *Reports 1951*, pp. 110–11.
18 *Reports 1954*, pp. 116–17.
19 *Reports 1950*, p. 107; *Reports 1951*, p. 109; *Reports 1952*, p. 106; *Reports 1953*, p. 110.
20 *Reports 1952*, p. 111.
21 *Reports 1946*, pp. 80–1.
22 Successive handbooks. Figure 19 is based on a student-unit file for 1947 and relates to full candidates only.
23 Based on matriculation full candidates for 1947 and population estimates from the 1947 Census of Population and Housing.
24 H. H. Hohne, *Success and Failure in Scientific Faculties of the University of Melbourne*, pp. 114–15.
25 University of Melbourne, *Report on a Conference on Careers between Victorian Secondary Schools and the University of Melbourne*, p. 38.
26 C. Sanders, *Student Selection and Academic Success in Australian Universities*, pp. 116–17.
27 Hohne, *Success and Failure*, pp. 3–5, 30, 119; Sanders, *Student Selection*, p. 125.
28 Hohne, *Success and Failure*, p. 118.
29 Quoted in H. Dow, *Memories of Melbourne University: Undergraduate Life in the Years since 1917*, p. 79.
30 Hohne, *Success and Failure*, p. 12.
31 R. Freeman Butts, *Assumptions Underlying Australian Education*, p. 53.
32 *Report of the Committee on Australian Universities* (Murray Report), p. 35.
33 Hohne, *Success and Failure*, pp. 103–10.
34 A. G. Phillips in Dow, *Memories of Melbourne University*, p. 26.
35 University of Melbourne, *Report on a Conference*, p. 34.
36 Gani, *The Condition of Science*, p. 41.

[37] Hohne, *Success and Failure*, p. 127.
[38] Blance, Senior school chemistry, p. 217; M. Cropley, 'The standardization procedure for HSC scores'.
[39] M. L. Heffernan, D. R. Stranks, K. Lee Dow et al., 'Matriculation Chemistry: the new 1966 course', p. 4.
[40] Heffernan, Stranks, Lee Dow et al., p. 5.
[41] K. J. Mappin, *Chemistry for Secondary Schools: the Atomic Structure Approach*.
[42] D. S. Stranks, M. L. Heffernan, K. Lee Dow et al., *Chemistry: a Structural View*.
[43] Stranks, Heffernan, Lee Dow et al., *Chemistry*, p. 2.
[44] Blance, Senior school chemistry, p. 158.
[45] L. E. Strong et al., *Chemistry*, vol. 2, pp. 27, 39–40.
[46] Strong et al., *Chemistry*, vol. 1, p. 3.
[47] M. Waring, *Social Pressures and Curriculum Innovation*, p. 124.
[48] For the views of the Nuffield chemistry reformer N. F. Halliwell on the 'straitjacket of acute success' and the 'straitjacket of chronic success' which hampered innovation, see Waring, *Social Pressures*, p. 114.
[49] Waring, *Social Pressures*, pp. 170–1, 205.
[50] VUSEB, *Circular to Schools*, no. 3, 1965; *Handbook 1968*, p. 106.
[51] *Handbook 1968*, p. 103.
[52] For Nuffield O-level students, see R. B. Ingle and M. Shayer, 'Conceptual demands in Nuffield O-level chemistry', pp. 182–3.

6 Structural Chemistry and its Social Beneficiaries

[1] Heffernan, Stranks, Lee Dow et al., 'Matriculation Chemistry', p. 4.
[2] Quoted by Blance, Senior school chemistry, pp. 183–4.
[3] P. Fensham, 'Science education: who is to learn and how?', p. 29.
[4] Heffernan, Stranks, Lee Dow et al., 'Matriculation Chemistry', p. 5, emphasis added.
[5] Enrolment rates derived from tables in successive examination handbooks.
[6] Cropley, 'The standardization procedure for HSC scores', p. 22; and *VISE News*, Bulletin no. 18, July 1980, p. 2.
[7] Honours rates derived from tables in successive examination handbooks.
[8] Blance, Senior school chemistry, p. 48.
[9] Unpublished HSC 1975 data.
[10] D. S. Anderson, 'Access to higher education and progress of students', pp. 125–6.
[11] Anderson, 'Access to higher education', p. 117.
[12] R. A. Fawns and R. Teese, *Students' Attitudes to their Schooling*.
[13] E. Richardson and R. W. Stanhope, 'Why do some secondary school pupils find science hard?'.
[14] T. W. Field, 'Cognitive style in science', pp. 32–3.
[15] I. V. H. Hansen, *Nor Free Nor Secular*, pp. 82–3.
[16] G. W. Bassett, *Teachers in Australian Schools 1979*, p. 148.
[17] Bassett, *Teachers*, pp. 157–8.
[18] M. J. Rosier, *Science Achievement in Australian Secondary Schools*, pp. 13, 25, 37.
[19] Unpublished tertiary admissions data, 1976.

7 Resisting Chemical Reform in the 1980s

1 VISE, *Policy Statement.*
2 L. Griffiths, 'HSC chemistry', pp. 30–1.
3 VISE, *Handbook [1978]*, p. 45.
4 D. Hyatt, 'Chemistry 1979', p. 4.
5 P. McTigue et al., *Chemistry, Key to the Earth.*
6 Blance, Senior school chemistry, p. 111.
7 VUSEB, *Circular to Schools*, no. 74, 1976, p. 2.
8 R. Milliken, 'Which schools cope best?', *National Times*, 8 July 1983, pp. 10–11; Brighton Grammar School, Prospectus and information papers, 1988.
9 A. L. H. Smith and R. N. Fox, *Questions in Chemistry*; E. D. Gardiner, *Problems in Physics.*
10 Wesley College, Prospectus and information papers, 1987.
11 Unpublished HSC results.
12 For 1966 results, see Hansen, *Nor Free Nor Secular*, p. 84.
13 VISE, *Handbook [1979]*, p. 145.
14 The dismissive attitude of the examiners to anything approaching meaning is captured in the comments, 'a lot of irrelevant information was supplied concerning the historical abundance of nitrogen and phosphorus in the universe', in VISE, *Report on HSC Assessment Program 1985*, p. 61.
15 Unpublished tertiary admissions data for 1990.

8 Chemistry and the Victorian Certificate of Education

1 Federation of Australian Scientific and Technological Societies, *The Response of the Federation of Australian Scientific and Technological Societies to the Government's Proposal for Tertiary Education, Training and Research.*
2 Trends are based on tables in successive examination handbooks.
3 Unpublished HSC data for 1985.
4 Physical Science Study Committee, *Physics.*
5 B. Selinger, *Chemistry in the Marketplace*; Victorian Curriculum and Assessment Board, *Chemistry Study Design* and *VCE Study Design, Chemistry Units 3 and 4.*
6 Unpublished HSC data 1990. Trends are based on tables in successive examination handbooks.
7 EOS 1994. Sample relates to students in Catholic schools (n=6982). For details, see R. Teese, M. Charlton, J. Polesel and M. Davies, 'Catholic secondary school students in Victoria: attitudes, achievement and destinations'.
8 EOS, 1994, Year 11 sample (n = 8961).
9 EOS, 1994, Year 11.
10 *Age*, 19 May 1990.
11 Former Vice-Chancellor David Penington, *Age*, 2 November 1989.
12 *Age*, 12 January 1989.
13 *Diamond Valley News*, 23 January 1990.
14 *Age*, 14 January 1986.

15 *Western Times*, 22 January 1986.
16 *Progress Press*, 4 April 1990.
17 *Age*, 12 January 1986.
18 *Brighton Grammarian 1986*, p. 105.
19 Unpublished VCE 1994 data.
20 N. Greenwood, 'Education through chemistry', *Education in Chemistry*, vol. 9, no. 1, 1972, quoted in Blance, Senior school chemistry, pp. 255–6.
21 VBOS, *Official Sample CATs 1995, Chemistry*, p. 22.
22 VBOS, *Official Sample CATs 1995*, p. 17.

9 Traditional Mathematics

1 Estimates relate to full candidates. Unpublished data from the matriculation examinations, 1947. See Teese, 'Curriculum hierarchy, private schooling and the segmentation of Australian secondary education', p. 406.
2 *Handbook of Public and Matriculation Examinations 1948*, pp. 366–9, 346–8.
3 Ibid., pp. 369–72.
4 For New South Wales, see G. M. Kelly, 'Thoughts on school mathematics', p. 81.
5 D. A. Quadling, 'Issues at secondary level', p. 174.
6 *Handbook 1948*, p. 366.
7 Cf. on the craft of discovery in the philosophy of George Polya, see P. J. Davis and R. Hersh, *The Mathematical Experience*, pp. 285–91.
8 *Reports 1948*, p. 110.
9 *Reports 1948*, p. 110.
10 'There should be greater insistence', the examiner in Pure Mathematics wrote in 1947, 'upon the principles and ideas of what is being taught, and less memorizing of special rules and formulae'. *Reports 1947*, p. 108.
11 *Reports 1948*, pp. 111–14.
12 *Reports 1948*, p. 113.
13 *Reports 1948*, p. 111.
14 *Reports 1949*, p. 133.
15 Unpublished matriculation data for 1947.
16 On the streaming of girls out of mathematics in the late pre-war years in country Victoria, see W. C. Radford, *The Educational Needs of a Rural Community*, p. 49; for the reduction in mathematics content for girls, see G. M. Dow et al., *Parent, Pupil and School: Victoria's Education System*, p. 50; for IQ tests at Melbourne Boys' High School, see *Educational Gazette and Teachers' Aid*, 15 November 1935.
17 P. G. Price, 'Opinion and fact in the organization of mathematics teaching', pp. 48–51.
18 *Reports 1949*, p. 119.
19 *Reports 1950*, p. 103.
20 The estimates by Ulam and by other mathematicians of the annual output of theorems are quoted in Davis and Hersh, *The Mathematical Experience*, pp. 20–1; A. Weil, *The Apprenticeship of a Mathematician*, p. 19.
21 Unpublished matriculation results 1947. See the examiner's comments quoted in note 19 above.

22 R. Selby Smith, 'A Victorian independent school: reflections on the development of Scotch College, 1953–1964', pp. 238–43.

23 *Reports 1948*, p. 107; *Reports 1949*, p. 132.

24 *Reports 1949*, pp. 99, 132.

25 *Reports 1949*, p. 116.

26 *Handbook of Public and Matriculation Examinations 1958*, pp. 347, 356, 394.

27 *Reports 1948*, pp. 48, 113–14.

28 *Reports 1948*, pp. 110–11.

29 Relating all passing students to the total number of 17-year-olds in the Victorian population, estimated from the teenage population aged 15–19 years at the 1947 census, as reported in *A Survey of the Distribution of the Population of Victoria*, p. 10.

30 Unpublished matriculation results 1947.

10 Reforming in the Shadow of the New Maths

1 *Reports 1950*, pp. 103–4.

2 Examination handbooks, successive years.

3 From a *Survey of General Ability of Pupils in Forms IV, V and VI of Victorian Secondary Schools 1962* cited in Badcock, 'The Secondary Division', pp. 554–5.

4 The historical exclusion of the teacher from the curriculum in the late nineteenth century in favour of exams is summed up by A. G. Howson: 'the growth of public examinations and increasing demands on the schools from the universities led to the codification of the curriulum and produced a situation in which the individual's powers as an innovator became seriously restricted.' See Howson, 'The diffusion of new ideas', p. 124.

5 P. Cribb, The New Maths 1959–1965. A lost opportunity for teaching reform, pp. 3, 47–70; M. A. Clements, *Mathematics for the Minority*, p. 47.

6 See reports by A. McMullen and H. Chong in *Australian Mathematics Teacher*, vol. 14, 1958, pp. 32–6 and vol. 18, 1962, pp. 50–62.

7 Howson, 'The diffusion of new ideas', p. 129.

8 See Organization for Economic Co-Operation and Development, *New Thinking in School Mathematics*, and Howson, 'The diffusion of new ideas', p. 129.

9 R. A. Reed quoted in Cribb, *The New Maths*, p. 45.

10 OECD, *New Thinking in School Mathematics*, pp. 105–18; B. Cooper, *Renegotiating Secondary School Mathematics*, pp. 158–67.

11 Kelly, 'Thoughts on school mathematics', p. 81.

12 Cribb, *The New Maths*, pp. 47–53; Fitzgerald, *The Secondary School at Sixes and Sevens*, p. 148.

13 VUSEB, *Handbook 1968*, pp. 275–87; M. Rosier, *Changes in Secondary School Mathematics in Australia, 1964–1978*, pp. 36–41; A. L. Blakers, 'Change in mathematics education since the late 1950s—ideas and realisation, Australia', pp. 150–1.

14 *Handbook of Directions 1968*, pp. 271–5.

15 L. Dawes, G. Bail and B. Daffey, *Modern Mathematics, Third Year*.

16 *Teachers in Australia*, pp. 33, 35.

17 K. M. Evans, 'The teaching of mathematics in Victoria', p. 69.

18 Cribb, *The New Maths*, pp. 74–5, 76–80.

19 For discipline clashes and resistance to reforms, see Cooper, *Renegotiating Secondary School Mathematics*, pp. 150–4, 250–66; L. Legrand, *Pour une politique démocratique de l'éducation*, pp. 133–6; Cribb, *The New Maths*, p. 15. On the target population of the reforms, see Marshall Stone's address to Royaumont in OECD, *New Thinking in School Mathematics*, pp. 20–1 and note Dieudonné's remarks to the seminar, in which he stressed, '*Nobody need be concerned, in secondary schools at least, with teaching the future professional mathematicians* (not to speak of the great ones), of which there may be one in 10,000 children. What is really at stake is the kind of mental picture of mathematics which will emerge in the minds of an *average* intelligent student after he has been subjected to the treatment for several years' in *New Thinking in School Mathematics*, p. 38 (original emphasis).

20 Clements, *Mathematics for the Minority*, pp. 48–9; Cooper, *Renegotiating Secondary School Mathematics*, pp. 250–66; Legrand, *Pour une politique*, pp. 136–42; Cribb, *The New Maths*, pp. 34–5, 59.

21 Quadling, 'Issues at Secondary level', p. 173.

22 For a contemporary summary on sources of variation in ability, see G. T. Evans, 'Mathematical Ability', pp. 8–15.

23 *Reports 1969*, pp. 216–17.

24 *Reports 1970*, pp. 198, 201.

25 *Reports 1970*, pp. 235.

26 *Reports 1971*, pp. 200.

27 *Reports 1971*, pp. 235–6.

28 OECD, *New Thinking in School Mathematics*, pp. 22–6, 48; Cribb, *The New Maths*, p. 85. On the inability of many teachers to cope with the changes, see M. A. Clements, L. A. Grimison and N. F. Ellerton, 'Colonialism and school mathematics', p. 70.

29 A. J. Bishop, *Mathematical Enculturation*, pp. 7–12.

30 R. Noss, 'Just testing: a critical view of recent change in the UK school mathematics curriculum', p. 159.

31 See D. M. Davison's review of C. W. Lucas, *General Mathematics for Senior Students* (1968) and C. W. Lucas and E. T. James, *Pure Mathematics for Senior Students*, and Cribb, *The New Maths*, p. 80.

32 *Reports 1971*, pp. 132.

33 *Reports 1971*, pp. 236.

34 Unpublished HSC data for 1975.

35 Failure rates from examination handbooks (successive years).

36 Davis and Hersh, *The Mathematical Experience*, p. 283.

37 Bernstein, 'Social Class, Language and Socialization', pp. 165–78.

38 See the fine address by Mother Brigid of the Loreto Convent, Toorak, in *Vinculum*, vol. 4, 1967, pp. 3–5.

39 On choice of mathematics options and post-school destinations, see R. V. Teese, 'Scholastic power and curriculum access: public and private schooling in post-war Australia' and 'Social selection and mathematics attainment: the geography of high school outcomes in Victoria at the end of post-war growth'.

40 For comparative results in the 1960s, see F. J. Hunt, *Resources and Achievements in Melbourne Secondary Schools*, pp. 75–102; for the greater 'public schools', see Hansen, *Nor Free nor Secular*, pp. 83–5.

41 Note 31 above.

42 W. J. Campbell, *Being a Teacher in Australian State Government Schools*, p. 14.

11 Pedagogical Freedom and Institutional Power in Mathematics Reform

[1] B. Thwaites (ed.), *On Teaching Mathematics*, p. 5.
[2] G. M. Kelly, 'Thoughts on school mathematics', p. 82.
[3] Bourdieu, Passeron and de Saint Martin, *Academic Discourse*.
[4] M. de Saint Martin, *Les fonctions sociales de l'enseignement scientifique*, pp. 115–19.
[5] Dieudonné in *New Thinking in School Mathematics*, p. 33.
[6] Dieudonné in *New Thinking*, p. 41.
[7] M. de Saint Martin, *Les fonctions sociales*, p. 114.
[8] J. Dieudonné, *Abrégé d'histoire des mathématiques 1700–1900*, vol. 1, p. 3.
[9] Dieudonné, *Abrégé d'histoire*, vol. 1, p. 11; see also Jean Dieudonné, *Mathematics—The Music of Reason*, p. 2.
[10] Dieudonné in *New Thinking*, p. 38.
[11] R. H. Cowban, 'Mathematical Association of Victoria—Presidential Address', p. 147.
[12] R. B. Potts, 'A case against the New Maths', pp. 36–7.
[13] E. R. Love, 'What is wrong with the teaching of school mathematics? A university view', pp. 18–19.
[14] G. B. Preston, 'What mathematics should be taught at school?', pp. 41–4.
[15] E. R. Love, 'What is wrong', pp. 18–19.
[16] M. A. Clements, 'A report on numeracy', pp. 100–11; S. Kudilczak, 'Survival mathematics', pp. 386–97.
[17] For the kinds of aptitudes to be cultivated in the low to average achievers, see Schools Council, *Mathematical Experience*, pp. 11–12.
[18] W. McDonell, 'Mathematics at school—how much?—of what kind?—for whom?', p. 106.
[19] D. Kennedy, 'Group 2 Mathematics—Mathematics at Work', pp. 12–13.
[20] Kennedy, 'Group 2 Mathematics', p. 12.
[21] P. Carter, 'Group 2 Mathematics—Business Mathematics', p. 13.
[22] S. F. Dooley, 'Group 2 Mathematics—Commercial Mathematics', pp. 14–15.
[23] Estimated from VCAB, *Statistical Information. VCE (HSC) Assessment Program 1990*.
[24] Estimated from examination handbooks (successive years).
[25] On General Mathematics, see R. More, 'An open letter', pp. 14–16; D. Clarke, 'Teachers: care versus content', p. 390; D. C. Kennedy, 'Is it still ad-VISE-able?', p. 7. On the comparative ease of General Mathematics, see the investigation by S. A. Elks in *Vinculum*, vol. 13, 1976, pp. 114–16; on teacher perceptions of relative difficulty, see the results of a survey in *Vinculum*, vol. 16, 1979, pp. 104–10; on General Mathematics as inadequate preparation for university, see N. Cameron in *Vinculum*, vol. 18, 1981, pp. 7–9.
[26] Participation and attainment differences are estimated from unpublished HSC data for 1985. On socio-economic status, mathematics and gender, see Stephen Lamb, 'Gender Differences in Mathematics Participation in Australian Schools: some relationships with social class and school policy', pp. 223–40, and 'Gender Differences in Mathematics Participation: an Australian perspective', pp. 105–

25. For teachers blaming peer group or individual differences, see Jane Kenway and Sue Willis, *Answering Back. Girls, Boys and Feminism in Schools*, p. 70.

27. For the effects on teaching of external examinations for Cambridge and Oxford, see H. B. Griffiths and A. G. Howson, *Mathematics, Society and Curricula*, pp. 32–3.

28. VISE, *Report on HSC Assessment Program 1984*, p. 168.

29. VISE, *Handbook for 1985 Year 12 Curriculum and Assessment*, p. 71.

30. For studies on language and mathematics in the Australian context, see N. Ellerton and M. A. Clements, *The Mathematics of Language: a Review of Language Factors in School Maths*; L. Dawe, 'Language and culture in the teaching of mathematics', pp. 230–47; J. Bickmore-Brand (ed.), *Language in Mathematics*; on cultural influences and mathematics attainment, see B. Atweh, T. Cooper and C. Kanes, 'The social and cultural content of mathematics education'; Robin Zevenbergen, 'Language, mathematics and social disadvantage: A Bourdieuian analysis of cultural capital in mathematics education', pp. 716–722; and R. R. Cocking and J. P. Mestre (eds), *Linguistic and Cultural Influences on Learning Mathematics*. On self-concept, see C. Flinn, Some determinants of students' course selection in mathematics.

31. For contemporary restatements of the demand for independent learners, see H. Freudenthal, *Mathematics as an Educational Task*, pp. 56–9, and Davis and Hersh, *The Mathematical Experience*, p. 283.

32. 'At the root of student problems is a breakdown of communication as it affects the learning process' (D. S. Anderson, 'Problems and performance of university students', p. 129); for an analysis of teaching and communication in contemporary France, see Bourdieu, Passeron and de Saint Martin, *Academic Discourse*.

33. Teese, 'Social selection and mathematics attainment'.

34. VISE, *Report on HSC Assessment Program 1983*, p. 150.

35. University of Melbourne, *Department of Mathematics Course Advice Book for 1990*; for contemporary research findings on the instructional efficiency of lectures, see D. A. Bligh, *What's the Use of Lectures?*.

36. D. Beswick, H. Schofield, L. Meek and G. Masters, *Selective Admissions under Pressure*; J. A. Bowden, G. N. Masters and P. Ramsden, 'Influence of assessment demands on first year university students' approaches to learning'; H. Schofield, *Selection Criteria and Social Diversity: An Evaluation of the Special Admissions Scheme*.

37. For the attempt to be academically elite without being socially elite, see University of Melbourne, *Minutes*, Academic Board Meeting, no. 8, 22 September 1983, and the views of former Vice-Chancellor David Caro, 'Some cause for optimism', *University of Melbourne Gazette*, vol. 40, no. 2, 1984, p. 4.

38. *Report on HSC Assessment Program 1983*, pp. 150–2; *Report on HSC Assessment Program 1984*, p. 167.

39. VISE, *Report on HSC Assessment Program 1983*, p. 151.

40. Unpublished HSC data 1985.

41. Selection Procedures Committee of the Academic Board, University of Melbourne, 'Undergraduate entrance requirements and selection for 1988 and beyond', unpublished, June 1985.

42. In 1986, a review of higher education efficiency in Australia concluded that 'generally speaking *institutions have not developed standard practices of*

systematic self-evaluation'. See CTEC, *Review of Efficiency and Effectiveness in Higher Education*, p. 17 [original emphasis]. The level of institutional management responsible for teaching was characterized by the 'absence of systematic and routine scrutiny of performance'. See Paul Bourke, *Quality Measures in Universities*, p. 23, and I. D. Thomas, 'Evaluation', pp. 254–6.

12 Mathematics for the Majority: Reform and Counter-Reform

1 G. Polya, *How to Solve It. A New Aspect of Mathematical Method*, p. 205.
2 On the liberation of mathematics from the natural sciences, see M. Kline, *Mathematics and the Physical World*, pp. 461–2, and his concerns over the modern 'undue emphasis on abstraction' (p. viii); for a modern statement of mathematics as an abstract science, see K. Devlin, *Mathematics: The Science of Patterns*, pp. 3–5.
3 VCAB, *Mathematics Study Design*.
4 Ibid.
5 On contemporary teaching, see L. Dawe, 'Language and culture in the teaching of mathematics', pp. 238–9.
6 Unpublished data from the VCE assessment program, 1992. For a detailed analysis of VCE mathematics participation and achievement in 1992, see R. V. Teese, M. Charlton and J. Polesel, *Curriculum Outcomes in Victoria: a Geographical and Gender Analysis*.
7 *Age*, 8 March 1990.
8 *Age*, 8 March 1990.
9 *Age*, 16 June 1993.
10 *Age*, 16 June 1993.
11 *Age*, 17 July 1992.
12 *Age*, 17 July 1992.
13 *Age*, 16 June 1993.
14 R. Teese, 'Seamless education and training', p. 22.
15 VBOS, *Mathematics VCE Study Guide*, pp. 9–10.
16 VBOS, *Mathematics VCE Study Guide*, pp. 9–10.
17 VBOS, *Mathematics VCE Study Guide*, pp. 9–10.
18 VTAC, *Bulletin*, no. 1, pp. 4–5.
19 For university attempts to impose an outmoded pedagogy on schools, see P. Martin, *The VCE Mathematics Experiment: An Evaluation*, p. 39. For teaching innovation in newer universities, see Roslyn Steele, 'School–tertiary interface', p. 174.
20 The Year 11 structure was simpler. In 1994 about 5 per cent of students in Year 12 took both Mathematical Methods and Further Mathematics.
21 Unpublished VCE data, 1994.
22 Educational Outcomes Survey, 1994.
23 The 'images' approach was prompted by the questionnaire employed in the survey of students using the library of the University of Lille, as reported in Bourdieu, Passeron and de Saint Martin, *Academic Discourse*, p. 131, though the images themselves, of course, were different.

24 Celia Hoyles, 'The pupil's view of mathematics learning', pp. 364–9.
25 G. W. F. Hegel, *Philosophy of Right*, §§199–200, pp. 129–30.
26 EOS, 1994.
27 EOS, 1996.
28 N. Duncan, VCE *Reasoning and Data* and VCE *Change and Approximation*.
29 Unpublished VCE data 1994.
30 Unpublished VCE data 1994.
31 Alan Bishop argues in his *Mathematical Enculturation*, p. 90, that the power of the 'pure mathematical research community' is waning. The revision of the VCE saw academics in engineering departments as well as mathematics departments combine against the previous reforms.
32 Placed under the tutelage of Monsieur Monbeig, who analysed grammar in the junior department of the Lycée Montaigne using algebraic notation, André Weil would later find nothing unfamiliar in the work of Chomsky. See his *The Apprenticeship of a Mathematician*, p. 20.
33 Destinations are derived from EOS, 1994.
34 For the distinction between vertical and lateral links, see D. A. Clowes, 'Community colleges and proprietary schools: conflict or convergence?', pp. 10–12.

13 Curriculum Hierarchy, Monopoly Access and the Export of Failure

1 For curriculum and social inequality, see P. Bourdieu, 'Cultural reproduction and social reproduction', pp. 494–5; P. Bourdieu and J-C. Passeron, *The Inheritors*, pp. 13–14 and n. 10 on p. 152, and P. Bourdieu and J-C. Passeron, *Reproduction in Education, Society and Culture*, p. 83; P. Bourdieu, *The State Nobility*, Part 1, ch. 1; I. F. Goodson, *School Subjects and Curriculum Change*, pp. 31–6, 199–200; F. Ringer, 'Introduction', pp. 8–9; F. Ringer, *Fields of Knowledge. French Academic Culture in Comparative Perspective, 1890–1920*, p. 35.
2 For the multiplier effect of streaming, see P. Bourdieu and J-C. Passeron, *Les Héritiers*, pp. 25–6, *The Inheritors*, pp. 13–14; *Reproduction*, p. 83; P. Bourdieu, 'The school as a conservative force: scholastic and cultural inequalities', p. 37; 'Cultural reproduction and social reproduction', p. 494; P. Bourdieu and L. Boltanski, 'Changes in social structure and changes in the demand for education', p. 206.
3 Into the competition for academic honours, the least advantaged social groups enter, as Bourdieu says, in broken ranks, so ensuring the reproduction of the social structure (Bourdieu, *La Distinction. Critique Sociale du Jugement*, pp. 184–5). By contrast, economically dominant groups compete through collective organization, conserving and augmenting individual resources and dispersing and diluting the resources available to weaker social groups unable to mobilize collectively through the school system or higher education.
4 EOS, 1996.
5 The development of dual-award vocational and general programmes in the Victorian Certificate of Education since 1994 has broken with this pattern.
6 EOS, 1996.

7 Unpublished VCE data, 1994.
8 Ibid.
9 Haileybury College Prospectus and other documents.
10 For unfeasibility, see Karmel Report, pp. 22–3; for the illegitimacy of generalized success, see, for example, *Age*, 29 June 1982.
11 Unpublished tertiary admissions data, 1995.

14 Power over the Curriculum, Historical Progress and Structural Reform

1 Unpublished tertiary admissions data, 1995; on the role of private schooling in retarding democratization, see G. Langouët, *La démocratisation de l'enseignement aujourd'hui*, p. 53.
2 Even the law course at Deakin—almost all places offered at Geelong—is dominated by private and Catholic schools, which together received 64 per cent of offers in 1995.
3 Unpublished tertiary admissions data, 1995.
4 Bourdieu, *La Distinction*, pp. 145–88; on the exposure of the education system to continual pressure to change, see Langouët, *La démocratisation*, p. 20.
5 EOS, 1996. On social progress in mass secondary education systems, see A. Heath and J. Ridge, 'Schools, examinations and occupational attainment', pp. 242–3, 254–5; A. F. Heath and P. Clifford, 'Class inequalities in education in the twentieth-century', p. 15; C. Baudelot and R. Establet, *Le niveau monte*; G. Langouët, 'Les années 80–90: quelle démocratisation?', p. 23; *La démocratisation*.
6 Examination handbooks, successive years. On the trend for boys, see R. Teese, 'Mass secondary education and curriculum access: a forty-year perspective on mathematics outcomes in Victoria'.
7 Rosier, *Changes in Secondary School Mathematics*, pp. 194–9.
8 R. Teese, G. McLean and J. Polesel, *Equity Outcomes*.
9 .Cf. *Report of the Taskforce on Pathways in Education and Training* (Deveson Report).
10 For structural diversity in tertiary education, see *Ministerial Review of the Provision of Technical and Further Education in the Melbourne Metropolitan Area* (Ramler Review), vol. 2, pp. 7–25.
11 For the West inquiry into higher education, see *Learning for Life*; on markets in Australian higher education and the aggravation of competition through credentialism, see S. Marginson, 'Markets in higher education: Australia', p. 23.
12 *Age*, 12 September 1994.

Bibliography

Abbreviations

ABS	Australian Bureau of Statistics
AISV	Association of Independent Schools of Victoria
HSC	Higher School Certificate
MU	Melbourne University
VCAB	Victorian Curriculum and Assessment Board
VCE	Victorian Certificate of Education
VISE	Victorian Institute of Secondary Education
VTAC	Victorian Tertiary Admissions Centre
VUSEB	Victorian Schools and Universities Examinations Board

ABS. *The Labour Force Australia. Historical Summary, 1966 to 1984.* Catalogue no. 6204.0. Canberra 1986.

ACE. *Teachers in Australian Schools. A report by the Australian College of Education*, ACE, Carlton 1967.

AISV. Report on the Survey of Parents, unpublished report, 1976.

Alexander, A. E., 'Some reflections on the teaching of chemistry in Australian universities', *VESTES*, vol. 3, 1960, pp. 36–40.

Anderson, D. S., 'Problems and performance of university students', in E. L. Wheelwright (ed.), *Higher Education in Australia*, Cheshire, Melbourne, 1965, pp. 129–57.

—— 'Access to higher education and progress of students', in G. S. Harman and C. Selby Smith (eds), *Australian Higher Education. Problems of a Developing System*, Angus & Robertson, Sydney, 1972, pp. 116–37.

Anderson, D. S. and Vervoorn, A. E. *Access to Privilege: Patterns of Participation in Australian Post-Secondary Education.* ANU Press, Canberra 1983.

Atweh, W. and Cooper, T., 'Hegemony in mathematics curricula: the effect of gender and social class on the organization of mathematics teaching for Year 9 students', in F. Furinghetti (ed.), *Proceedings of the 15th International Psychology of Mathematics Education Conference*, Assisi, 1991, pp. 88–95.

Aughterson, W. V., Aughterson, J. and Stirling, G. M. *A Handbook of English for Junior and Intermediate Pupils in Victorian Secondary Schools.* Whitcombe & Tombs, Melbourne n.d. [first edn, *c.* 1934].

Badcock, A. M., 'The Secondary Division', in L. J. Blake (ed.), *Vision and Realisation: A Centenary History of State Education in Victoria.* Education Department, Melbourne, 1973, pp. 435–603.

Bainbridge, Bill, 'To each according to his need', *English in Australia*, vol. 1, 1965, pp. 48–55.

Ballard, P. B. *Teaching and Testing English.* University of London Press, London 1959.

Barcan, A. *A History of Australian Education.* Oxford University Press, Melbourne 1980.

Bassett, G. W. *Teachers in Australian Schools 1979.* The Australian College of Education, Melbourne 1980.

Bate, Weston. *Light Blue Down Under. The History of the Geelong Grammar School.* Oxford University Press, Melbourne 1990.

Baudelot, C. and Establet, R. *Le niveau monte.* Seuil, Paris 1989.

Bernstein, B., 'Social class, language and socialization', in P. P. Giglioli (ed.), *Language and Social Context*, Penguin, Harmondsworth, 1972, pp. 157–79.

Bessant, B. and Spaull, A. D. *Teachers in Conflict.* Melbourne University Press, Carlton 1972.

Beswick, D., Schofield, H., Meek, L. and Masters, G. *Selective Admissions under Pressure.* University of Melbourne, Centre for the Study of Higher Education, Parkville 1984.

Biaggini, E. G. *English in Australia: Taste and Training in a Modern City.* Melbourne University Press, Carlton 1933.

Bickmore-Brand, J. (ed.). *Language in Mathematics.* Australian Reading Association, Carlton South 1990.

Bishop, Alan. *Mathematical Enculturation. A Cultural Perspective on Mathematics Education.* Kluwer Academic, Dordrecht 1988.

Blainey, Geoffrey. *A Centenary History of the University of Melbourne.* Melbourne University Press, Carlton 1957.

Blakers, A. L., 'Change in mathematics education since the late 1950s—ideas and realisation, Australia', *Educational Studies in Mathematics*, vol. 9, 1978, pp. 147–58.

Blance, Annette R., Senior School Chemistry in Victoria—Syllabus Prescription and Pressure for Change, M.Ed. thesis, University of Melbourne, 1984.

Blane, Dudley, Rejoinder in *Age*, 20 March 1990.

Blane, D., Maurer, A. and Stephens, M., 'The essentials of mathematics education', in P. Costello, S. Ferguson, K. Slinn et al. (eds), *Facets of Australian Mathematics Education*, Australian Association of Mathematics Teachers, Blackburn, 1984, pp. 45–53.

Bligh, D. A. *What's the Use of Lectures?* Penguin, Harmondsworth 1972.

Bourdieu, P. *Academic Discourse. Linguistic Misunderstanding and Professorial Power*, trans. R. Teese. Polity Press, Cambridge and Stanford 1994.

—— 'Cultural reproduction and social reproduction', in J. Karabel and A. H. Halsey (eds), *Power and Ideology in Education*, Oxford University Press, New York, 1977, pp. 487–511.

—— 'Intellectual field and creative project', in M. F. D. Young (ed.), *Knowledge and Control. New Directions for the Sociology of Knowledge*, Collier–Macmillan, London, 1978, pp. 161–88.

—— *La Distinction. Critique sociale du jugement*. Minuit, Paris 1979.

—— *La noblesse d'État. Grandes écoles et esprit de corps*. Minuit, Paris 1989.

—— 'The school as a conservative force: scholastic and cultural inequalities', in J. Eggleston (ed.), *Contemporary Research in the Sociology of Education*, Methuen, London, 1974, pp. 32–46.

—— *The State Nobility. Elite Schools in the Field of Power*, trans. L. C. Clough. Polity Press, Cambridge 1996.

Bourdieu, P. and Boltanski, L., 'Changes in social structure and changes in the demand for education', in S. Giner and M. S. Archer (eds), *Contemporary Europe: Social Structure and Cultural Patterns*, Routledge & Kegan Paul, London, 1978, pp. 197–227.

Bourdieu, P. and Champagne, P., 'Les exclus de l'intérieur', *Actes de la Recherche en Sciences Sociales*, vol. 91/92, 1992, pp. 71–5.

Bourdieu, P. and Passeron, J-C. *Les héritiers. Les étudiants et la culture*. Minuit, Paris 1964.

Bourdieu, P. and Passeron, J-C. *The Inheritors. French Students and their Relation to Culture*, trans. R. Nice. University of Chicago Press, Chicago 1979.

Bourdieu, P. and Passeron, J-C. *La Reproduction. Éléments pour une théorie du système d'enseignement*. Minuit, Paris 1970.

Bourdieu, P. and Passeron, J-C. *Reproduction in Education, Society and Culture*, trans. R. Nice. Sage, London and Beverly Hills 1977.

Bourdieu, P. et al. *La misère du monde*. Seuil, Paris 1993.

Bourke, Paul. *Quality Measures in Universities*. AGPS, Canberra 1986.

Bowden, J. A., Masters, G. N. and Ramsden, P., 'Influence of assessment demands on first year university students' approaches to learning', *Research Working Papers*, no. 87.3, Centre for the Study of Higher Education, University of Melbourne, Parkville 1987.

Bowden, Lord, 'The Universities', in J. Wilkes (ed.), *Tertiary Education in Australia*, Angus & Robertson, Sydney 1965, pp. 31–65.

Brighton Grammar. *The Brighton Grammarian 1986*.

—— Prospectus. 1988.

Brock, W. H. *The Fontana History of Chemistry*. Fontana, London 1992.

Butts, R. Freeman. *Assumptions underlying Australian Education*. ACER, Hawthorn 1970.

Caldwell, B. and Hayward, D. K. *The Future of Schools. Lessons from the Reform of Public Education.* Falmer, London 1997.

Callander, W. F. and Heywood, S. B., 'Matriculation Expression: the course and the examination', *Idiom*, vol. 3, 1964, pp. 33–6.

Cameron, N., 'Coping (or copping it) with General Mathematics', *Vinculum*, vol. 18, 1981, pp. 7–9.

Campbell, W. J. *Being a Teacher in Australian State Government Schools.* AGPS, Canberra 1975.

Caro, D., 'Some cause for optimism', *University of Melbourne Gazette*, vol. 40, 1984, p. 4.

Carter, P., 'Group 2 Mathematics—Business Mathematics', *Vinculum*, vol. 18, 1981, p. 13.

Chong, H., 'Model mathematical programmes in action', *Australian Mathematics Teacher*, vol. 18, 1962, pp. 50–62.

Christian, G. D. *Analytical Chemistry.* Xerox College Publishing, Waltham, Mass., 1971.

Clarke, D., 'Teachers: care versus content', in Ann Maurer (ed.), *Conflicts in Mathematics Education*, Mathematics Association of Victoria, Parkville, 1984, pp. 388–95.

Clarke, M. L. *Greek Studies in England 1700–1830.* Adolf M. Hakkert, Amsterdam 1986 [reprint of Cambridge University Press edn, 1945].

Clements, M. A. (Ken). *Mathematics for the Minority. Some historical perspectives of school mathematics in Victoria*, rev. ed. Deakin University Press, Geelong 1992.

—— 'A report on numeracy', *Vinculum*, vol. 12, 1975, pp. 100–11.

Clements, M. A. (Ken), Grimison, L. A. and Ellerton, N. F., 'Colonialism and school mathematics', in N. F. Ellerton and M. A. (Ken) Clements (eds), *School Mathematics: the Challenge to Change*, Deakin University Press, Geelong, 1989, pp. 50–78.

Close, R. W., 'Some problems in present-day mathematical education', *Australian Mathematics Teacher*, vol. 19, 1963, pp. 49–53.

Clowes, D. A., 'Community colleges and proprietary schools: conflict or convergence?', in D. A. Clowes and E. M. Hawthorne (eds), *Community Colleges and Proprietary Schools: Conflict or Convergence*, Jossey-Bass, San Francisco, 1995, pp. 5–15.

Coates, J. G., Reading Habits and Interests of Victorian Boys and Girls, M.Ed. thesis, University of Melbourne, 1942.

Cocking, R. R. and Mestre, J. P. (eds). *Linguistic and Cultural Influences on Learning Mathematics*, L. Erlbaum Associates, Hillsdale, NJ, 1988.

Connell, W. F., Francis, E. P. and Skilbeck, E. E. *Growing up in an Australian City.* ACER, Hawthorn 1966.

Cowban, R. H., 'Presidential Address, 1971', *Vinculum*, vol. 8, 1971, pp. 145–53.

CONASTA, 'The teaching of physical sciences in girls' schools. Statement by the Conference of Australian Science Teachers' Associations', *Australian Science Teachers' Journal*, vol. 33, 1965, p. 68.

Cooper, B. *Renegotiating Secondary School Mathematics. A Study of Curriculum Change and Stability.* Falmer, London 1985.

Cribb, Peter, 'Learning mathematical language', *Vinculum*, vol. 13, 1976, pp. 122–6.

—— The New Maths 1959–1965. A Lost Opportunity for Teaching Reform, M.Ed. thesis, University of Melbourne, 1986.

Cropley, M., 'The Standardization Procedure for HSC Scores', *VISE Circular*, July 1979, pp. 17–24.

—— 'Standardization—What's the Score?', *VISE News*, 18 July 1980, pp. 1–4.

—— *Statistical Moderation: a guide.* VISE, Melbourne 1981.

CTEC. *Review of Efficiency and Effectiveness in Higher Education.* AGPS, Canberra 1986.

Curriculum and Examinations in Secondary Schools (Norwood Report), HMSO, London 1943.

Dainville, François de. *L'Éducation des jésuites (XVIe–XVIIe siècles).* Minuit, Paris 1978.

Dale, Leigh. *The English Men. Professing Literature in Australian Universities.* Association for the Study of Australian Literature, Toowoomba 1997.

Davey, P., 'Financing of education', in R. B. Scotton and H. Ferber (eds), *Public Expenditure and Social Policy in Australia*, Longman Cheshire, Melbourne, 1978, pp. 38–86.

Davis, P. J. and Hersh, R. *The Mathematical Experience.* Harvester, Brighton, Sussex 1981.

Davison, D. M., 'Review of Lucas' *General Mathematics for Senior Students* (1968)', *Vinculum*, vol. 5, 1968, pp. 185–7.

Dawe, L., 'Language and culture in the teaching of mathematics', in L. Grimison and J. Pegg (eds), *Teaching Secondary School Mathematics: Theory into Practice*, Harcourt Brace, Sydney, 1995, pp. 230–47.

Dawes, L., Bail, G. and Daffey, B. (eds). *Modern Mathematics—Third Year.* Jacaranda, Milton, Queensland, 1973

DEET. *National Report on Australia's Higher Education Sector.* AGPS, Canberra 1993.

Delves, Tony, 'English as She is not taught', *English in Australia*, vol. 3, 1966, pp. 33–40.

—— *Issues in Teaching English.* Melbourne University Press, Carlton 1972.

Dening, Greg. *Xavier: A Centenary Portrait.* The Old Xaverians' Association, Armadale 1978.

Devlin, K. M. *The Science of Patterns. The Search for Order in Life, Mind and the Universe.* Scientific American Library, New York 1994.

Dieudonné, Jean (ed.). *Abrégé d'histoire des mathématiques 1700–1900*, Hermann, Paris, 1978.

—— *Mathematics—The Music of Reason*, trans. H. G. and J. C. Dales, Springer-Verlag, Berlin 1992.

Dixon, John. *Growth through English*. Oxford University Press for the National Association for the Teaching of English, London 1975.

Docherty, J., 'The Technical Division', in L. J. Blake (ed.), *Vision and Realisation: A Centenary History of State Education in Victoria*. Education Department, Melbourne, 1973, pp. 607–787.

Dooley, S. F., 'Group 2 Mathematics—Commercial Mathematics', *Vinculum*, vol. 18, 1981, pp. 14–15.

Dow, Gwyneth M. et al. *Parent, Pupil and School. Victoria's Education System*. Cassell, Melbourne 1966.

Dow, Hume (ed.). *Memories of Melbourne University: Undergraduate Life in the Years since 1917*. Hutchison, Melbourne 1983.

Doyle, R. (ed.). *New Perspectives 87. Approaches to Year 12 Group 1 English*. Coghill Publishing, Malvern 1986.

Duggan, Tom, 'Does school maths add up?', *Age*, 16 June 1993.

Duncan, N. *VCE Change and Approximation: CATs 3 and 4, questions and worked solutions*, rev. ed., Coghill, Malvern 1992.

—— *VCE Reasoning and Data: CAT 3 and CAT 4, questions and worked solutions*, rev. ed., Coghill, Malvern 1992.

Dunn, S. S., 'Examinations', in R. W. T. Cowan (ed.), *Education for Australians*, Cheshire, Melbourne, 1964, pp. 162–92.

Durkheim, Emile. *L'Évolution pédagogique en France*. PUF, Paris 1969.

Eagleton, Terry. *Criticism and Ideology. A Study in Marxist Literary Theory*. Verso, London 1992.

—— *Literary Theory: An Introduction*. Blackwell, Oxford 1996.

Education Department Victoria. *Report of the Minister of Education, 1972–1973*. Melbourne 1973.

—— *Report of the Minister of Education, 1975–1976*. Melbourne 1976.

—— *Report of the Minister of Education, 1976–1977*. Melbourne 1977.

Elks, S. A., 'HSC mathematics', *Vinculum*, vol. 13, 1976, pp. 114–16.

Ellerton, N. and Clements, M. A. (Ken). *The Mathematics of Language: a Review of Language Factors in School Maths*. Deakin University, Geelong 1991.

Encel, Sol. *Equality and Authority. A Study of Class, Status and Power in Australia*. Cheshire, Melbourne 1970.

English, June, 'Brunswick Girls' High School: a personal view', in L. F. Claydon (ed.), *The Urban School*, Pitman Pacific Books, Carlton, 1975, pp. 119–41.

Evans, G. T., 'Mathematical ability', *Australian Mathematics Teacher*, vol. 19, 1963, pp. 8–15.

Evans, Ifor. *English Literature: Values and Traditions*. Unwin, London 1962.

Evans, K. M., 'The teaching of mathematics in Victoria', *Australian Mathematics Teacher*, vol. 18, 1962, pp. 68–70.

Fabius, A. J., 'Mathematics as the study of structure', *Australian Mathematics Teacher*, vol. 19, 1963, pp. 25–35.

Fawns, R. A. and Teese, R. *Students' Attitudes to their Schooling.* Schools Commission, Canberra 1979.

Fennema, E. and Sherman, J., 'Sex-related differences in mathematics achievement, spatial visualization and affective factors', *American Educational Research Journal*, vol. 14, 1977, pp. 51–71.

Fensham, P. J. (ed.). *Rights and Inequality in Australian Education.* Cheshire, Melbourne 1970.

—— 'Science education: who is to learn and how?', *Australian Science Teachers' Journal*, vol. 15, 1969, pp. 29–34.

Field, T. W., 'Cognitive style in science', *Australian Science Teachers' Journal*, vol. 18, 1971, pp. 27–35.

Fifteen to Eighteen. Report (Crowther) of the Central Advisory Council for Education—England. HMSO, London 1959.

Findlay, J. J. *The School: an Introduction to the Study of Education.* Thornton Butterworth, London 1932.

Fitzgerald, R. T. *The Secondary School at Sixes and Sevens.* ACER, Hawthorn 1970.

Flinn, Christine., Some determinants of students' course selection in mathematics, M.Ed. thesis, University of Melbourne, 1984.

Flower, F. D. *Language and Education.* Longman, Green & Co., London 1966.

Fogarty, R. *Catholic Education in Australia, 1806–1950.* Melbourne University Press, Carlton 1959.

Fomin, F. and Teese, R., 'Public finance to private schools: the argument of the Karmel Report and later policy', *Melbourne Working Papers*, vol. 3, 1981, pp. 184–200.

French, E. L., 'The humanities in secondary education', in A. Grenfell Price (ed.), *The Humanities in Australia: A Survey with special Reference to the Universities*, Angus & Robertson, Sydney, 1959, pp. 34–55.

Freudenthal, Hans. *Mathematics as an Educational Task.* Reidel, Dordrecht 1973.

Gani, J. *The Condition of Science in Australian Universities.* Pergamon, London 1963.

Gardiner, E. D. *Problems in Physics. SI Edition.* McGraw-Hill, Sydney 1971.

Gasking, D. A. T. *Examinations and the Aims of Education.* Melbourne University Press, Carlton 1945.

Gerth, H. H. and Mills, C. Wright (eds). *From Max Weber. Essays in Sociology*, Routledge & Kegan Paul, London 1970.

Girls, School and Society. Report for the Schools Commission. Canberra 1975.

Goodson, I. F. *School Subjects and Curriculum Change.* Croom Helm, London 1983.

Gordon, P. and Lawton, D. *Curriculum Change in the Nineteenth and Twentieth Centuries.* Hodder & Stoughton, London 1978.

Government Statist. *A Survey of the Distribution of the Population of Victoria. Based on the Census, 30th June, 1954*. Government Printer, Melbourne 1956.

Gramsci, Antonio. *Selections from the Prison Notebooks*, ed. and trans. Q. Hoare and G. N. Smith, International Publishers, New York 1971.

Green, H. A., Jorgensen, A. N. and Gerberich, J. R. *Measurement and Evaluation in the Secondary School*. Longman, Green & Company, New York 1949.

Gregory, R. G. and Sheehan, P., 'Poverty and the collapse of full employment', in R. Fincher and J. Nieuwenhuysen (eds), *Australian Poverty, Then and Now*, Melbourne University Press, Carlton, 1998, pp. 103–26.

Griffiths, H. B. and Howson, A. G. *Mathematics, Society and Curricula*. Cambridge University Press, London 1974.

Griffiths, Leila, 'HSC Chemistry', *Lab-Talk*, vol. 19, 1975, pp. 30–1.

Grimison, L. and Pegg, J. (eds). *Teaching Secondary School Mathematics. Theory into Practice*. Harcourt Brace, Sydney, 1995.

Gurrey, P. *Teaching English Grammar*. Longman, Green & Co., London 1962.

Haileybury College. *Haileybury College, Australia*. Haileybury College, Melbourne, 1987.

Halsey, A. H., Heath, A. F. and Ridge, J. M. *Origins and Destinations. Family, Class and Education in Modern Britain*. Clarendon Press, Oxford 1980.

Hambly, A. N., 'Chemistry feels the winds of change', *Australian Science Teachers' Journal*, vol. 29, 1964, pp. 53–9.

Hamerston, Michael T., The Public Examination of English in Victoria: A Study of One External Influence on the Secondary School English Curriculum, 1944–1974, M.Ed. thesis, Melbourne University, 1980.

Hannan, W., Hannan, L. M. and Dow, G. M., 'Literature in the Secondary School', *Idiom*, vol. 2, 1970, pp. 3–15.

Hansen, I. V. H. *Nor Free Nor Secular. Six Independent Schools in Victoria: A First Sample*. Oxford University Press, Melbourne 1971.

—— *Young People Reading*. Melbourne University Press, Carlton 1973.

Hart, K. M., Kerslake, D., Brown, M. L., Ruddock, G., Küchemann, D. E. and McCartney, M. *Children's Understanding of Mathematics: 11–16*. John Murray, Oxford 1986.

Hartog, P. J. *Examinations and their Relation to Culture and Efficiency*. Constable & Co., London 1918.

Hartog, P. J. and Rhodes, E. C. *The Marks of Examiners*. Macmillan & Co., London 1936.

Heath, A. F. and Clifford, P., 'Class inequalities in education in the twentieth century', *Journal of the Royal Statistical Society*, Series A, vol. 153, Part 1, 1970, pp. 1–16.

Heath, A. and Ridge, J., 'Schools, examinations and occupational attainment', in June Purvis and Margaret Hales (eds), *Achievement and Inequality in Education*, Routledge & Kegan Paul, London, 1983, pp. 239–57.

Heffernan, M., Stranks, D. R., Lee Dow, K., McTigue, P. T. and Withers, G. M., 'Matriculation chemistry. The new 1966 course', *Lab-Talk*, vol. 3, 1964, pp. 4–5.

Henderson, R. F. (ed.). *Youth Unemployment*. Proceedings of the Second Academy Symposium, November 1977. Academy of the Social Sciences in Australia, Melbourne 1977.

Hegel, G. W. F. *Philosophy of Right*, trans. T. M. Knox. Oxford University Press, London 1967.

Hohne, H. H. *The Prediction of Academic Success*. ACER, Melbourne 1951.

—— *Success and Failure in Scientific Faculties of the University of Melbourne*. ACER, Melbourne 1955.

Holbrook, David. *English in Australia Now*. Cambridge University Press, Cambridge 1973.

Hopkins, J., 'Coming ready or not!', *Vinculum*, vol. 17, 1980, pp. 14–15.

Hore, T., Linke, R. D. and West , L. H. T. (eds). *The Future of Higher Education in Australia*, Macmillan, South Melbourne 1978.

Howson, A. G., 'The diffusion of new ideas', in G. T. Wain (ed.), *Mathematical Education*, Van Nostrand Reinhold, New York, 1978, pp. 124–39.

Howson, G., Keitel, C. and Kilpatrick, J. *Curriculum Development in Mathematics*. Cambridge University Press, London 1982.

Hoy, Alice. *A City Built to Music. The History of University High School, Melbourne, 1910 to 1960*. University High School, Melbourne 1961.

Hoyles, Celia, 'The pupil's view of mathematics learning', *Educational Studies in Mathematics*, vol. 13, 1982, pp. 349–72.

Hughes, N. E., 'Thinking in school mathematics: a woman replies', *Australian Mathematics Teacher*, vol. 10, 1954, pp. 28–32.

Hunt, F. J. *Resources and Achievements in Melbourne Secondary Schools*. Monash University, Clayton 1972.

Hunter, Ian. *Culture and Government. The Emergence of Literary Education*. Macmillan, Basingstoke 1988.

Hyatt, Don, 'Chemistry 1979', *Lab-Talk*, vol. 23, 1979, pp. 2–5.

Ingle, R. B. and Shayer, M., 'Conceptual demands in Nuffield O-level chemistry', *Education in Chemistry*, vol. 8, 1971, pp. 182–3.

Ivanhoe Girls' Grammar School. Staff Reference Manual 1988.

Jenkins, E. W. *From Armstrong to Nuffield. Studies in twentieth-century science education in England and Wales*. John Murray, London 1979.

Johnson, Lesley. *The Cultural Critics. From Matthew Arnold to Raymond Williams*. Routledge & Kegan Paul, London 1979.

Jones, W. *Secondary School Mathematics and Technological Careers.* ACER, Hawthorn 1988.

Kelly, G. M., 'Thoughts on school mathematics', *Australian Mathematics Teacher,* vol. 18, 1962, pp. 81–6.

Kline, Morris. *Mathematics and the Physical World,* Thomas Y. Crowell Coy., New York 1959.

—— *Mathematics in Western Culture.* Allen & Unwin, London 1954.

Kennedy, D. C., 'Is it still ad-VISE-able?', in Sue Ferguson (ed.), *Mathematics for the 80s,* Mathematics Association of Victoria, Parkville, 1979, p. 7.

—— 'Group 2 Mathematics—Mathematics at Work', *Vinculum,* vol. 18, 1981, pp. 12–13.

Kenway, J. and Willis, S. *Answering Back. Girls, Boys and Feminism in Schools.* Allen & Unwin, Sydney 1997.

Kudilczak, S., 'Survival mathematics', in S. Ferguson (ed.), *Mathematics for the 80s,* Mathematical Association of Victoria, Parkville, 1979, pp. 386–97.

Kyle, N. *Her Natural Destiny: The Education of Women in New South Wales.* New South Wales University Press, Kensington 1986.

Lamb, Stephen, 'Cultural consumption and the educational plans of Australian secondary school students', *Sociology of Education,* vol. 62, 1989, pp. 95–108.

—— 'Cultural selection in Australian secondary schools', *Research in Education,* vol. 43, 1990, pp. 1–14.

—— 'Gender differences in mathematics participation in Australian schools: some relationships with social class and school policy', *British Educational Research Journal,* vol. 22, 1996, pp. 223–40.

—— 'Gender differences in mathematics participation: an Australian perspective', *Educational Studies,* vol. 23, 1997, pp. 105–25.

Langouët, G., 'Les années 80–90: quelle démocratisation?', *L'Orientation Scolaire et Professionnelle,* vol. 22, 1990, pp. 3–24.

—— *La démocratisation de l'enseignement aujourd'hui.* ESF, Paris 1994.

Learning for Life. Review [West] of Higher Education Financing and Policy. A Policy Discussion Paper. AGPS, Canberra 1997.

Lee Dow, Kwong. *Teaching Science in Australian Schools,* Melbourne University Press, Carlton 1971.

Léger, A. *Enseignants du secondaire.* PUF, Paris 1983.

Legrand, L. *Pour une politique démocratique de l'éducation.* PUF, Paris 1977.

Linke, R. *Regional Analysis of Socioeconomic Trends in Educational Participation.* ANU Press, Canberra 1988.

Love, E. R., 'What is wrong with the teaching of school mathematics?', in T. H. MacDonald (ed.), *Mathematics Teaching in Schools: a Critique,* Primary Education, Richmond, 1975, pp. 15–20.

Lowe, Ian, 'Problem-solving in mathematics education', *Vinculum*, vol. 1981, pp. 6–10.

Lublin, Jacqueline, 'Where Angels fear to Tread', *Idiom*, vol. 8, 1970, p. 10.

MacDonald, T. H., 'Conflicts and Criticism about Mathematics Teaching', in T. H. MacDonald (ed.), *Mathematics Teaching in Schools: a Critique*, Primary Education, Richmond, 1975, pp. 5–14

Mack, J., 'One step back, two steps forward', in P. Costello, S. Ferguson, K. Slinn et al. (eds), *Facets of Australian Mathematics Education*, Australian Association of Mathematics Teachers, Blackburn, 1984, pp. 54–7.

Mackay, Lindsay D., 'Teacher characteristics affecting student changes in PSSC', *Australian Science Teachers' Journal*, vol. 16, 1970, pp. 74–7.

Mappin, K. J. *Chemistry for Secondary Schools: the Atomic Structure Approach*. Cheshire, Melbourne 1963.

Marginson, S., *Markets in Education*. Allen & Unwin, Sydney 1997.

—— 'Markets in higher education: Australia', in J. Smyth (ed.), *Academic Work: The Changing Labour Process in Higher Education*, Society for Research into Higher Education and Open University Press, Buckingham 1995.

Martin, P. J. *The VCE Mathematics Experiment: An Evaluation*. Deakin University, Geelong 1993.

Maslen, Geoffrey. *Understanding the New VCE*. The Education Library, Melbourne 1990.

Mathieson, Margaret. *The Preachers of Culture. A Study of English and its Teachers*. George Allen & Unwin, London 1975.

McDonell, Win., 'Will mathematics outlast HSC?', *Vinculum*, vol. 13, 1976, pp. 35–9.

McLaren, John, 'From examination to discourse', *English in Australia*, vol. 3, 1966, pp. 12–20.

—— 'Humanities in Australian higher education', in Stephen Murray-Smith (ed.), *Melbourne Studies in Education 1979*, Melbourne University Press, Carlton, 1979, pp. 6–44.

McTigue, P. T. (ed.). *Chemistry, Key to the Earth*, 2nd edn. Melbourne University Press, Carlton 1986.

Medley, J. D. G., 'The present and future of Australian universities', John Murtagh Macrossen Memorial Lecture for 1945. Queensland University Press, Melbourne 1945.

Melbourne Grammar. Information Sheet 1978.

—— *Grammar Newsletter*, no. 36, October 1988.

Melbourne Girls' Grammar School. Outline of Courses 1987/88.

Melbourne University. Department of Mathematics Course Advice Book for 1990, August 1989.

—— *Public Examinations Papers, 1946–47.*

—— *Report on a Conference on Careers between Victorian Secondary Schools and the University of Melbourne*, Carlton 1956.

—— *Reports of Examiners. Public and Matriculation Examinations*. Carlton, successive years.

—— Undergraduate entrance requirements and selection for 1988 and beyond, unpublished document of the Selection Procedures Committee of the Academic Board, June 1985.

Menkilowski, A., 'Whither Business Mathematics', in Ken Clements (ed.), *Whither Mathematics*, Mathematics Association of Victoria, Parkville, 1990, pp. 104–5.

Ministry of Education. *The Road to the Sixth Form*. HMSO, London 1951.

Ministry of Education Victoria. *VCE: a higher education for life*. Melbourne n.d. [1990].

More, R., 'An open letter', *Vinculum*, vol. 18, 1981, pp. 14–16.

Moss, J. D. *Towards Equality: progress by girls in mathematics in Australian secondary schools*. ACER, Hawthorn 1982.

Müller, D. K., Ringer, F. and Simon, B. *The Rise of the Modern Educational System: Structural Change and Social Reproduction, 1870–1920*. Cambridge University Press and Maison des Sciences de l'Homme, Cambridge and Paris 1987.

Murison, D. M., 'HSC English—where is it going?', *Idiom*, vol. 8, 1973, pp. 3–8.

Musgrave, P. W. *From Humanity to Utility: Melbourne University and Public Examinations 1856–1964*. ACER, Hawthorn 1992.

—— *Knowledge, Curriculum and Change*. Melbourne University Press, Carlton 1973.

—— *Society and the Curriculum in Australia*. Allen & Unwin, Sydney 1979.

—— *Whose Knowledge? A Case-Study of the Victorian Universities and Schools Examinations Board, 1964–79*. Falmer, London 1988.

National Council of Teachers of Mathematics, 'An argument for action. Recommendations for school mathematics of the 1980s', *Vinculum*, vol. 17, 1980, pp. 10–15.

Newman, M. A., 'Maths and the second language child', in P. Costello, S. Ferguson, K. Slinn et al. (eds), *Facets of Australian Mathematics Education*, Australian Association of Mathematics Teachers, Blackburn, 1984, pp. 149–56.

Noss, R., 'Just testing: a critical view of recent change in the UK school mathematics curriculum', in N. F. Ellerton and M. A. (Ken) Clements (eds), *School mathematics: the Challenge to Change*, Deakin University Press, Geelong, 1989, pp. 155–69.

OECD. *New Thinking in School Mathematics*. Paris 1961.

Oertel, S., 'Do mathematics students become mathematicians?', *Vinculum*, vol. 9, 1972, pp. 175–6.

Ozolins, Uldis, 'Victorian HSC examiners' reports: a study of cultural capital', *Melbourne Working Papers*, vol. 3, 1981, pp. 142–83.

Palmer, D. J. *The Rise of English Studies*. Oxford University Press, Oxford 1965.

Persse, M. C. *Well-Ordered Liberty. A Portrait of Geelong Grammar School 1855–1995*. Cliffe Books, Melbourne 1995.

Pitman, A., 'Mathematics education reform in its social, political and economic contexts', in N. F. Ellerton and M. A. (Ken) Clements (eds), *School Mathematics: the Challenge to Change*, Deakin University Press, Geelong, 1989, pp. 101–19.

Polya, G. *How To Solve It. A New Aspect of Mathematical Method*, 2nd ed. Doubleday Anchor, New York 1957.

Potts, R. B., 'A case against the New Maths', *Vinculum*, vol. 11, 1974, pp. 36–7.

Power, C., Robertson, F. and Beswick, D. *Access to Higher Education: Participation, Equity and Policy*. National Institute of Labour Studies, Adelaide 1985.

Price, P. G., 'Opinion and fact in the organization of mathematics teaching', *Australian Mathematics Teacher*, vol. 3, 1947, pp. 48–51.

Preston, G. B., 'What mathematics should be taught at school?', in ACER, *Primary Mathematics Conference. Report of a Conference, University of Melbourne, 1975*. ACER, Hawthorn, 1975, pp. 38–45.

PSSC. *Physics*, 2nd edn. D. C. Heath, Boston 1966.

Quadling, D. A., 'Issues at Secondary Level', in G. T. Wain (ed.), *Mathematical Education*, Van Nostrand Reinhold, New York, 1978, pp. 169–80.

Radford, Joan. *The Chemistry Department of the University of Melbourne. Its Contribution to Australian Science, 1854–1959*. The Hawthorn Press, Melbourne 1978.

Radford, W. C. *The Educational Needs of a Rural Community*. Melbourne University Press, Carlton 1939.

Report [Murray] of the Committee on Australian Universities, Government Printer, Canberra 1957.

Report [Blackburn] of the Ministerial Review of Postcompulsory Schooling. Government Printer, Melbourne 1985.

Report [Deveson] of the Taskforce on Pathways in Education and Training. Government Printer, Melbourne, 1992.

Response of the Federation of Australian Scientific and Technological Societies to the Government's Proposal for Tertiary Education, Training and Research, Canberra 1988.

Review [Ramler] of the Provision of Technical and Further Education in the Melbourne Metropolitan Area, Education Victoria, Melbourne, 1997.

Richardson, E. and Stanhope, Roy W., 'Why do some secondary school pupils find science hard? A study involving 1700 pupils in Forms

I–VI in five NSW schools', *Australian Science Teachers' Journal*, vol. 17, 1971, pp. 66–74.

Richmond, W. Kenneth. *Culture and General Education, A Survey*. Methuen, London 1963.

Ringer, Fritz K., 'Cultural transmission in German higher education in the nineteenth century', *Journal of Contemporary History*, vol. 2, 1967, pp. 123–38.

—— *Education and Society in Modern Europe*. Indiana University Press, Bloomington 1979.

—— *Fields of Knowledge. French Academic Culture in Comparative Perspective, 1890–1920*. Cambridge University Press and Maison des Sciences de l'Homme, Cambridge and Paris 1992.

Room, T. G., 'Mathematics at school and university', *Australian Mathematics Teacher*, vol. 16, 1960, pp. 27–30.

Roper, Tom. *The Myth of Equality*. National Union of Australian University Students, North Melbourne 1970.

Rosier, M. J. *Science Achievement in Australian Secondary Schools. Some School Results from the IEA Science Project*. ACER, Hawthorn 1973.

—— *Changes in Secondary School Mathematics in Australia, 1964–1978*. ACER, Hawthorn 1980.

Rowe, A. P. *If the Gown Fits*. Melbourne University Press, Carlton 1960.

Saint Martin, Monique de. *Les fonctions sociales de l'enseignement scientifique*. Cahiers du Centre de Sociologie Européenne, no. 8. Mouton, Paris 1971.

Sanders, C., 'The Australian universities', in R. W. T. Cowan (ed.), *Education for Australians. A Symposium*, Cheshire, Melbourne, 1964, pp. 121–41.

—— *Student Selection and Academic Success in Australian Universities*. Government Printer, Sydney 1948.

Sargent, J. and Carozzi, B. W., 'Evaluation and English', *Idiom*, vol. 1, 1970, pp. 8–16.

Schoenheimer, H., 'Henry Schoenheimer criticizes HSC English', *Idiom*, vol. 7, 1972, pp. 3–7.

Schofield, H. *Selection Criteria and Social Diversity: An Evaluation of the Special Admissions Scheme*. Centre for the Study of Higher Education, University of Melbourne, Parkville 1988.

Schools Commission. *Commonwealth Standards for Australian Schools. Recurrent Resource Goals*. AGPS, Canberra 1984.

Schools Council. *Mathematical Experience. Mathematics for the Majority Series*. Chatto & Windus, London 1970.

Schools in Australia. Report [Karmel] of the Interim Committee of the Australian Schools Commission. AGPS, Canberra 1973.

Schools Inquiry Commission (Taunton Report). *British Parliamentary Papers, 1867–68*.

Scotch College. *Great Scot*, July 1983, March 1986.
—— A Guide to Scotch College, 1988/1989.
—— *The Scotch Collegian 1986*.
Secondary Education. A report of the Advisory Council on Education in Scotland. HMSO, Edinburgh 1947.
Selby Smith, R., 'A Victorian independent school: reflections on the development of Scotch College, 1953–1964', in E. L. French (ed.), *Melbourne Studies in Education 1965*, Melbourne University Press, Carlton, 1966, pp. 225–50.
Selinger, Ben. *Chemistry in the Marketplace*, 5th edn. Harcourt Brace, Sydney 1998.
Spaulding–Morrison Report. *The Training of Secondary School Teachers, especially with reference to English. Report of a Joint Committee of the Faculty of Harvard College and of the Graduate School of Education*. Harvard University Press, Cambridge, Mass., 1942.
St Leonard's College. *St Leonard's College World School, Melbourne. Prospectus* [1988].
Smith, A. L. H. and Fox, R. N. *Questions in Chemistry. A Comprehensive, Developmental and Relevant Course*, 2nd edn, McGraw-Hill, Sydney 1980.
'Some thoughts on mathematics teaching' [Mother Brigid of Loreto Convent], *Vinculum*, vol. 4, 1967, pp. 3–5.
Spaull, A. and Hince, K. *Industrial Relations and State Education in Australia*. A. E. Press, Melbourne 1986.
Srivastava, D. M., 'Mathematics for school leavers and employment', *Vinculum*, vol. 16, 1979, p. 68.
—— 'Future of the Year 12 mathematics courses', *Vinculum*, vol. 16, 1979, pp. 104–10.
Steel, Roslyn, 'School–tertiary interface', in Jill O'Reilly and Sue Wettenhall (eds), *Mathematics: Inclusive, Dynamic, Exciting, Active, Stimulating*, Mathematics Association of Victoria, Parkville, 1991, pp. 173–4.
Sumner, R. J. and Wilson, N. L., 'A survey of science interests of secondary school students', *Australian Science Teachers' Journal*, vol. 18, 1977, pp. 64–6.
Sureties, Brian, 'English teaching in the sixties and seventies', in B. H. Bennett and J. A. Hay (eds), *Directions in Australian Secondary School English*, Longman, Camberwell, Vic., 1971, pp. 47–8.
Teese, R., 'Australian private schools, specialization and curriculum conservation', *British Journal of Educational Studies*, vol. 37, 1989, pp. 235–52.
—— 'Le conservatisme social du marché universitaire australien', *Actes de la Recherche en Sciences Sociales*, vol. 70, 1987, pp. 83–6.
—— 'Curriculum hierarchy, private schooling and the segmentation of Australian secondary education, 1947–1985', *British Journal of Sociology of Education*, vol. 19, 1998, pp. 401–17.

—— 'Mass secondary education and curriculum access: a forty-year perspective on mathematics outcomes in Victoria', *Oxford Review of Education*, vol. 20, 1994, pp. 93–110.

—— 'Scholastic power and curriculum access: public and private schooling in post-war Australia', *History of Education*, vol. 24, 1995, pp. 353–67.

—— 'Seamless Education and Training', in *Ministerial Review of Metropolitan TAFE*, Paper no. 6, Education Victoria, Melbourne, 1997.

—— 'Social selection and mathematics attainment: the geography of high school outcomes in Victoria at the end of post-war growth', *History of Education Review*, vol. 24, 1995, pp. 55–73.

—— 'The traditional structure of the university market in Australia', *Australian Universities' Review*, vol. 29, 1986, pp. 17–21.

Teese, R. and Fawns, R. 'Social and attitudinal differences amongst high school students', unpublished report for the Schools Commission, 1982.

Teese, R., Charlton, M. and Polesel, J. 'Curriculum outcomes in Victoria: a geographical and gender analaysis', Educational Outcomes Research Unit, University of Melbourne, 1995.

Teese, R., Charlton, M., Polesel, J. and Davies, M. 'Catholic secondary school students in Victoria: attitudes, achievement and destinations', unpublished report, Educational Outcomes Research Unit, University of Melbourne, 1996.

Teese, R., McLean, G. and Polesel, J. *Equity Outcomes*, AGPS, Canberra 1993.

Tertiary Education in Australia (Martin Report), Government Printer, Canberra 1964–65.

Thwaites, Bryan (ed.). *On Teaching Mathematics*. Pergamon, Oxford 1961.

Tickell, W. G., 'How can schools develop the ability of critical thinking?', *Idiom*, vol. 7, 1972, pp. 3–19.

Ulam, S. M. *Adventures of a Mathematician*. Scribner, New York 1976.

UNESCO. *The Teaching of English*. Australian UNESCO Seminar, University of Sydney, May–June 1972. AGPS, Canberra 1973.

VBOS. 'Assessment Advice for 1994 School Assessed Common Assessment Tasks', *VCE Bulletin*, Supplement, February 1994.

—— *Chemistry VCE Study Design. Units 3 and 4*. Carlton 1993.

—— *Chemistry VCE Study Design*. Carlton 1994.

—— *English VCE Study Design*. Carlton 1994.

—— *English VCE Study Design 1997–2000*. Carlton 1996.

—— *Enhancing their Futures. Report of the Committee of Review [Lee Dow] on the Victorian Certificate of Education*. Carlton 1997.

—— *Literature VCE Study Design*. Carlton 1994.

—— *Mathematical Methods. CATs 2 and 3: Written examinations Booklets*. Carlton 1996.

—— *Mathematics: Further. CATs 2 and 3: Written examinations Booklets*. Carlton 1996.

—— *Mathematics: Specialist. CATs 2 and 3: Written examinations Booklets*. Carlton 1996.

—— *Mathematics VCE Study Design 1997–2000*. Carlton 1996.

—— *Official Sample CATs English 1994*. Collins Dove, North Blackburn 1994.

—— *Official Sample CATs English 1996*. HarperSchools, North Blackburn 1996.

—— *Official Sample CATs Chemistry 1996*. HarperSchools, North Blackburn 1996.

—— *Official Sample CATs Mathematical Methods 1995*. HarperSchools, North Blackburn 1995.

—— *Official Sample CATs Mathematical Methods 1996*. HarperSchools, North Blackburn 1996.

—— *Official Sample CATs Mathematics: Further 1995*. HarperSchools, North Blackburn 1995.

—— *Official Sample CATs Mathematics: Further 1996*. HarperSchools, North Blackburn 1996.

—— *Official Sample CATs Mathematics: Specialist 1996*. HarperSchools, North Blackburn 1996.

—— *Reports to teachers containing reports from Chief Assessors and State Reviewers on VCE CATs 1984*. Carlton 1995.

—— *Statistical Information, Victorian Certificate of Education, Assessment Program*. Carlton, successive years.

—— *VCE Administrative Handbook*. Carlton, various years.

VCAB. *Statistical Information, Victorian Certificate of Education, Assessment Program*. Carlton, successive years.

—— *Chemistry VCE Study Design*. Carlton, 1991.

—— *Chemistry Course Development Support Material*. Carlton 1991.

—— *Mathematics Study Design*. Carlton 1990.

VISE. *Policy Statement. Curriculum and Assessment in Year 12*. Melbourne, 1978.

—— *VISE News,* Bulletin no. 31, July–August 1982.

—— *Handbook for 1984 Year 12 Curriculum and Assessment*. South Melbourne 1983.

—— *Handbook for Year 12 Curriculum and Assessment*. South Melbourne, successive years.

—— *Towards a revised policy on curriculum and assessment in the Victorian Year 12 HSC program. A Paper for Discussion*. Melbourne 1984.

—— *VISE News,* Bulletin no. 49, March 1985.

—— *VISE News,* Bulletin no. 52, November–December 1985.

—— *Report on HSC Assessment Program*. South Melbourne, various years.

—— *Viewprints,* no. 6, April 1986.

Volk, Valerie, 'The place of the prescribed books in the H.S.C. English Expression course', *Idiom,* vol. 6, 1971, pp. 4–6.

VTAC. *Bulletin,* no. 1, 1995.

VUSEB, *Circular to Schools* (various issues).

—— *Handbook of Directions and Prescriptions.* Melbourne (various years.).

—— *Matriculation Examination 1968.* Carlton n.d.

—— *Matriculation Examination 1969.* Carlton n.d.

—— *Reports of Examiners. School Leaving Examination. HSC Examination* (various years).

Walden, R. and Walkerdine, V. *Girls and Mathematics. From Primary to Secondary Schooling.* University of London, London 1988.

Walkerdine, Valerie. *The Mastery of Reason. Cognitive Development and the Production of Rationality.* Routledge, London 1988.

Walkerdine, V. and Lucey, H. *Democracy in the Kitchen. Regulating Mothers and Socializing Daughters.* Virago, London 1989.

Waring, Mary. *Social Pressures and Curriculum Innovation. A Study of the Nuffield Foundation Science Teaching Project.* Methuen, London 1979.

Watson, R., McLaren, R. and Fraser, D. *Change and Approximation. Mathematics Today: Senior Series.* McGraw-Hill, Roseville 1990.

Weil, André. *The Apprenticeship of a Mathematician,* trans. Jennifer Gaga, Birkhäuser, Basel 1992.

Wesley College. *The Lion,* April 1983, March 1985.

—— 'Letter to Parents'. February 1984.

—— 'The Senior College'. Pamphlet, February 1987.

—— *Wesley College Chronicle,* Prahran Campus, December 1987.

White, Paul, 'An introduction to teaching calculus', in L. Grimison and J. Pegg (eds), *Teaching Secondary School Mathematics. Theory into Practice.* Harcourt Brace, Sydney, 1995, pp. 165–85.

Wilkinson, Ian R., 'Frederick McCoy—first science professor at the University of Melbourne', *History of Education Review,* vol. 25, 1996, pp. 54–70.

—— 'Science in Victorian secondary schools in the late nineteenth century', *History of Education Review,* vol. 17, 1988, pp. 63–78.

Williams, Doug, 'Teachers: the beginnings of creation', in P. Costello, S. Ferguson, K. Slinn et al. (eds), *Facets of Australian Mathematics Education,* Australian Association of Mathematics Teachers, Blackburn, 1984, pp. 80–100.

Williams, Raymond. *Drama from Ibsen to Eliot,* rev. edn. Peregrine Books, Harmondsworth, 1964.

Withers, G. and Cornish, G., 'Assessment in practice: competitive or non-competitive?', *VISE Occasional Paper,* no. 11, May 1984.

Zevenbergen, Robin, 'Language, mathematics and social disadvantage: a Bourdieuian analysis of cultural capital in mathematics education', in C. Kanes, M. Goos and E. Warren (eds), *Teaching Mathematics in New Times*, Mathematics Education Research Group of Australasia, Brisbane, 1998, vol. 2, pp. 716–22.

Index